ST. MICHAEL'S COLLEGE SERIES

— 3 —

COVER: Giovan Battista Salvi "Il Sassoferrato" (1609-1685), *Madonna*

Saints and the Sacred

Proceedings of
A St. Michael's College Symposium
(25-26 February, 2000)

Edited by
Joseph Goering, Francesco Guardiani, Giulio Silano

LEGAS

New York   Ottawa   Toronto

© 2001 **LEGAS** No part of this book may be reproduced in any form, by print, photoprint, microfilm, microfiche, or any other means, without written permission from the publisher.

Canadian Cataloguing in Publication Data

Main entry under title:
    Saints and the sacred: proceedings of a St. Michael's College symposium (25-26 February, 2000)

(St. Michael's College Series: 3)
Includes bibliographical references and index.
Text in Portuguese, French and English.
ISBN 1-894508-17-3

1. Christian saints—Congresses.   I. Guardiani, Francesco, 1949-   II. Silano, Giulio, 1955-   III. Goering, Joseph, 1947-   IV. Series.

BT970.S25 2001   270'092'2   C2001-901123-7

For further information and for orders:

LEGAS

P. O. Box 040328	3 Wood Aster Bay	2908 Dufferin Street
Brooklyn, New York	Ottawa, Ontario	Toronto, Ontario
USA 11204	K2R 1B3	M6B 3S8

Printed and bound in Canada

A THIRD ST. MICHAEL'S COLLEGE SYMPOSIUM

We seem to have done it again. As we make ready to hold our fourth Symposium, on Mystics, Visions, and Miracles, we also make the presses groan (can one still speak this way? do presses still groan?) with the labour of producing the Proceedings of our third, on Saints and the Sacred.

We have made clear from the inception of this little enterprise that one of our aims in holding these Symposia, apart from our obvious enjoyment of the fellowship which they express and engender, is to single out broad topics for discussion which, directly or indirectly, help those of us who are at St. Michael's in various capacities to ponder what the College has been and may become.

As the Catholic College within the University of Toronto, St. Michael's has a privileged claim to ponder the stories, myths, representations of those who have preceeded us in the Church and who have been found to be such exemplary embodiments of the sacred that, with an adjective usually reserved for God alone, they are themselves called holy. So it was good for the symposiasts to meet at a place named after a saint in order to praise, or study the praise, or decry the praise of famous men and women of God from various Christian ages and traditions, and even from non-Christian ones. What better way for a Catholic College to begin a new Christian millennium than by doing such a thing?

To such a degree did this seem an enthusing activity to the participants that the choice of the subject of the fourth Symposium was to made to flow directly from the pleasant experience of the third. And so we affirm once more (as an article of faith, as it were) that the St. Michael's yearly Symposium is here to stay as a small reminder of what we are and do in our College.

Indeed, as we see things unfolding around us in the wider academic community, we are reinforced in the conviction that initiatives like ours are absolutely necessary for the well-being of the humanities within the University, and need to be encouraged and cherished. As the importance of the University looms ever larger in the dominant sectors of our society and economy, there is not a concomitant growth of the space devoted to humane pursuits. The College constitutes a little space within which these pursuits can still find a welcome, and so we mean to enjoy extending and receiving the hospitality of our Symposium for as long as we may.

Meanwhile, let us send these Proceedings on by noting with gratitude the grumpily generous support which Principal Joseph Boyle has extended to this undertaking.

    Joseph Goering
    Francesco Guardiani
    Giulio Silano

Contents

Introduction: An Idea of Sanctity   9

JACALYN DUFFIN
*Saints Cosmas and Damian of Toronto:
Origin and Meaning of the Medical Cult of Divine Twins*   11

AWAD EDDIE HALABI
*Tradition and the tombs of the Prophet Moses:
The Medieval Islamic Period*   25

DOMENICO PIETROPAOLO
The Zodiac Saints   35

REINER JAAKSON
Wilderness as Sacred Place   61

RANDALL A. ROSENFELD
*Santa Caterina da Bologna (1413-1463), Her Violeta,
and a Late-Medieval Contemplative Practice*   71

SERGIY KUZMENKO
The Life of St. Andrew the Fool and Cult of Holy Fools in Byzance   97

PETER COFFMAN
*Eadburg of Repton and Southwell Minster:
Norman Shrine-Church for a Saxon Saint?*   105

ERIC GRAFF
*Holier than thou, or how the betters get the goods:
an early Bridgettine pioneer's letter home*   123

CHRISTOPHE POTWOROSKI
The Theologian and the "Little Way" 135

MAIRI COWAN
*Mungo's Miracles: St. Kentigern, the City Crest of Glasgow,
and Medieval Scottish Traditions of Sanctity* 147

JOSEPH GOERING
The Virgin and the Grail: A Forgotten Twelfth-Century Cult 163

FRANCESCO GUARDIANI
A Christological Metamorphosis in a Baroque Poem 185

GIULIO SILANO
*Popes and Lawyers on the Papal Canonization
of Saints and its Reasons* 199

INTRODUCTION: AN IDEA OF SANCTITY

We would not even try to define sanctity, to say what sanctity is. Definitions are always dangerous, and all the more so when they presume to contain something as sublime as sanctity. And so we renounce the attempt to recall various definitions drawn from various disciplines, various dictionaries, in various languages – a complicated thing, while sanctity is simple, "simple" as the opposite of the "banal." As the pope has recently had occasion to say, let it suffice to qualify sanctity as the message which convinces, without the need for words, and to note that, for Christians, it is the living reflection of the face of Christ.

"Ah, to have two years to study theology!" McLuhan once said, without any intention, really, of stopping what he was doing to invest years in the study of theology. He felt, perhaps, that he could get as close to the practical side of sanctity as a good theologian could. And we, little, practical, Christian philosophers certainly think so because, again, we believe that sanctity is a simple thing, and if not simple to define, then simple to experience.

A profound simplicity is the constant quality that appears in the greatest saints (or, shall we say, in the most revered of them), from Francis of Assisi to Thérèse de Lisieux, regardless of the historical period in which they lived, of their social status, their sex, their field of activity,

Sanctity is simple and is also easy, in the sense, at least, that it appears as effortless, for the saints, as breathing or talking or walking in the most comfortable of circumstances. We do not need to bring into the picture the serene expressions of martyrs offered to us for meditation from the traditional iconography to convince ourselves of this other ever-present quality of human sanctity.

We just need to think of the effortless dramatic actions of the saints as an expression of a life that is not merely natural, a life that goes beyond human nature, a life that, therefore, becomes supernatural, and so most fully human.

Jacopone da Todi, a mystic writer of the thirteenth century, embraced sanctity when he discovered that his dead wife (a victim of an accident from the collapse of a floor during a party) was wearing a hairshirt. The radiant, happy, and apparently worldly woman in a well-to-do family had a secret, saintly life which she lived, with excruciating pain, effortlessly.

Other qualifiers of sanctity that describe it without the ambition of defining it could include "graceful" and "happy," as innumerable examples, even of those saints caught in the mystical throes of the dark night, could indicate. Sanctity, then, as a simple, effortless, graceful, and happy condition, seems to be a human ideal to which all human persons might aspire. It is to encourage this aspiration as broadly and generously as possible that the present pope surprises us with an ever lenghtening list of new saints, all of them invitations to a life of simple, effortless, gracefully demanding happiness.

JACALYN DUFFIN

SAINTS COSMAS AND DAMIAN OF TORONTO: ORIGIN AND MEANING OF THE MEDICAL CULT OF DIVINE TWINS

ABSTRACT. Since 1987, the Little Italy parish of Saint Francis of Assisi marks the September 27 feast day of Saints Cosmas and Damian with a special mass and a musical parade in the shadow of the presitigious Toronto Hospital. This paper will explore the origin and significance of the celebration of the twin physicians. This research has been amplified by visits to the festivals and interviews with donors, priests, organizers, and pilgrims. At least three other Italian immigrant communities have developed feast day celebrations to the doctor saints in the mid-twentieth century: Manhattan, Utica, and Howard Beach (all in N.Y state). Rivalry with Utica, in particular, was an important trigger for the Toronto event. Testimony of the organizers suggests that the popularity of the celebration is growing. That of the pilgrims describes healing of physical ailments often continuous with (or following) conventional hospital treatment. The analysis invites a reconsideration of the nature of healing, magic, and miracle in our time.

I am an historian of medicine, not an expert on saints, and I have joined today's symposium looking for advice on a compelling project that, perhaps, I should not be pursuing. In this paper, I will briefly tell how I came to be interested in the twin healers, Saints Cosmas and Damian. Then I will trace their cult from its origins to the New World. My sources include liturgical and lay literature, interviews with priests and donors, and surveys of feast-day pilgrims that I have been conducting over the last seven years at five North American festivals devoted to these saints. Today, I will concentrate on the findings from the Toronto event and its rival in Utica, N.Y., situating them within four theories from religion and comparative mythology. I will conclude by advancing an hypothesis about the recurring phenomenon of healing twins. This work-in-progress is slow and somewhat perverse since it can best be advanced on only one day a year!

Saints and the Sacred - A St. Michael's College Symposium
Joseph Goering, Francesco Guardiani, Giulio Silano eds. Ottawa: Legas, 2001

When I was a medical student in the early 1970s, I lived in Toronto's little Italy. My landlady was younger than I, but she already had three children and always wore black. Early in the morning, I could hear her footsteps and those of women like her, young and old, all dressed in mourning, walking to mass at the nearby church. Ten years ago, while visiting the same neighbourhood, I noticed a poster on a telephone pole announcing the festival of the doctor saints, Cosmas and Damian. I was fairly certain no such celebration had existed thirty years ago. Was it new or had I simply failed to notice it? Where did it come from, and why? What follows are the preliminary answers to these questions.

According to the *Acta Sanctorum*, Cosmas and Damian were twin physicians martyred in the early fourth century persecutions of the Roman Emperor, Diocletian. Evidence pertaining to their lives is vague and problematic.[1] Nevertheless, the record states that the brothers performed miraculous cures and always refused payment for their work; hence, they called the "Anargyroi" (those who take no money). When the hour of martyrdom came, their bodies proved particularly resilient to destruction: they were tossed in the sea but angels retrieved them; they were crucified for hours without effect; they were set alight at the stake but the flames did not consume them; they were shot with arrows but the arrows turned back on the archers. Finally, they were beheaded.[2]

Within a century, Cosmas and Damian were venerated throughout the Roman Empire. Shrines were established in Constantinople, Athens, Ravenna, and Rome.[3] The list of their widely transported relics suggests a mass of organic material far in excess of that which would normally comprise two human bodies.[4] Their miracles continued after their deaths. Many were cures effected while patients slept and dreamt in church sanctuaries, a process strikingly similar to the incubation cures of ancient temple medicine and the cult of Asklepios.[5] The most famous of the posthumous cures is the miracle of the "black leg": the saints removed the putrefying leg of a white man who slept in their basilica and replaced it with the leg of a dead "moor" recently interred in the local cemetery. Surgical journals are fond of citing the Anargyroi as patrons of transplantation.[6]

---

[1] David-Danel; Delehaye, 1931 and 1962; Deubner; Julien and Ledermann; Julien, Ledermann and Touwaide; Skrobucha; Stiltingo; Wittmann.
[2] Grabar; Ward-Perkins.
[3] Deichmann; Wittmann, 22-23,
[4] Stiltingo, 441-459; Wittmann, 80-81.
[5] Jackson; Rousselle; Sudhoff; Temkin.
[6] See for example, Lehrman.

Towns and shrines have been dedicated to the medical saints, as have academic, secular, and professional groups of surgeons, physicians, and pharmacists. Scholarly works examine their active festivals in Italy and Sicily and their iconography.[7] David-Danel has shown how the various images of the saints reflect the development of medicine itself: with the palm branch, they have held books, spatulae, pots of ointment, scalpels, urinals, blood-letting instruments, and test tubes.[8]

How and why did Cosmas and Damian come to Toronto? In this city and elsewhere, veneration seems to belong to Italian immigrant communities, and some explanations can be found in the recent sociological studies of immigrant Italians and popular Catholicism among them.[9] I wanted to know if there were something special about these doctor saints? Officials of St Francis of Asissi Church on Grace street referred me to the former parish priest, Father Rafaello (Ralph) Paonessa and to the donor family.

Lively festivals are a feature of the yearly cycle of the St. Francis parish: at Christmas, a life-sized, illuminated crèche occupies an outer wall of the church and carols are played on a loudspeaker; at Easter, a passion play receives media attention. Celebration of the feast day of Cosmas and Damian began in 1987. On September 27, or the nearest Sunday to it, a special mass ends with a procession of people who are profoundly religious, some who are sick, and some who have sick friends or relatives; they are led by life-sized, polychrome, wooden statues. Police stop traffic on two major streets to allow the procession to pass. Over a decade, the celebration grew to a triduum—or three days of masses, and St Michael the Archangel has joined in the devotions. This is the first festival dedicated to the medical saints in Canada.[10]

The inspiration came from Ersilia Jannetta (Mrs Di Gregorio). Ersilia came to Canada in 1953 from Campobasso, and has now retired from working as a babysitter. She was one of twelve children born to a midwife and a former monk. Her family attended local religious celebrations, including the Cosmas and Damian festival in Isernia, but they were devoted to all the saints. When Ersilia came to Canada, she felt the absence of the medical saints in particular and vowed to bring them to

---

[7] Wittmann, 32-37. A host of guidebooks provide details of local festivals. For example, Martellotta; Vacca.
[8] David-Danel.
[9] Iacovetta; Orsi; Carroll, 1986, 1989, and 1992; Zucchi, 25, 137-140.
[10] Sites of pilgrmage and thaumaturgic healing are numerous in Canada, especially in Quebec. See Boglioni and Lacroix.

Toronto. After saving for many years, her family provided the funds for the purchase and air-transport of the statues from Rome. Ersilia showed me tangible evidence of the first Toronto miracle: a carefully wrapped cane and written testimonial of a woman who had been healed of a knee ailment and spared surgical amputation. In leaving her cane with Ersilia, the woman said, "The saints help me, I help the saints." Ersilia told me that modern medicine, doctors, and hospitals were good, but they do not provide hope; the Anargyroi bring hope to everyone when the medicine runs out.[11]

Father Ralph Paonessa is an enthusiastic priest dedicated to church traditions. He denies his own influence and credits the festival's success to the keen and intense devotion of the donor family. Having had small contact with his exuberant charm, I find his modest statement difficult to believe. I asked him about the relation of the statues to the celebration. He explained that they were necessary accoutrements, like the proper set for a grand opera. Alluding to the tremendous social function of the ceremonies, he told me that "hard feelings" arose as people in Utica, New York, complained about the loss of Toronto pilgrims who used to attend a feast there and seemed to have stolen the idea.[12]

The Utica Celebration

Obviously something had been happening in upstate New York, that was directly related to the founding of the Toronto cult. I have twice attended the Cosmas and Damian celebration at the church of St Anthony of Padua in Utica, and I have spoken with its organizer, Deacon William Dischiavo, whose paternal grandmother was a founder.[13] Established by Italian immigrants in 1912, a year after the founding of their church, the Utica festival was modeled on the same celebration in their home Alberobello, southern Italy. Signora Dischiavo (née Gerardi) was born in Foggia, Italy, and came to the United States in 1904 with her parents, three sisters, and one brother. Her family worked in the cotton mills. No special attention was given to the medical saints in Foggia, but she was deeply devoted to them and to the patron of the parish from her late teens until her death at age 90 in 1983. Deacon Dischiavo remembers her intense prayers during a particularly wet celebration in the

---

[11] Interview with Ersilia Jannetta her daughter, Mary Colanardi, as translator, 15 February 1992.
[12] Interview with Rafaello Paonessa, priest St Lawrence the Martyr church, Scarborough, 13 March 1992.
[13] Interview with Deacon William Dischiavo, 18 July 1994; Cimino.

1950s when he was seven or eight years old: it had rained all night and the ground was sodden; his grandmother knelt in the mud praying fervently for his older brother who was severely afflicted with polio. The brother lived with only minor sequelae.

Since its inception, the Utica celebration has taken the form of one or more masses, a candlelight procession, and a daytime parade. Presently there are three masses: one for the sick on Friday, another on Saturday evening followed by a solemn candlelight procession through the neighbourhood streets, and a third on Sunday morning also followed by a procession, which is more festive, like a secular parade. Images of the saints abound, on banners at private homes and as statues in or near the church. Since the late 1940s, additional masses are held outdoors to accommodate the large crowds. A permanent outdoor altar was rebuilt twice, most recently in 1984 and at that time yet another set of statues in Carerra marble was commissioned from Rome. On the back of the outdoor altar is the double-winged caduceus (of Mercury) used by the American Medical Association: a wonderful juxtaposition of religious and professional symbolism complete with cultural slippage.

Deacon Dischiavo claims that Utica has the largest festival in North America. In the 1960s, attendance lagged and "only fourteen or fifteen busloads" of pilgrims would attend. During the early 1990s, however, ten to twelve thousand pilgrims attended annually, arriving in seventy or eighty busses. My survey of eighty-eight Utica pilgrims shows that the majority (80%) come every year, At least half travel six hours or more from the Ontario cities of Toronto, Guelph, Mississauga, Hamilton, Niagara Falls, Welland and St. Catherines. I asked these pilgrims why they do not celebrate in Toronto. They respond that the Utica festival is older, bigger, and more authentic, partly because it demands a greater financial and physical sacrifice. Others come from elsewhere in New York State; nearly a third of pilgrims are relative newcomers to the Utica festival.

For the celebration on 24 and 25 September 1994, hotels as far as forty-five minutes away were being booked in early July. When asked to account for the recent resurgence in popularity of the Utica celebration, Deacon Dischiavo immediately recognized the leadership of the "immigrants" who courageously built a life in a new land without forgetting the traditions of home. He believes that in disillusionment with modern ways, people are interested in "getting back to their roots" and returning to spirituality.[14] Like the Toronto priest, he recognizes the social and economic functions served by the celebration and influx of visitors: traditional foods, decoration of homes, music and dancing, and the chance to greet old friends.

I asked if there had been miracles. Deacon Dischiavo replied that his brother's healing from polio may have been assisted by the prayers of his grandmother for the intercession of the saints; however, he admitted that he has not asked his brother's own opinion of the cure. Other cures are inferred from the discarded casts and crutches left behind or gifts of gold, now worth an amount so considerable that they are kept in the church safe. Two Utica physicians participate enthusiastically in the procession. But Dischiavo cautioned that the healings are as much spiritual as physical.

When I asked why Torontonians still come to Utica, Dischiavo explained that approximately twenty years ago, in an effort to promote the Utica celebration, he placed an advertisement in a Toronto newspaper. That year, one bus left Toronto to join the other twenty to thirty buses travelling to Utica. The next year Torontonians filled three buses; the following year, fifteen.[15] After a few years of making the tiring journey, people in Toronto thought it might be easier to celebrate at home. Overworked and not lacking for pilgrims, Deacon Dischiavo did not betray the "hard feelings" that had been described in Toronto. As for why many Torontonians continue to make the trip to Utica when they could celebrate at home, he echoed the responses to my survey: people want "the sacrifice of pilgrimage"–"the journey" he said, "is part of the prayer."

The Surveys

To explore the advent of the medical saints to Toronto and other North American sites, I conducted surveys of pilgrims. My interest is in the twentieth century devotions, but the theories I found on the transmission of traditions forced me to consider the ancient past. In constructing the survey questions, I wished to be able to situate answers in light of four theoretical explanations, all of which seemed to make some sense with respect to these festivals: a genealogical theory of religions

---

[14] See for example, Simons.
[15] Another source enumerated 14 Toronto busses in 1983. Julien, 1985, p. 56.

and three theories from comparative mythology, the diffusion model, a psychoanalytic model, and a sociological model.[16]

1. ***Genealogy***. The pagan roots of Christianity have been explored as often as its Judaic roots. At least two parallels are uncontested and widely popularized: first, connections between Artemis (or Diana) in Ephesus and Mary, the mother of Jesus; and second, links between the healing god Asklepios (Aesculapius) and Jesus.[17] Even the early Church fathers recognized how the pagan practice of hero worship could be related to the Christian veneration of martyr saints.[18] In some places, people venerated deities from both religions at once.[19]

Like other saints, Cosmas and Damian find specific parallels in the pagan religion, in practices and in individuals. Two parish priests readily described them to me.[20] First, as mentioned already, some cures suggest incubation. Second, the practice of leaving votives was adopted in the fourth century C.E. and continues today at healing shrines. Third, pagan temples often became churches; those of the doctor saints were sometimes built in the defunct healing temples, or Asklepeia.[21] The Roman basilica to Cosmas and Damian occupied the Forum temple to Romulus. Fourth, the saintly attributes and functions of Cosmas and Damian are linked to the Greek and Roman Dioscuroi, the twin heroes, Castor and Pollux, born to Leda and Zeus who had assumed the form of the swan. The aforementioned basilica to Cosmas and Damian within the walls of the Roman forum is only a few meters from the temple to Castor and Pollux. Between the two temples lay the fountain of Juturna, a well capable of miraculous cures.[22]

This genealogical association of the saints with other divine twins may be part of a wider phenomenon, called "universal dioscurism."[23] Twin healers, called the Asvins or Näsatyas, are found in the Hindu pantheon. Germanic tribes venerated twin healers and Baltic tradition also claimed a pair of heroic twins. These observations have led to the hypothesis that twin gods may have been part of the prototypical religion

---

[16] For a summary of these perspectives, see Larson; Littleton 1966 (p. 33-38) and 1974.
[17] Campbell and Mohr, 180; Temkin, 75, 80; Ferngren.
[18] Brown; Theodoret.
[19] Harris, 63.
[20] Father Gregory of Toronto, September 1996, and Father F. J. Evans of Howard Beach, Long Island, N.Y., 12 August 1998.
[21] Jackson; Travlos, 127-137
[22] Grant, 82-90.
[23] Ward. Harris described the connection of the Dioscuri to the saintly pair Florus and Laurus.

of the Indo-European peoples.[24] Cosmas and Damian could be descended from a long, unbroken line of divine twins that has traversed several religions. But efforts to relate them to other twin gods are fraught with contradictions and lacunae.[25]

2. **Geographic model.** Much evidence supports diffusion from Italy (possibly via Utica, N.Y.) as an explanation for the coming of Cosmas and Damian to Toronto. Eighty per cent or more of Italians who live in Toronto came from southern Italy or Sicily,[26] where the saints are venerated with the most elaborate festivals.[27] My surveys show that the Toronto and Utica pilgrims also originated in the south of Italy. Cosmas and Damian are Eastern saints: their earliest following was in Byzantium. This diffusion model might be extended further back to the recognized link between ancient Greek culture and southern Italy, where mass was conducted in Greek until the eleventh century.

3. **Psycholanalytic model.** The psychoanalytic theory holds that myths function to preserve social and psychological stability. A psychoanalytic focus on the symbolic meaning of twins may help explain the extension of the cult. When asked if it was important that the saints were twins, seventy per cent of forty-six pilgrims in Toronto and a majority elsewhere said "yes." The powerful natural events of birth, life, illness, and death threaten moral, social, and psychological order. Twin healers may have been repeatedly discovered and rediscovered in different cultures and different times. According to the interpretation of the Apocryphal Acts of Thomas, Thomas was the mortal twin of the divine Jesus, a tradition said to signify the existence of an earlier cult of twins in that province.[28]

The existence of twin deities who cannot be linked to Indo-European origins supports this view: for example, the Egyptian gods, Isis and Osiris, one living, one dead, brother and sister gods of medicine, healing, death, and after-life. Twins represent fertility, an excess of

---

[24] Perrot, 1976, 17. A semantic relationship has been postulated between "Näsatyas" and the French word for birth "naissance" and the German verb to recover, "genesen."
[25] Amundsen; Brown; Harris; Jackson; Ward, 18; Wittman, Fig. 33, opp. 177.
[26] Bagnell; Harney; Jansen, 1986 and 1987.
[27] According to Martellotta, 1986, (p. 143), the sites and dates of origin of the most popular celebrations of the "santi medici" in Italy are Alberobello (1636), Bitonto (14thC), Elena (Gaeta), Isernia (1130), Maglie (Lecce), Matera (1230), Napoli (1604), Oria (8thC), Ravello (15thC), Anela (Sassari).
[28] See Gärtner; Perrot, 30; Pick.

vitality, and, in a sense, extra- or re-birth.[29] They may signify the triumph of life-giving order over the chaos of death. Like some anthropomorphized Yin and Yang, mythic twins may rehearse natural dualities in human existence: sickness and health; life and death; or in medical existence: diagnosis and non-diagnosis; therapeutic success and failure.

4. *Sociological model.* The sociological model implies that the saints fulfill active social functions peculiar not only on this cult, but to religious healing in general. That the saints are doctors is more important to pilgrims than their status as twins. When asked if it was important that the saints are doctors, sixty to eighty per cent of all pilgrims in all places responded "yes." Some thought I was mad to ask the question. "Of course, the saints are doctors!" they said, "good ones too!" Americans often told me (jokingly) that these saintly medics charge no fees.

About half the pilgrims in both Toronto and Utica said they knew of miracles; some qualified the answer by saying that they had heard of them, believed in them, or were "still waiting." A few provided first-hand accounts. Again like the ancient temple cures, dreams frequently figured in these stories, but almost all were healings from physical illness—and they took place in hospitals.[30] Many other pilgrims said that they attended the festival because of illness in themselves or a family member. In other words, they were consulting the doctor saints.

My problems in interpretation relate to the nature of the sources, which tend to participate in and obscure the social function of all healing cults. As with any historical endeavour, writer bias colours not only the analysis but also the selection of evidence. In the case of the medical saints, authors seem to be either absolute believers or absolute skeptics; there is little middle ground.[31] Thus the erudite Bollandist, Delehaye, went to some lengths to refute the suggestion that the twin saints have a genealogical connection to pagan deities.[32] Others look on the veneration of saints as a kind of magical corruption introduced into the purity of the early church. They contend that after the persecutions ended, the religion became popular with so-called "nominal Christians," who retained their pagan traditions, as opposed to the more devout early Christians, who had severed connections with their past, welcomed illness as

---

[29] Ward 1968 and 1970.
[30] 3 of 3 in Toronto; 8 of 11 in Utica; and 5 of 6 in Manhattan.
[31] On these problems, see Van Dam, 84-86.
[32] Delehaye, 1904 and 1962.

a good, and were ready to be eaten by lions.[33] Some even suggest that the expanding Church deliberately and dishonestly promoted devotion to homologous figures simply to enhance its appeal.[34]

Several scholars have attempted to distinguish between medicine, magic, and miracle.[35] But I doubt that anyone has made these distinctions successfully with respect to other people, let alone other cultures. Since Hippocrates at least, western medicine has self-consciously defined itself by its opposition to magic and religion. But Hippocratic medicine was used by both Christians and pagans in a manner that complemented and interpreted the articles of faith. Since the earliest times, societies have kept a place for parallel forms of religious healing. Ours does too, although only a few medical historians have noticed.[36]

Sick people partake of all the traditions around them.[37] The fuzzy boundaries between these categories are falsely sharpened by doctors, priests, and, indeed, by historians of medicine who tend to focus on one or another category, as if it were entirely distinct from the others.[38] To a believer of one faith, other religious practices are magical. To a confident physician, all other forms of practice, including earlier medicines, are magical.

Magic used to be portrayed as the first step along continuum through religion to science–a trend reified by an older generation of medical historians who saw the magic of "primitive" medicine steadily swept away by the march of science. Recent scholarship has tried to avoid this positivistic perspective through the conceptual vehicles of social function and "placebo effect"; some go so far as to acknowledge, if not recommend, ritual in practice.[39] But no healers in the late twentieth century choose to call themselves "magicians". Even self-identified professional magicians are known to all–not as healers or wizards–but as kindly deceivers of children.

The problem with magic is the word–a word readily applied to the "story" told by someone else, from another culture or another time.[40] If

---

[33] Amundsen, 1986; Amundsen and Ferngren, 1986; Ferngren, 1992. Jesus was often described as a healer, but Ferngren maintains that until the fourth century, this title referred to healing of the soul not of the body.
[34] See for example, Carpenter 1971, 201, 205; Harris.
[35] Kee; Lloyd; Temkin; Thomas.
[36] Numbers; Risse.
[37] See for example, Berland.
[38] Canguilhem.
[39] Eamon; Preston; Souverbie; Webster.
[40] These ideas are informed by K.M. Hunter's work on narrative structure in medicine.

the illness story told by a patient does not correspond to the story told by an observer, then the observer will likely label the process as "magic." But a story told about an illness is, in a sense, the construction of a disease; and therapies must be consistent with the perceived concept of that disease.

Cosmas and Damian turn out to be active consultants in a health care smorgasbord. The separation of medicine, magic, and miracle is an artifact of scholarship. For the Ersilia Jannettas of this world, they are one. And they are one for thousands who find help from the medical saints or at healing shrines elsewhere in Canada and around the world. Perhaps medicine, magic, and miracle are united not only for this particular social group, but also for the academics jogging across the campus, for the purveyors of holistic medicine, and for the consumers of tofu. Modern medicine offers indifferent probability and cold technology; the thaumaturgic saints promise hope against hope.

Ironically, then, it may be the miracle of modern medicine that provides greatest impetus for the continuing miracles of faith. Herein may lie the best explanation for how, on a specific day next September, you will find new statues of ancient twins making their way down a Toronto street.

WORKS CITED

Amundsen, Darrel W. "The Medieval Christian Tradition." *Caring and Curing. Health and Medicine in the Western Religious Traditions.* Eds. Ronald L. Numbers and Darrel W. Amundsen. New York and London: Macmillan, 1986. 65-107.

Amundsen, Darrel W., and Gary B. Ferngren. "The Early Christian Tradition." *Caring and Curing. Health and Medicine in the Western Religious Traditions.* Eds. Ronald L. Numbers and Darrel W. Amundsen. New York and London: Macmillan, 1986. 40-60.

Bagnell, Kenneth. *Canadese. A Portrait of the Italian Canadians.* Toronto: Macmillan, 1989.

Berland, Warren. "Can the Self Affect the Course of Cancer: Unexpected Cancer Recovery: Why Patients Believe They Survive." *Advances; The Journal of Mind Body Health* 11.4 (1995): 5-19.

Boglioni, Pierre, and Benoît Lacroix. *Les pèlerinages au Québec.* Québec: P U Laval, 1981.

Brown, Peter. *The Cult of the Saints: Its Rise and Function in Latin Christianity.* Chicago: U of Chicago P, 1981.

Campbell, Joseph, Bill Moyers, and Betty Sue Flowers (ed.). *The Power of Myth.* New York: Doubleday, 1988.

Canguilhem, Georges. "Histoire des religions et histoires des sciences." *Mélanges Alexandre Koyré*. Vol. 2. Paris: Hermann, 1964. 69-87.

Carpenter, Edward. *Pagan and Christian Creeds. Their Origin and Meaning*. New York: Harcourt Brace and Company, 1971.

Carroll, Michael P. *The Cult of the Virgin Mary: Psychological Origins*. Princeton: Princeton University Press, 1986.

_____. *Catholic Cults and Devotions: A Psychological Inquiry*. Montreal and Kingston: McGill Queen's U P, 1989.

_____. *Madonnas That Maim: Popular Catholicism in Italy since the Fifteenth Century*. Baltimore and London: Johns Hopkins U P, 1992.

Cimino, Stephen F. *St. Anthony of Padua Church, 1911-1986*. Utica, N.Y.: St. Anthony of Padua Church, 1987.

David-Danel, Marie-Louise. *Iconographie des saints médecins Côme et Damien*. Lille: Morel et Corduant, 1958.

Deichmann, Friedrich Wilhelm. *Ravenna, Hauptstadt des spätantiken Abendlandes*. 3 vols. Stuttgart: Franz Steiner, 1989.

Delehaye, Hippolyte. "Castor Et Pollux Dans Les Légendes Hagiographiques (Essay Review)." *Analecta Bollandiana* XXIII (1904): 427-32.

_____. "Commentarius perpetuus in martyrologium hieronymianum." *Acta Sanctorum*. November, vol. II part 2. Bruxelles: J. de Meester et filii, Actorum Bollandianorum, 1931. 528-30.

_____. *The Legends of the Saints*. Trans. Donald Attwater. New York: Fordham U P, 1962.

Deubner, Ludwig. *Kosmas und Damien. Texte und Einleitung* [1907]. Leipzig: Aalen Scienta Verlag, 1980.

Eamon, W. "Technology as Magic in the Late Middle Ages and the Renaissance." *Janus* 70 (1983): 171-203.

Ferngren, Gary B. "Early Christianity as a Religion of Healing." *Bulletin of the History of Medicine* 66 (1992): 1-15.

Gärtner, Bertil. *The Theology of the Gospel of Thomas*. London: Collins, 1961.

Grabar, André. *Martyrium. Recherches sur le culte des reliques et l'art chrétien antique*. London: Variorum, 1972.

Grant, Michael. *The Roman Forum*. London: Weidenfeld and Nicolson, 1970.

Harney, Robert F. "Toronto's Little Italy." *Little Italies in North America*. Eds. Robert F. Harney and J. Vincenza Scarpacci. Toronto: Multicultural History Society of Ontario, 1981. 41-62.

Harris, J. Rendel. *The Dioscuri in Christian Legends*. London: C.J. Clay and Cambridge U P, 1903.

Hunter, Kathryn Montgomery. *Doctors' Stories: The Narrative Structure of Medical Knowledge*. Princeton, N.J.: Princeton U P., 1991.

Iacovetta, Franca. *Such Hardworking People: Italian Immigrants in Post-War Toronto*. Montreal and Kingston: McGill-Queen's University Press, 1992.

Jackson, Ralph. *Doctors and Diseases in the Roman Empire*. Norman and London: U of Oklahoma P, 1988.

Jansen, Clifford J. *Factbook on Italians in Canada.* Toronto: Department of Sociology York U, 1987.

Jansen, Clifford J. *Italians in a Multicultural Canada.* Canadian Studies Series Vol. 1. Lewiston and Queenston: Edwin Mellen P, 1988.

Julien, Pierre. *Saint Côme et Saint Damien, patrons des médecins, chirurgiens, et pharmaciens.* Paris: Louis Pariente, 1980.

──────────. "Côme et Damien, hier et aujourd'hui: quelques questions." *Saint Côme et Saint Damien. Culte et iconographie.* Eds. Pierre Julien and François Ledermann. Zurich: Juris Druck, 1985. 43-62.

Julien, Pierre, and François Ledermann, eds. *Saint Côme et Saint Damien. Culte et iconographie. Colloque, Mendriso, September 29-30, 1985.* Zurich: Juris Druck & Verlag, 1985.

Julien, Pierre, François Ledermann, and Alain Touwaide. *Cosmo e Damiano dal culto popolare alla protezione di chirurghi, medici, e farmacisti: Aspetti e immagini.* Milan: Antea edizioni, 1993.

Kee, Howard Clark. *Medicine, Miracle, and Magic in New Testament Times.* Cambridge: Cambridge U P, 1986.

Larson, Gerald James. "Introduction; the Study of Mythology and Comparative Mythology." *Myth in Indo-European Antiquity.* Eds. Gerald James Larson, C. Scott Littleton and Jaan Puhvel. Berkeley, Los Angeles, London: U of California P, 1974. 1-16.

Lehrman, Arthur. "The Miracle of Cosmas and Damien." *Plastic and Reconstructive Surgery* 94 (1994): 218-21.

Littleton, C. Scott, ed. *The New Comparative Mythology. An Anthropological Assessment of the Theories of Georges Dumézil.* Berkeley: U of California P, 1966.

Littleton, C. Scott. "Georges Dumézil and the Rebirth of the Genetic Model. An Anthropological Appreciation." *Myth in Indo-European Antiquity.* Eds. Gerald James Larson, C. Scott Littleton and Jaan Puhvel. Berkeley: U of California P, 1974. 169-79.

Lloyd, Geoffrey E.R. *Magic, Reason, and Experience. Studies in the Origins and Development of Greek Science.* Cambridge: Cambridge U P, 1979.

Martellotta, Angelo. *Memorie istoriche ed il presente nel culto dei SS. Medici ricorrendo il 350° anniversario della devozione Alberobellese.* Alberobello, 1986.

Numbers, Ronald L. " Garrison Lecture, 1997: Faith, Hope, and Charity; The Religious Roots of American Health Care," *Bulletin of the History of Medicine.* forthcoming.

Orsi, Robert Anthony. *The Madonna of 115th Street: Faith and Community in Italian Harlem.* New Haven and London: Yale U P, 1985.

Perrot, Jean. *Mythe et littérature sous le signe des jumeaux.* Paris: Presses Universitaires de la France, 1976.

Pick, Bernard. *The Apocryphal Acts of Paul, Peter, John, Andrew and Thomas.* Chicago: Open Court Publishing, 1909.

Preston, J. J. "Necessary Fictions: Healing Encounters with a North American Saint." *Literature and Medicine* 8 (1989): 42-62.

Risse, Guenter B. *Mending Bodies; Saving Souls: A History of Hospitals.* New York and Oxford: Oxford U P, 1999.
Rouselle, Robert. "Healing Cults in Antiquity." *Journal of Psychohistory* 12.Winter 1985 (1984-5): 339-52.
Simons, Marlise. "Spiritual Values. Why Catholics Are Flocking to Shrines." *Globe and Mail* 14 October 1993, A21.
Skrobucha, Heinz. *The Patrons of the Doctors.* Trans. Hann Hermann Rosenwald. Pictoral Library of Eastern Church Art, Vol. 7. Recklinghausen, West Germany: Aurel Bongers, 1965.
Souverbie, M.-T. "Magie et médecine." *Histoire de la Médecine* 20 mars 1970: 3-43.
Stiltingo, Joanne. "De SS Cosma, Damiano, Anthilmo, Leontio et Euprepio Mm. Aegis in Cilicia." *Acta Sanctorum.* Vol. September vol. VII. Antwerp. 428-78.
Sudhoff, Karl. "Healing Miracles of SS. Cosmas-Damian and Cyrus-John." *Essays in the History of Medicine.* Ed. Fielding H. Garrison. New York: Medical Life Press, 1926. 219-21.
Temkin, Oswei. *Hippocrates in a World of Pagans and Christians.* Baltimore: Johns Hopkins U P, 1991.
Theodoret de Cyr. *Thérapeutique des maladies helléniques.* Trans. Pierre Canivet. Vol. 2. 2 vols. vols. Paris: Cerf, 1958.
Thomas, Keith Vivian. *Religion and the Decline of Magic.* New York: Charles Scribner's Sons, 1971.
Travlos, J. *Pictorial Dictionary of Ancient Athens.* London: Thames and Hudson, 1971.
Vacca, Domenico. *Reading the Life of the Holy Doctors: Cosma and Damiano.* Trans. N.Y. English translation "with ecclesiastical approval" by Joseph De Candia of Howard Beach, N.Y. Bitonto: np, 1973.
Van Dam, Raymond. *Saints and Their Miracles in Late Antique Gaul.* Princeton, N.J.: Princeton U P, 1993.
Ward, Donald J. "The Separate Functions of the Indo-European Divine Twins." *Myth and Law among the Indo-Europeans.* Ed. Jaan Puhvel. Berkeley, London, Los Angeles: U of California P, 1970. 193-202.
Ward, Donald. *The Divine Twins. An Indo-European Myth in Germanic Tradition.* Berkeley: U of California P, 1968.
Ward-Perkins, J.B. "Memoria, Martyr's Tomb and Martyr's Church." *Journal of Theological Studies* N.S. XVII, Pt. I (1966): 20-37.
Webster, C. *From Paracelsus to Newton: Magic and the Making of Modern Science. The Eddington Memorial Lectures.* Cambridge: Cambridge U P, 1982.
Wittmann, Anneliese. *Kosmas und Damien. Kultausbreitung und Volksdevotion.* Berlin: E. Schmidt, 1967.
Zucchi, John E. *Italians in Toronto: Development of a National Identity, 1875-1935.* Montreal and Kingston: McGill Queen's U P, 1988.

Awad Eddie Halabi

Tradition and the Tombs of the Prophet Moses: The Medieval Islamic Period*

ABSTRACT This paper investigates the origins of both the Islamic shrine and annual festival of the Prophet Moses (al-Nabi Musa), from its earliest recorded evidence in the mid-thirteenth century until the period of Ottoman conquest in 1516. Seven kilometers south-west of Jericho, the Egyptian Mamluk Sultan al-Malik al-Zahir Runk al-Din Baybars(1223-1277) constructed a dome over a tomb which Islamic popular tradition had identified as the tomb of the Prophet Moses. Baybars also encouraged a local annual festival celebrating the Prophet Moses, which involved a pilgrimage from Jerusalem to the Moses shrine. The concern that Christian forces could retake Jerusalem encouraged Sultan Baybars to promote the Prophet Moses festival, which attracted Muslim worshippers from the villages and towns of Palestine to Jerusalem. Thus, the local, popular and relatively minor shrine in the Judean desert commemorating the Prophet Moses was transformed to become a significant, state-sponsored shrine, which attracted Muslim worshippers from throughout Palestine. By examining the contemporary chronicles discussing Sultan Baybars' construction of the shrine, and the earliest performances of the festival, we can then appreciate how a local, popular shrine was appropriated to address the concerns of state officials. Ultimately, the shrine and the festival reveal a great deal about the dynamics existing between popular religious beliefs and state-sponsored religious practices.

Introduction:

During the earliest period of Islamic history, Muslim worshippers and scholars debated the location of the tomb of the Prophet Moses (*al-Nabi Musa*). Eventually, Muslim worshippers honoured a number of sites where Moses was supposedly interred. Understanding how beliefs in these several tombs arose requires appreciating the blending of "popular" and scholarly tradition revering the *bilad al-Sham* ("Greater Syria")[1] as the land of Islam's Jewish and Christian biblical prophets.

---

* When translating from Arabic, I have forgone using diacritical marks. For most Arabic plurals, I have simply added an "s" to the original singular form of the word.
[1] This region denotes the contemporary states of Syria, Lebanon, Jordan, Israel and the borders of British Mandate Palestine (1923-1947).

Saints and the Sacred - A St. Michael's College Symposium
Joseph Goering, Francesco Guardiani, Giulio Silano eds. Ottawa: Legas, 2001

Within the *bilad al-Sham* lay *al-ard al-muqaddasa*, the "Holy Land," where God delivered His divine message to the Christian and Jewish communities (*ahl al-Kitab*) before He bestowed His Final Revelation on the Prophet Muhammad, the "Seal" (*khatam*) of the Prophets (*al-Qur'an* XXXIII: 40).[2] The tradition of honouring Greater Syria as the Holy Land is the context for understanding how ordinary Muslim worshippers as well as scholars attributed various sites for the tomb of Moses.

Islamic Tradition and the Holy Land:

The way in which Muslim scholars, such as the transmitters of sayings of the Prophet Muhammad, historians, exegetes, and geographers, conceived of Islam's historical relationship to the other revealed religions arose from the *Qur'an* itself (Duri, 21; Khalidi, 69).

Principally, the *Qur'an* constructed a vision of history which was, as A. Duri remarks, "...a succession of prophetic missions - all essentially a single message preached by various prophets, the last of whom, Muhammad, was the *khatam* (the Seal)." (Duri, 21) The *Qur'an*'s own depictions of the Final Revelation given to Muhammad as being the true singular divine message originally imparted to God's earlier prophets, unaltered by the sectarian schisms within Christianity and Judaism, is clearly expounded in a verse from *Surat al-Baqara* (The Cow):

> They say: "Become Jew or become Christians, and find the right way". Say: "No. We follow the way of Abraham the upright, who was not an idolater." Say: "We believe in God and what has been sent down to us, and what had been revealed to Abraham and Ishmael and Isaac and Jacob and their progeny, and that which was given to Moses and Christ, and to all other prophets by the Lord. We make no distinction among them, and we submit to Him. (II: 135-136)

In the attempt to elaborate and clarify the historical discourse in the *Qur'an* about the Jewish and Christian prophets, Muslim story-tellers and scholars drew upon Jewish and Christian legends and tales, or in some cases exact references from the biblical texts themselves, of biblical characters and events. (Schwarzbaum, 34-39; Heller).

One type of literature which reflected the *Qur'an*'s view of Islam's historical relationship to the biblical peoples is the *Adab al-Isra'iliyyat* (Israelite or Children of Israel Literature), stories which focused on the biblical Jewish people, or didactic and edifying tales set within the historical period of ancient Israelites (*`Ahd Bani Isra'il*). Storytellers, mystics, and

---

[2] All citations and translations are taken from Yusif Ali's *al-Qur'an*.

chroniclers of Islamic and pre-Islamic history were known to have narrated these tales. (Vajda, 211-212; Binner, 1988a, 400-401).

The most prominent compiler of this literature was the early eighth century Yemenite of Persian descent Wahb Ibn Munabbih (d. 732), who collected the tales and myths of the Jewish people from seventh century compilers, and gathered additional tales through his own contacts with the "People of the Book.." (referring to Christians and Jews; Schwarzbaum, 58; Khoury)

Later writers and `ulama' (doctors of law) expunged Wahb Ibn Munabbih's stories of their folkloric elements, and pejoratively depicted the entire genre of *Isra'iliyyat* literature as "popular" stories (sing. *qissa*, pl. *qisas*) dismissed by "serious" chroniclers or *hadith* compilers. (Brinner 1988a, 401) Yet, Wahb Ibn Munabbih's ability to uphold the world-view of the *Qur'an* – of Mankind witnessing a universal unfolding of prophetic missions – strongly encouraged many Muslim worshippers and some writers living in the *bilad al-Sham* area to posit this region as the fulcrum between the religion of the Final Revelation – Islam – and the religion of the earlier revelations – Christianity and Judaism.

A complement to the literature on the biblical Jews were the written tales focusing on the histories or stories of the pre-Islamic Prophets, known collectively as the *Qisas al-Anbiya'* (Stories of the Prophets), compiled by writers such as Ahmad al-Tha`labi, in his `*Ara'is al-Majalis* and the versions of the *Qisas* written in the name of Muhammad b. `Abd Allah al-Kisa'i.

These hagiographies initially arose within Islamic discourse as orally transmitted tales narrated by storytellers to an audience at a mosque or the court of a ruler. Generally, the storyteller's (sing. *qass*, pl. *qussas*) technique was to interpolate references about prophets mentioned in the *Qur'an* to his own embellished narrative. (Pinault, 735-736) For instance, al-Kisa'i's discussion of "The Creation of the Earth, Mountains and the Seas" is an extended collation of qur'anic references (XLI:9; XXI:31; II:24; etc.) alongside his own extraneous narrative (Kisa'i, 26). For Muslim worshippers, these popular stories enhanced a tradition they had cultivated of identifying biblical prophets and events mentioned in the *Qur'an* with the areas generally encompassing Greater-Syria (Brinner, 1988b, 466; Nagel, 176).

A final literary tradition which specifically stressed the importance of Jerusalem in the Greater-Syria region was the *Fada'il al-Quds*, the Praise Literature of Jerusalem. This panegyric prose borrowed from a wide variety of literary genres, such as oral traditions attributed to Muhammad or to those close to him, *Qur'an*ic exegesis, legends or popular stories, and historical compendiums, to elevate the status of Jerusalem in Islam. This praise literature highlighted the prominent figures and significant events in Islamic, Judaic, and Christian religious traditions associated with Jerusalem. Examples include stories and sayings eulogising the Jewish Temple; miracles performed by Jesus; praises of Jerusalem for being designated the first *qiblah* (direction of prayer, *Qur'an* II: 136-139); and the popular association of Jerusalem and the Temple Mount with the *al-Masjid al-Aqsa* (the distant mosque, *al-Qur'an* XVII: 1), the place to which Muhammad was transported during his Night Journey (*Lailat al-Isra'*; Hirschberg, 314-335; Sivan, 266-267).

Clearly, the Israelite Literature, Stories of the Prophets, and the Praise Literature of Jerusalem celebrated Islam's historical lineage in the Christian and Jewish bibles. For Muslim worshippers and scholars in the *bilad al-Sham* region, they expressed their belief in this tradition by associating the Greater Syria region as the Holy Land, the home of Islam's biblical prophets.

The tenth century geographer Muhammad b. Ahmad al-Muqaddasi is representative of the Muslim geographers who conceived of *bilad al-Sham* as containing Islam's biblical past. In his chapter on the province of Syria (*iqlim al-Sham*), a variant of the term *bilad al-Sham*, the author extols the regions' religious heritage: "Syria," he writes, "is the land of prophets, the abode of righteous men, the home of the Saints!... [it is] the Holy Land (*al-ard al-muqaddasa*)..." Guided by the *Qur'an*'s historical narrative of the Christian and Jewish prophets, he continues by enumerating the regions important figures, such as: Abraham, Job, David, Solomon, Isaac and his mother; Jacob, Saul; Goliath; Jeremiah, Zechariah, and Jesus. The author adds that within this province was, "...the tomb of Moses...as well as other holy places without number, and conspicuous excellences" (242-247).

Yet, it is important to recognize that although the tales of biblical prophets and the veneration of Jerusalem were components of a religious tradition adhered to by the Muslim faithful within *bilad al-Sham*, and by some outside it (Hasson, 366), many Muslim scholars, failed to accept either tradition. For the Muslim scholars critical of these traditions, they regarded stories of the prophets and the veneration of Jerusalem as *bid`a*, knowledge of Islam which is not based on the traditional sources of Islamic education – the *Qur'an* and the *Sunna* (the actions of the Prophets; Goitein, 141).

Nonetheless, these genres permeated the belief systems of Muslim worshippers and filtered into the literary works of some scholars. The ability for these stories and the religious traditions they promoted to circulate and to enter the "popular consciousness" of Muslim worshippers and scholars, especially in the *bilad al-Sham* area, contributed to the founding of various shrines and sites honouring the life and death of Moses.

The tombs of the Prophet Moses in Islamic Literature:

Muslim worshippers and scholars learned of biblical figures through the *Qur'an*, for example Moses preaching to the Pharaoh of Egypt (XX:8-99); hearing God speak from the burning bush (XX:12; LXXIX:16); and receiving the divinely inscribed tablets (VII:139). An important lacuna in this narration is the discussion of Moses' death. According to the Hebrew biblical account, Moses died in the land of Moab after ascending Mount Nebo, without having entered the Holy Land, being buried in a location unknown to the Children of Israel (Deuteronomy XXXIV: 1-10).

Therefore, one source for the debate amongst Muslim writers concerning the location of Moses' tomb appeared in response to an oral tradition or saying of Muhammad (*hadith al-nabawi*). In the accounts of Moses' death, we encounter an *hadith* in which Muhammad described seeing Moses' tomb situated at the side of the road under the red hill (*al-Kathib al-Ahmar*) during his Night Journey (*Lailat al-Isra'*, XVII:1) from Mecca to Jerusalem. Muhammad conveyed to his companions: "If I were there with you, I would have showed you his tomb next to the road at the Red Hill (*fa-law kuntu thamma li-araytukum qabrahu ila janibi al-tariqi `inda 'l-kathibi al-ahmari*). This saying is cited by many of the most notable compilers of Prophetic traditions, such as Muhammad al-Bukhari (Vol. IV, 407, No. 616), Ibn al-Hajjaj Muslim (Vol. IV, 1368-1373), `Ali al-Nasa'i (Vol. I, 363) and Ahmad Ibn Hanbal (Vol. III, 120 and Vol. V, 362-365).[3]

Thus, confronted with the absence of a qur'anic account of Moses' death, and presented with a vague topographical reference in a saying of Muhammad, Muslim writers relied on geographic areas mentioned prominently in the qur'anic narration of Moses' life to determine the location of his tomb. Significantly, Muslim scholars and worshippers

---

[3] These traditions are dealt with extensively by A. El'ad in, "Some Aspects of the Islamic Traditions Regarding the Site of the Grave of Moses."

interpreted all the areas cited in the qur'anic account of Moses' life, such as the desert, Jericho, and Midyan, as found within the *bilad al-Sham* region. As such, for Muslim writers already familiar with an Islamic tradition of associating the *bilad al-Sham*/Greater-Syria region with the *al-ard al-muqaddasa*/the Holy Land, debating the site of Moses' tomb became a natural extension of this tradition.

The writings of medieval Muslim geographers best demonstrate the linkage Muslim scholars forged between *bilad al-Sham* and Islam's biblical legacy. In the *Surat al-Ma'idah* (The Feast), the *Qur'an* tells of how God forced the Jewish people to wander the desert for forty years, in punishment for their poor faith in God and his prophet Moses (V: 21-26). While a number of tenth century geographers place the desert as a region lying roughly between Syria and Egypt, it is the twelfth century geographer Muhammad b. Muhammad Idrisi who invoked a religious inflection, writing that the desert: "...is called *fahs al-tih* (the Wilderness of the Wanderings), for it was here that the Children of Israel wondered in the time of Moses." (21). The grand thirteenth century geographical dictionary of `Abdallah Yaqut similarly reverts to the historical narrative in the *Qur'an*:

> ...and it [the desert] is the place where Moses, peace be upon him, and his people, went astray (*dalla*)...and it is said that the tribe of Israel (*bani Isra'il*) entered the desert and there was no one over the age of sixty or under the age of twenty, and they all died in the course of forty years, and none of them emerged from it who entered it with Musa...except Yush` b. Nun [Joshua, Num. 1: 4] and Kalab b. Yufunna [Caleb son of Jephunneh, Num. 13: 6] rather, they got out immediately afterward. (Vol. II, 69)

The thirteenth century geographer Muhammad al-Qazwini adds that it was in the desert during the wanderings of Moses and his people that Moses struck twelve springs (*al-Qur'an* II: 60), one for each of the twelve tribes (*al-asbat*) of Israel. (Qazwini, 174)

Similarly, other geographic areas were related to the qur'anic account of Moses' life. In his treatment of Midyan, present-day north-west Saudia Arabia, al-Yaqut quotes various transmitters who identified the region as the place where Moses struck springs of water for his people to drink (Yaqut, Vol. V, 77). Qazwini writes of Jericho (*Ariha*) as the village of the *al-`Amaliqah* (Amalekites) which Joshua and Kaleb succeeded in conquering (Joshua 1: 1) after the Children of Israel wandered in the desert for forty years (*al-Qur'an* V: 26; Qazwini,142-143). Clearly, medieval Muslim geographers adopted the traditions recognising the

Greater Syria region as the Holy Land – the land of Islam's biblical heritage – when discussing the qur'anic narration of Moses' life.

The veneration for this prophet, of course, existed within the larger cultural spectrum in Sunni and Shi`i Islam of revering the tombs of holy persons.

Without the funds to finance the construction of a mosque or to provide remuneration for a cleric, and usually living at some distance from towns or cities, local peasant and bedouin religious practices involved designating specific sites as places of veneration, for example, the tomb of a Sufi shaykh, a cave reputed to be inhabited by the spirits of a holy person, as well as the tombs of Judaic, Christian or Islamic personalities (Cannan).

Tombs of Moses in the Greater-Syria Region:

The Islamic tradition which linked the *bilad al-Sham* region to Islam's biblical lineage, along with the universal[4] Islamic practice of the veneration of saints, resulted in Muslim worshippers identifying various sites as the tomb of Moses.

Damascus, the main centre of *bilad al-Sham*, became known for several of these tombs.[5] The famed eleventh century chronicler of Syria, `Ali al-Raba`i, related that the tomb of Moses was near Damascus, (49-50), while Ibn `Asakir quoted a tenth century source who considered it at *al-Ghuta*, the plain located south of Damascus, near *al-Qadam* Mosque (Vol. II, 22; Ibn Jubayr, 282). According to a tradition recorded by Ibn Hibban, Muhammad witnessed Moses standing in his tomb praying, between `*Aliya* and `*Uwayliya*, a site also near *al-Qadam* mosque (230); but the twelfth century chronicler Ibn `Asakir, placed the tomb in the town of al-Qati`, near Damascus. (Vol. II, 94)

While the Damascus sites may have attracted much interest, other areas in the Greater-Syria region became more immediately associated with the qur'anic discussion of Moses' life, and as a consequence, Moses' tomb. The Persian traveller `Ali al-Harawi visited Jerusalem during the Crusader period, and it appears he is the first chronicler to mention the tomb of Moses near Jericho before the Mamluk Egyptian Sultan Baybars (ruled 1260-1277) converted it into a shrine. "Jericho (Riha)," he writes, "is a village (*qaraya*) [and] in it is a tomb they say is for Moses. It appears that Jericho is the city of *al-Jabbarin* (i.e the Canaanites) men-

---

[4] The term is Meri's, 44.
[5] Joseph Sadan discusses the sources citing many of these tombs in his, "Le Tombeau de Moise a Jéricho et a Damas."

tioned in the *Qur'an* [V: 22]." (Harawi, 18) A second writer to mention the Jericho tomb was the jurist, historian and transmitter of Prophetic traditions al-Hafiz Diya al-Maqdasi (d. 1245), who is also the first to associate the Jericho tomb with the oral tradition of Muhammad seeing Moses' tomb at the "Red Hill." "It is well known (*ishtahara*)," claimed al-Maqdasi, "that Moses' tomb is in the Holy Land and it is near Jericho. And it is said that the tomb of Moses is at the Red Hill (*al-kathib al-ahmar*) and its road." (Ibn Jama`ah Abu al-Baqa', folio 110)

However, even Harawi mentioned tombs other than the Jericho site, which were similarly related to the *Qur'an's* accounts of Moses' life. During his travels, Harawi later writes that in the land of Moab, the mountainous region lying on the east banks of the Dead Sea, "... is a village called Shayhan; in it is a tomb (*qabr*) which a light (*nur*) descends on it [and] which the people see. It is on a mountain and they maintain that it is the tomb of Moses." (19) As Muslim geographers had already associated the Moab region with the desert where the Children of Israel wandered for forty years, and as Christian and Jewish tradition had recognized the mountains near Shayhan as the biblical Mount Nebo, Muslim worshippers naturally developed adoration for this area, too. The geographer al-Qazwini claims that a valley in the Moab region known by worshippers as the Valley of Moses (*Wadi* Musa) is the place where Moses descended and struck twelve springs for the twelve tribes of Israel before God ended his life (*thumma qubida* Musa; 279). And finally, the chronicler Muhammad Ibn Shaddad writes that another tomb of Moses could be found in the Moab area in the village of Irbid, near the present-day capital of Amman . (275-276)

Conclusion:

A natural evolution for the esteem Islamic tradition had for the Holy Land was the many popular shrines venerating Moses in the *bilad al-Sham*. The tombs at Damascus and its environs, Irbid, Jericho, the Valley of Moses, or the village of Shayhan, were areas either mentioned explicitly in the qur'anic reference to Moses life or were areas which worshippers and scholars recognized as the Holy Land.

These unsophisticated, primitive shrines, evolving from a rural peasant religious tradition, should not belie the significance powerful figures in Islamic societies were willing to attribute to them. The Egyptian Sultan Baybars constructed a dome over the Jericho tomb and built an adjoining mosque in 1269. This ruler sought to consolidate Jerusalem and its vicinity as a land endowed with Islam's biblical legacy, especially in the period after the Crusader presence in the Middle East. Sultan Baybar's recognition of a minor shrine in the southern Syrian desert was one means to herald Islamic authenticity in the Holy Land, testifying to the role local religious practices played in the eyes of rulers and scholars.

WORKS CITED

Ali, Ahmed. (1984). *Al-Qur'an: A Contemporary Translation*. Princeton: Princeton University Press.
Brinner, W.M. (1998a). Isra'illiyyat. *Encyclopedia of Arabic Literature*: 400-401, Vol. I. Edited by Julie Scott Meisami and Paul Starkey. London: Routledge Press.
_____. (1988b). Legends of the Prophets. *Encyclopedia of Arabic Literature*: 465-466, Vol. I.
Al-Bukhari, Muhammad (d. 869) (1979). *Sahih al-Bukhari*. Medina.
Duri, A. (1983). *The Rise of Historical Writing Among the Arabs*. Edited and translated by Lawrence I. Conrad. Princeton: Princeton University Press.
El'ad, A. (1988). Some Aspects of the Islamic Traditions Regarding the Site of the Grave of Moses. *Jerusalem Studies in Arabic and Islam*, Vol. XI: 1-15.
Encyclopaedia of Islam, (2nd Edition). Edited by H.A.R. Gibb, et al. Leiden: Brill.
Encyclopedia of Arabic Literature. (1988). Edited by Julie Scott Meisami and Paul Starkey. London: Routledge Press.
Canaan, Taufik. (1927). *Mohammedan Saints and Sanctuaries in Palestine*. London: Luzac.
Goitein, S.D. (1966). *Studies in Islamic History and Institutions*. Leiden: E.J.Brill.
al-Harawi, `Ali b. Abi Bakr (d. 1215). (1953). *Al-Asharat ila Ma`rifat al-Ziyarat*. Ed. by Janine Sourdel-Thomine. Damascus: Institut Francais de Damas.
Hasson, I. (1987). Jerusalem in the Muslim Perspective: The *Qur'an* and Tradition Literature, in *The History of Jerusalem: The Early Islamic Period*, pp. 283-313. Edited by. J Prawer. Jerusalem: Yad Izhak Ben-Zvi.
Heller. (1934). The Relation of the Aggada to Islamic Legends. *Moslem World*, Vol. XXIV: 273-296.
Hirschberg, J.W. (1951). The Sources of Moslem Traditions Concerning Jerusalem. *Rocznik Orientalistyczny*, XVII: 314-350
Ibn `Asakir, `Ali Ibn Hasan. (d. 1177). (1955). *Ta'rikh Madinat Dimashq*. Forty-Two Volumes. Damascus: Matba'at al-`Ilmi al-Arabi.
Ibn Hibban (d. 965). (1970). *Kitab al-Majruhin*. Haydarabad: al-Matba`ah al-`Aziziyah.
Ibn Jubayr, Muhammad ibn Ahmad (d. 1217). (1907). *Rihla*. Leyden: Gibb.
Ibn shaddad (d. 1235). (1962). *Al-A`laq al-Khatira fi Dhikhr Umara' al-Sham wa'l-Jazira*. Damascus: French Institute for Arabic Studies.
Idrisi, al-Sharif (d. 1165). (1970-1984). *Nuzhat al-Mushtaq fi Ithtiraq al-Afaq*. Edited by E. Ceurlli et al. Naples.

Khalidi, Tarif. (1994). *Arabic Historical Thought in the Classical Period.* Cambridge: Cambridge University Press.

Khoury, R.G. (1972). *Wahb Ibn Munabbih, Der Heidelberger Papyrus PSR Heid Arab 23*, 2 Vols. Wiesbaden: O. Harrasowitz.

Kisa'i, Muhammad ibn Muhammad. (1978). *The Tales of the Prophets of al-Kisa'i*, Translated from the Arabic with Notes by W. M. Thackston, Jr.. Boston: Twayne Publishers.

Meri, Josep (1999). "The Islamic Cult of Saints and Medieval Popular Culture," *al-`Usur al-Wusta*, October: 34-44.

Muqaddasi, Muhammad b. Ahmad (d. 946). (1897-1910). *Ahsan al-Taqasim fi Ma`rifat al-Aqalim.* English Translation from the Arabic and Edited by G.S.A. Ranking and R.F. Azoo. Calcutta Asiatic Society of Bengal.

Al-Muslim Ibn al-Hajjaj (d. 875). (1995). *Sahih al-Muslim.* Beruit.

Nagel, T. Al-Kissa al-Anbiyya. *Encyclopaedia of* Islam, (2nd Edition): 180-181.

Najam al-Din, Ibn Jama`ah Abu al-Baqa' (d. after 1496). *Al-Durr al-Nazim fi Akhbar Saidna Musa al-Kalim.* El-Escorial Library, Spain.

Al-Nasa'i `Ali (d. 830). (1985). *Kitab Sunan al-Nasa'i.* Bombay.

Pinault, D. (1988). Story-telling. *Encyclopaedia of Arabic Literature:* 735-737, Vol. II.

Qazwini, Ibn Muhammad (d. 1283). (1960). *Athar al-Bilad wa Akhbar al-`Ibad*, Beirut: Dar al-Sadir.

Al-Raba`i, *Fada'il al-Sham wa-Dimashq* (d. 1052). (1950). Damascus: Matba'at al-`Ilm al-Arabi

Sadan, Joseph. (1981). Le Tombeau de Moise a Jéricho et a Damas. *Revue des Études Islamiques.* Vol. XLIX: 59-99.

Sivan, Emmanuel. (1975). The beginnings of the *Fada'il al-Quds* Literature. *Israel Oreintal Studies*, 1:263-271).

Schwarzbaum, Haim. (1982). *Biblical and Extra-Biblical Legends in Islamic Folk-Literatur.* Verlag fur Orientkunde.

Tha`labi, Ahmad ibn Muhammad (d. 1035). (1928) `*Ara'is al-Majalis fi Qisas al-Anbiya'.* Cairo.

Vajda, G. (1960). "ISRA'ILIYYAT," *Encyclopaedia of* Islam, (2nd Edition), pp. 211-212

Yaqut, al-Hamawi (d. 1229). (1866). *Mu`jam al-Buldan.* Ed. F. Wustenfeld. Leipzig.

DOMENICO PIETROPAOLO

THE ZODIAC SAINTS

ABSTRACT The purpose of this paper is to examine some of the issues involved in the imaginative interpretation of the sacred in post-Trentine Catholicism, analysed in relation to the traditional use of allegory as a tool of cultural appropriation and dominance, and in the context of the growing tension between science and religion. The chief points of access to these issues will be found in the sacramental theory of signification taught by the authors of Roman catechism and in the stellar cartography of Julius Schiller.

In a memorable passage in his discussion of Spenser, C. S. Lewis describes how this great allegorical poet of Protestantism is more likely than not to seem pro-Catholic to an innocent reader, on account of the fact that the images with which he constructs his allegorical machinery appear to describe Catholic practices more closely than Protestant ones. More sophisticated readers, confident of Spenser's Protestantism and yet certain of the Catholic appearance of his allegories, might instead be induced to conclude that the poet could not appear other than Catholic, because all Christian allegory is necessarily Catholic, even when it is found in a Protestant poem. However the truth of the matter, Lewis is quick to point out, "is not that allegory is Catholic, but that Catholicism is allegorical"[1] Its institutional order and its devotional practices are seen as tangible representations of the invisible world, concrete analogues of transcendence, embodiments of the spirit in a universe of matter, wherein they appear as allegorical entities, like similes "seen from the other end."[2] To regard a text or a material object as an allegory is to confer upon it the status of an imaginative analogue of an intangible truth, to transform it into the concrete pole of a simile designed to give abstract ideas material presence by implication. Since the allegorist is

---

[1] C.S. Lewis, *The Allegory of Love* (Oxford: Oxford University Press, 1936; rpt. 1977), p. 322.
[2] *Ibid.*, p. 125. This is in fact the way Lewis defines allegory.

somehow already in possession of that truth, to allegorise is also to appropriate material objects as channels of signification through which that truth may be brought within ordinary reach in the world of the living. It is, moreover, to colonise other areas of culture and nature as signs of the glory of God, to annex them to the patrimony of the received tradition and to control the way we may understand their place in the scheme of things, delivering them from any bondage they may have previously had to other masters. From this perspective, the Catholic world is a world of allegorical images designed to give experiential presence to the world of transcendence and therefore to enable us to use our limited human senses as points of access to the amorphous infinity that lies, or that is believed to lie, beyond them.

We need not agree with all the implications of the position assumed by Lewis, particularly with regard to the modern world, but there can be no doubt that in the years of the Counter Reformation, a period mesmerised by the quick development of the baroque aesthetic and by controversial progress in the sciences, the allegorical colonisation of culture is a major activity of Catholicism. The early modern history of the Catholic world is marked by a hitherto unknown spirit of militancy, both defensive and aggressive, that left the imprint of Rome in all areas of culture. The title of my paper refers, in a general way, to stellar cartography, an area of research which, though still under the symbolic domain of ancient paganism, was then being reshaped in response to the most advanced ideas in science, art, and religion, as the discipline that surveyed the boundary between this and the other worlds. In a more specific way, my title refers to the work of Julius Schiller, who laboured to release the night sky from Greek and Babylonian mythology and to colonise it on behalf of the Church, reconfiguring all the constellations as saints and sacred symbols, beginning with the twelve Zodiac houses, which he redrew as the twelve apostles. Thus in his maps the spring constellations of Aries, Taurus, and Gemini, are reassigned to St Peter, St Andrew, and St James the Greater[3]; the summer constellations of Cancer, Leo, and Virgo have become those of St. John, St Thomas (doubting) and St James the Less;[4] the autumn houses of Libra, Scorpio and Sagittarius are reconfigured as St Philip, St Bartholomew and St Matthew[5]; the first two winter houses, Capricorn and Aquarius, now belong to St Simon and St Judas Thaddeus, while Pisces, the last house

---

[3] Constellations XXII, XXIII, and XXIV respectively.
[4] Constellations XXV, XXVI, and XXVII respectively.
[5] Constellations XXVIII, XXIX, and XXX respectively.

of the winter Zodiac, under whose aegis we hold our conference, has been reconfigured as St Matthias, the elected successor of Judas Iscariot.[6] Outside the ecliptic of the sun, at least eight degrees north and south of the celestial equator, other notable changes include Orion as St Joseph, Pegasus as the Archangel Gabriel, Cassiopea as Mary Magdalen, Andromeda as the Holy Sepulchre, Eridanus as the river Jordan, the Ship of the Argonauts as Noah's Ark, Auriga as St Jerome, and, among the less grandiose figures, the modest Delphinus as the Water Pot of Cana just prior to the first miracle of Jesus.

First published in 1627, Schiller's *Coelum Stellatum Christianum*[7] is a collection of maps that together constitute a gigantic vault, conceived much like those of contemporary baroque churches, on which are depicted the champions and symbols of Christian sanctity watching over the affairs of men from the edge of reality. The intended sociological function of this colonisation of the night sky was clearly to condition, on the one hand, the way in which stargazers might relate the constellations to history, no longer a disjointed narrative of legends and myths unenlightened by faith, but the linear history of salvation, along which they too aspired to journey under the guidance of the saints, and, on the other hand, the manner in which they might understand the unfolding of their personal destinies under the influence of the stars. It seemed possible, in other words, to give a sense of physical orientation to the instinctive upward glance implicit in Christian prayer and at the same time to appropriate astrology, transforming the mysterious power of governance that the stars were thought to have over the lives of men into the benevolent guidance of the saints, silently pointing out to them the way to salvation.

Julius Schiller was not the first to propose raising the apostles to the ecliptic or to transform the traditional meaning of the Zodiac allegories into moral virtues. As Richard Hinckley Allen pointed at the end of the nineteenth century, before Schiller the Venerable Bede had suggested that the signs of the Zodiac be transformed into signs of the apostles, with John the Baptist summoned to fill the place of Judas, while more recently Giordano Bruno had proposed that the signs be reinterpreted as allegories of moral excellence.[8] But whether Schiller knew or not that

---

[6] Constellations XXXI, XXXII, and XXXIII respectively.
[7] Augustae Vindelicorum: Praelo Andreae Apergeri, 1627.
[8] *Star-Names and Their Meanings* (1899), re-issued as *Star Names: Their Lore and Meaning* (New York: Dover, 1963), p. 28. The allusion is to Bede's *Corona seu Circulus Sanctorum Apostulorum* and Bruno's *Spaccio della bestia trionfante*.

he was walking in the footsteps of Bede, whose orthodoxy was beyond suspicion, and that his allegories of moral guidance resonated with echoes of Giordano Bruno, who had been burned at the stake in times uncomfortably close to the present, is ultimately of no concern to us. Historically, what is significant is that Schiller was the first scientific cartographer actually to Christianize the heavens, and, what is more, the one to inaugurate the flurry of theological and artistic activity that took place in the studios of stellar cartography in the seventeenth century, when, largely under his influence, others attempted their own Christian redepiction of the night sky. Theologically, echoes of Bruno notwithstanding, there is nothing in his scheme that could render it suspect to the Church. On the contrary, Schiller has no doubts that the only view of Christianity suitable for his maps is the hierarchical one on which the Church was based, and that is why the most prominent area of the sky, that part of it which determines how life is influenced on Earth, the area that all stargazers were invited to watch so as to determine how to exercise their judgement wisely in their daily lives, was placed under the tutelage of the apostles, taken as a group and therefore including such figures as St Matthias (Pisces) and St James the Less (Virgo), who, in the firmament of great Christian saints, could hardly figure as stars of the first magnitude. The Roman Catechism had made it perfectly clear that issues of orthodoxy are ultimately a matter of authority, that, though it was presided over by the Holy Ghost, the Church was ministered by the successors of the apostles, to whom the divine spirit of guidance and governance was first imparted and from whom it had come down to their successors in a line of uninterrupted continuity.[9] The apostles, however humble some of them may have remained in the history of Christianity, represent the origin of the Church, the foundations on which the rest was built. So in Schiller's cartography the apostles gird the universe, give both relative location and meaning to the planets and to the stars, and mediate the influence of heaven to the earth below. As an added bonus, Schiller's by far most prominent non-Zodiacal constellation is Noah's Ark (constellation XL), which the Roman Catechism presents as the most important allegory of the Old Testament, recommending that pastors use it as a source of instruction. "It was built by the command of God, in order that there might be no doubt that it was a symbol of the Church, which God has so constituted that all who enter therein through baptism, may be safe from danger of eternal death,

---

[9] *The Catechism of the Council of Trent*, translated by John A. McHugh and Charles J. Callan (Rockford, Illinois: Tan Books and Publishers, 1982), p. 107.

while such as are outside the Church, like those who were not in the ark, are overwhelmed by their own crimes."[10] Nulla salus extra ecclesiam.

All these factors taken into account, Schiller no doubt anticipated enduring success. He was wrong, of course: within fifty years or so, mainstream celestial cartography forgot all about him, as did the other areas of culture that he had brought to his studio. This is at first a most surprising fact. From a purely astronomic point of view, Schiller's maps were perhaps the most accurate and up to date, with respect to both number and relative position of the stars. His atlas, for example, is the first to record the great nebula of Andromeda, which in Schiller's scheme figures on the edge of the constellation of the Holy Sepulchre. On the whole, Schiller's atlas was a considerable improvement on the *Uranometria* of Johann Bayer (Augsburg 1603), an improvement in part achieved by Schiller with the help of the ageing Bayer himself. And yet Bayer's atlas, which does not have any saints on it, remained for a long time the prototype and the standard of excellence in the field. Two planispheres of Schiller were published, with new engravings, by Andreas Cellarius in his *Atlas Coelestis seu Harmonia Macrocosmica* in 1660 alongside other projections without the saints,[11] but after that date knowledge of Schiller's atlas wanes very rapidly. The saints, in fact, brought down his stature as an astronomical cartographer and ultimately determined his total disappearance from history. Unlike England, where scientific research and theology intentionally sought each other's enlightenment in the same institutions, as exemplified best perhaps by Cambridge in the age of Newton, Catholic countries were to witness, in the second half of the seventeenth and in the whole of the eighteenth centuries, formidable tension between the two fields, even if, in the wake of the trial of Galileo, the hostility did not give rise to many vociferous debates. That is no doubt why the whole flurry of biblical pictography and interpretation which accompanied stellar map making in the first half of the seventeenth century slowly came to a halt, and why its proponents sank soon after into oblivion. As a consequence Julius Schiller, Philip Zesen (Latinised as Caesius), Jeremias Drexelius, William Drummond and many others who laboured to bring religion and stellar cartography into each other's debt, in Catholic and Protestant countries

---

[10] *Ibid.*, p. 107.
[11] These are bound to become somewhat popular in our own times, since they have been reprinted as greeting cards (from the copy in the British Library) by Pomegranate Publications (n. 429).

alike, are now mere names.[12] Our culture is separated from theirs by an unbridgeable abyss—so much so that, when we read in John Donne's *A Litanie* (IX) a prayer to the "illustrious Zodiacke / of twelve apostles, which ingirt this all," and when we meet in *Paradise Lost* a reference to the "translated saints" (III, 460), we can hardly hear the echo of conversations over their maps.[13]

Yet, despite its relatively short life, Schiller's Christian cartography was at the time an entirely logical development for both science and religion. A map of the celestial vault is the spatial counterpart of a calendar, not only in the scientific sense that the latter could not be constructed without the former, but in the practical sense of their intended function, which is to enable us to find orientation in time and space. However, when stellar cartography had still an entirely mythological appearance, the calendar was also a device for spiritual orientation. The Christian dominance of the calendar in the Renaissance is so well known that it does not require any comment—suffice it to say that the calendar was then little more than a list of saints, in relation to which it was possible to determine when to worship and when to attend to other matters. Unlike modern calendars, which fix temporal location by means of abstract and equal segments of neutral time, sixteenth- and seventeenth-century calendars are still only a matter of fixed and movable liturgical events, in which differences in time are viewed and calculated as a function of specific days of worship. Yet in a curious mixture of Christian and pagan symbolism, the calendar makers of the time routinely included the symbols of the Zodiac next to the names of the months, not only on wall calendars, which had just been introduced and which were becoming popular very quickly, but also on those in books of hours, which were closer to prayer and meditation than they were to the practical tasks of daily living.[14]

No doubt these symbols had become so trite that they did not represent any risk of religious distraction, not even when they were printed in such a spiritual setting as a book of hours, but it is perfectly reasonable to expect that in the militant climate of the time someone should desire to Christianise the Zodiac everywhere, on calendars, on maps of the heavens, and in the imaginations of all stargazers, so that when they

---

[12] On the biblical school of stellar cartography, see Allen, p. 28 *et passim*.
[13] Respectively from the editions of Donne's *The Divine Poems* by Helen Gardner (Oxford: 1952) and of Milton's *The Complete Poetical Works* by C. Bush (Boston: 1965).
[14] On the relationship between calendars and zodiac signs, Francesco Maiello, *Storia del calendario:La misurazione del tempo, 1450-1800* (Torino: Einaudi, 1994), pp. 112-114.

looked at the night sky they should also see the saints that gave structure and meaning to the days of the year. And it is entirely logical that such a person would begin his work of conversion by transforming the visual paradigms and the vocabulary of professional astronomers, since stellar atlases were published chiefly for them, as aids to telescopic navigation and as charts on which they could record their own observations and from which they could construct descriptive names for all newly discovered stars. A Christian atlas implied a Christian nomenclature. Polaris in Ursa Major, to cite the first example in Schiller's chart of names and technical specifications, becomes "stella maris, dextera manus" in the constellation of the Archangel Michael.[15] To raise one's eyes to Polaris was automatically to see the profile of Archangel Michael on the dark vault of the sky and to think simultaneously of the Virgin Mary, celebrated as the star of the sea in the popular hymn "Ave maris stella."

This may seem like a bit of trivial erudition, but the fact is that the Roman Catechism severely reprimanded parents who insisted on giving their children classical pagan names, and instructed that one of the functions of baptism was to enable the child to acquire the name of a saint, of a person "of eminent sanctity" so that he might be stimulated by his name to imitate him in the practice of virtue.[16] Though its scale is different and the subjects in question are stars rather than children, the operation undertaken by Schiller was essentially the same: to rename the constellations, to give them new images in the likeness of the saints, and to cause the astronomers using his maps in their explorations of the night sky to give Christian names to new stars, all on the assumption that this would slowly but systematically remove from the culture's field of awareness all the traces of non-Christian symbolism that had been traditionally associated with the observation of the stars.

Allegorical catasterism, or the elevation of objects and human beings to the stars as the final step in the creation of a living mythology, involves a complex form of visual signification, which is based on the possibility of hybridising concepts and images from various sources, and which therefore flourishes best in a culture where the arts and sciences are not consciously kept apart but are purposely brought together in the pursuit of goals that they cannot achieve by working in isolation. I cannot here explore with you, with any degree of rigour, the epistemological factors that make this possible and the institutional conditions that make it desirable in certain periods of history. But even without such an analy-

---

[15] *Coelum Stellatum Christianum*, p. 131.
[16] *The Catechism of the Council of Trent*, p. 197.

sis, it may perhaps be granted, for the sake of the argument, that the culture of the baroque period is one whose components transfuse readily into each other, giving rise to hostilities when the light coming from one area shows errors in the other, but also and more frequently bringing about an enrichment of each other's creative potential. Such conditions are presupposed by the invention of opera and of the oratorio, the construction of sculptural fountains, and the pictorial recasting of the constellations, among other typically baroque phenomena.

Among the conceptual parameters of this form of visual signification there must be, firstly, the conviction that society is held together by a bond of sensible signs, a principle that is central to the Catholic idea of community, as had been recognised by St Augustine and reasserted in the catechism of the Council of Trent, where it is given as a premise of sacramental theology.[17] Secondly, there must be a pervasive sense that material reality is a ciphered message, something which we certainly know to be true for baroque science, witness Galileo's concept of the book of nature and of Kepler's geometric view of astrophysical harmony, but also and more obviously for the baroque verbal and pictorial arts, where it was probably derived from a Neoplatonist substratum in the inherited culture.[18] Thirdly, there must be a widespread conviction that language, at the most general level of conception as an instrument of communication involving any or all of the human senses, is a system of artificial and material signs through which, almost as if their very opacity were a transparent filter, we focus upon and grasp abstract ideas. This, too, is fundamental to the culture of Catholicism, and especially so in the baroque period, in which it was disseminated by the Roman Catechism as another premise of sacramental theology.[19] Fourthly, there

---

[17] Augustine discusses the issue in *Contra Faust*. Lib. Ix, c, ii. The Roman Catechism puts it thus: "A fourth reason why the institution of the Sacraments seems necessary is that there may be certain marks and symbols to distinguish the faithful; particularly since, as St. Augustine observes, no society of men, professing a true or a false religion, can be, so to speak, consolidated into one body, unless united and held together by some bond of sensible things." *The Catechism of the Council of Trent*, p. 149.

[18] See, for example, Cristoforo Giarda, *Liberalium Disciplinarum Icones Symbolicae Bibliotecae Alexandrinae* (1626), and the following commentaries: E.H. Gombrich, "Icones symbolicae," *Journal of the Warburg and Courtauld Institutes* XI (1948), pp. 162-192; Robert Klein, "The Theory of Figurative Expression in Italian Treatises on the Impresa," in *Form and Meaning: Writings on the Renaissance and Modern Art*, translated by Madeline Jay and Leon Wieseltier (Princeton, New Jersey: Princeton University Press, 1979), pp. 20-24.

[19] *The Catechism of the Council of Trent*, p. 145: "Other signs are not natural, but conventional, and are invented by men to enable them to converse one with another, to convey their thoughts to others, and in turn to learn the opinions and receive the advice of other

must be a credible means of conceiving the progressive rarefaction of matter to the point where it vanishes into transparency, without losing its presence and yet without becoming spirit, but leaving the impression that it has become spirit. This principle, familiar enough to students of Vico, is an abstract statement of the intellectual operation involved in the philosophy of Euhemerus, who could debunk the gods and reduce paganism to atheism by claiming that they were none other than images of deified powerful men. In the Middle Ages Euhemerism was at times invoked by the fathers in their polemic against paganism, but there was no reason why it could not now be used to raise the saints to the symbolic heaven of the stars.[20]

These conditions, theoretical and historical, favoured Schiller's catasterism of the Apostles. The Roman Catechism had stated that figures of the saints, of crosses and other sacred objects were artificial signs with the power to signify the sacred but not with the power to accomplish what they signified, which is a prerogative only of the sacraments.[21] Therefore, so long as one did not fall prey to the temptation of sacramental empowerment, the allegorical catasterism of the saints was a desirable cultural acquisition because of the great multitudes of people that were bound to be affected by it. All forms of catasterism, pagan as well as Christian, are iconic allegories capable of being grasped in their entirety by simple inspection and susceptible of complete recollection without effort: one looks at them and automatically sends the mind wandering after the implications of the simile visible through their transparency, with the consequence that the narrative which necessarily results from the search unfolds entirely within, as an immanent experience of consciousness that requires no further contact with the material world. Stargazers who configure images of saints where the eyes see only distant stars perform a signifying action that remains wholly within the privacy of their minds, and any experience of moral conversion that they may undergo is produced entirely by that action rather than by any sacramental power of the signs themselves.

The immanence of that action, however, does not mean that the experience has no social dimension. On the contrary, it is a special prerogative of allegories to speak quietly within, though with the voice of

---

men. The variety and multiplicity of such signs may be inferred from the fact that some belong the eyes, many to the ears, and the rest to the other senses."
[20] On the use of Euhemerism in medieval apologetics see John D. Cooke, "Euhemerism: A Medieval Interpretation of Classical Paganism, " *Speculum* 2, n. 4 (1927), pp. 396-410.
[21] *The Catechism of the Council of Trent*, p. 146.

an entire community. The personal conversion that they seek to bring about is always a return to the ways of the community, real or idealised though the community may be. Allegory can hardly be conceived other than as a function of community discourse. Its ideological thrust is necessarily to reaffirm the values of a society and simultaneously to tighten the grip that the community has on the individual. Allegory is, among other things, an instrument for the annexation of individuals to a community held together, as Augustine had said, by its sensible signs. These considerations enable us to approach in a meaningful way what is by far the most interesting aspect of Schiller's maps, namely the convex direction of their curvature. In the seventeenth century stellar maps could be constructed as flat projections of either a concave or a convex surface, the stars being imagined either on the inside or on the outside of a geocentric globe. In either case the globe figured as the boundary of reality, or as Kepler once defined it, as the skin of the world,[22] beyond which it was not possible to venture and still remain in the realm of reality. In the context of a pagan world-view, the direction of the curvature could not have any serious consequences: the map was simply a practical instrument without metaphysical implications. But when the signs had been transformed into Christian allegories, the situation was quite different, since beyond the physical world there was the world of divine transcendence. Geometrically a convex surface is one that bulges towards the point of observation and therefore implies the presence of an observer on the other side of space. By showing the Christianised constellations in this manner Schiller is offering their beholders the fiction that they can project themselves into the realm of transcendence and imaginatively assume the perspective of God, even as they retain the human vantage point of men looking at the stars from the surface of the earth.

When this situation is regarded as a lived experience of single individuals in a community of believers, we observe, in the first place, the individuals vicariously overcoming both the immanence of their efforts and the material limits of their being by apparently projecting their consciousness into the region of transcendence, while they look at the stars from below and hence retaining full awareness of their own, their community's, and their world's material finitude. In the second place, we know that the dialectical movement of their consciousness, from the concavity of the real starry heaven to the convexity of the one that shapes their imaginative experience of it, is ultimately a form of intro-

---

[22] Johannes Kepler, *Epitome of Copernican Astronomy* and *Harmonies of the World*, translated by Charles Glenn Wallis (Amherst, New York: Prometheus Books, 1995), p. 15.

spection, since when they assume the fictionally-transcendent point of view and, as it were, look down on the constellations, through the transparency of the saints they must also see themselves in the act of looking up, whereas when they experience their human perspective, the saints frame for them their imaginative projection of themselves as transcendent observers, as a community which is already in a fictional heaven, an imaginative Church Triumphant rather than a real Church Militant. In the third place, we note that whereas to the consciousness of the earthbound observers the saints are points of access to the realm of transcendence, with which they appear to be co-substantial and in unmediated contact, to the consciousness of the pseudo-transcendent observers they appear far below and separated by an infinite chasm, almost as if the globe of the universe were looked at from heaven through the wrong end of the telescope—a reminder, no doubt, that though through a form of Christian Euhemerism the saints have been rarefied and raised to the edge of reality, they are still on this side of the boundary and knowable only as men and women of this world, their faces made visible to the imagination by the light of the stars rather than the light of glory.

Aesthetically, this experience of consciousness, in which the mind is given the illusion of contact with transcendence through an action that is exclusively immanent, an experience in which our focus of awareness is made to slide back and forth along the dialectic that links our physical to our imaginative power of vision, in which the constellations of the saints figure as a gateway to heaven and yet are as far from it as light is from glory, in which the inner and the outer surfaces of reality continuously undermine each other's claim to primacy in our consciousness, and in which, moreover, what is represented is the act of representation itself, in a manner that allows the observer to be simultaneously in and out of the picture—all of this is exquisitely baroque, in conception and in execution. It is a phenomenon made possible by a culture sustained by the effort to lock together into a single creative act science, art, philosophy, and religion, on the principle that when they come together they enrich each other to opulence and when they come apart they can restrict each other's movement down to paralysis.

ILLUSTRATIONS

1. Constellatio XXII   St. Peter   (Aries)
2. Constellatio XXIII   St. Andrew   (Taurus)
3. Constellatio XXIV   St. James the Greater (Gemini)
4. Constellatio XXV   St. John   (Cancer)
5. Constellatio XXVI   St. Thomas   (Leo)
6. Constellatio XXVII   St. James the Less   (Virgo)
7. Constellatio XXVIII   St. Philip   (Libra)
8. Constellatio XXIX   St. Bartholomew   ((Scorpio)
9. Constellatio XXX   St. Mattew   (Sagittarius)
10. Constellatio XXXI   St. Simon   (Capricorn
11. Constellatio XXXII   St. Judas Thaddeus   (Aquarius)
12. Constellatio XXXIII   St. Matthias   (Pisces)
13. Constellatio XXXIV   Noah's Ark   (Ship of the Argonauts)

CONSTELLATIO XXII.

CONSTELLATIO XXIII.

CONSTELLATIO XXIV.

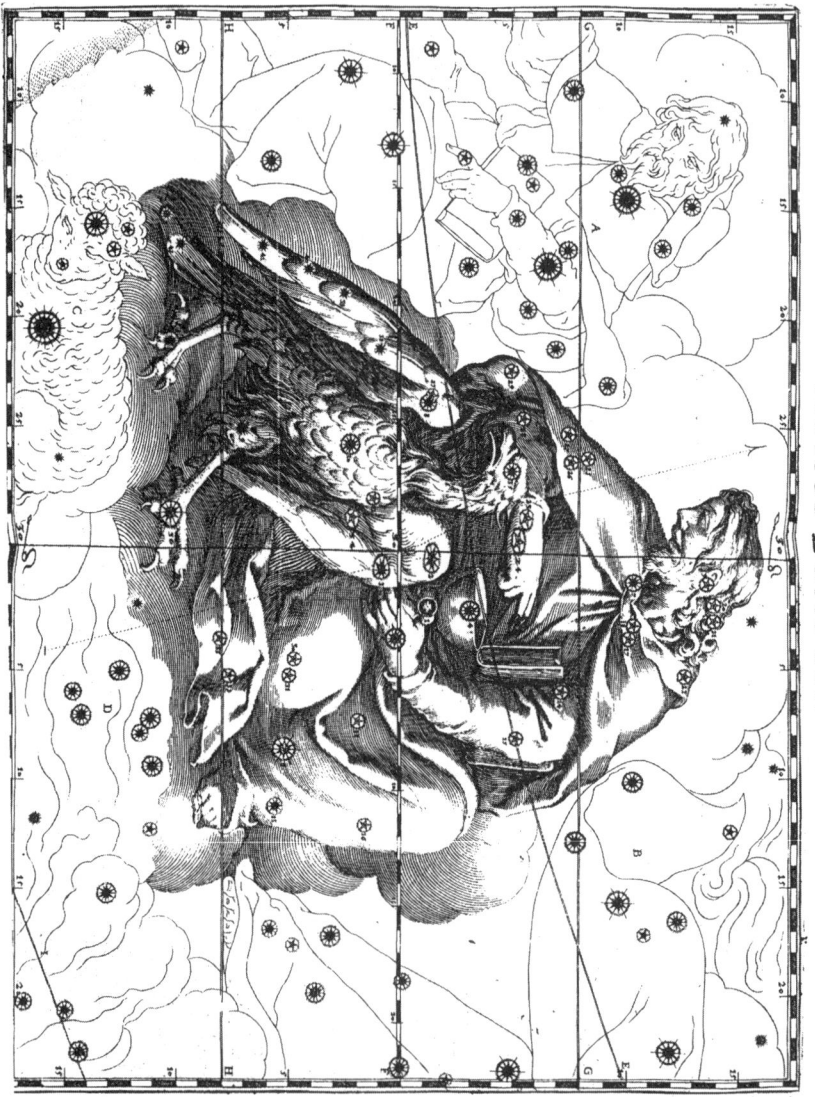

CONSTELLATIO XXV.

CONSTELLATIO XXVI.

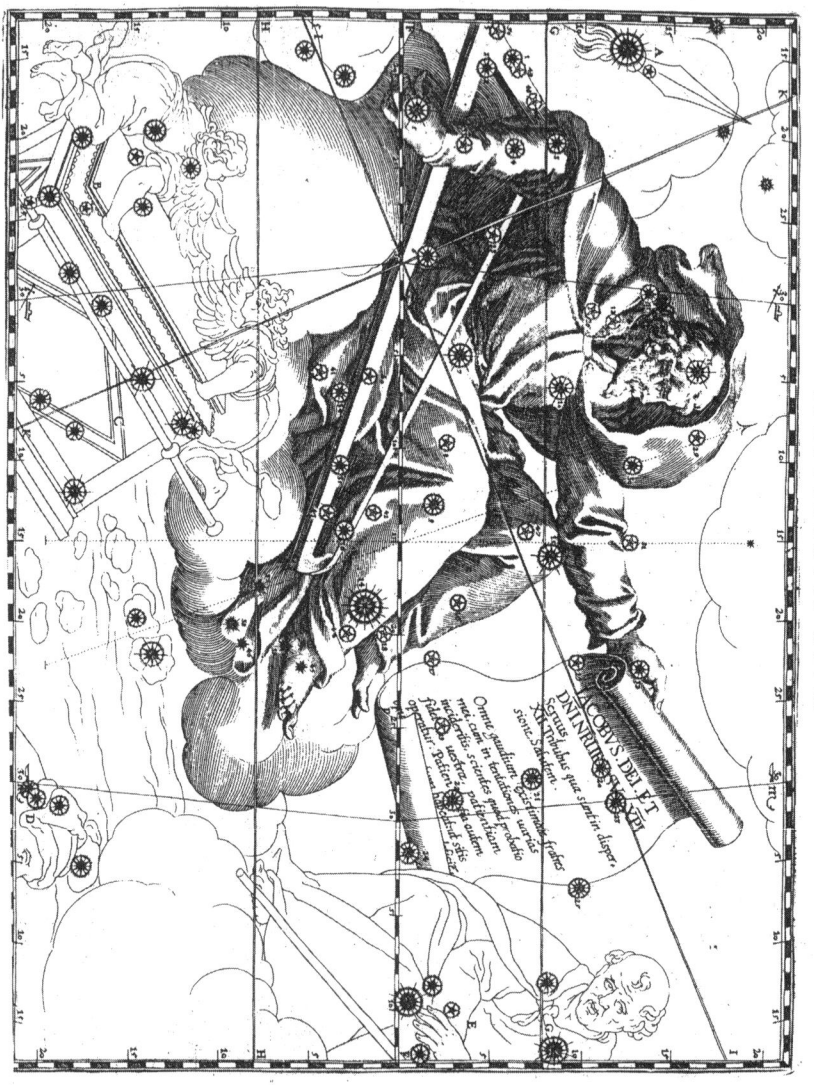

CONSTELLATIO XXVII.

D. N. IACOBVS. DEI. ET
Servus. *
XI. Tribubus quæ sunt in disper-
sione, Salutem.
Omne gaudium existimate fratres
mei, cum in tentationes varias
incideritis: scientes quod probatio
fidei vestræ patientiam autem
opus habet. Patientia autem
opus perfectum habet.

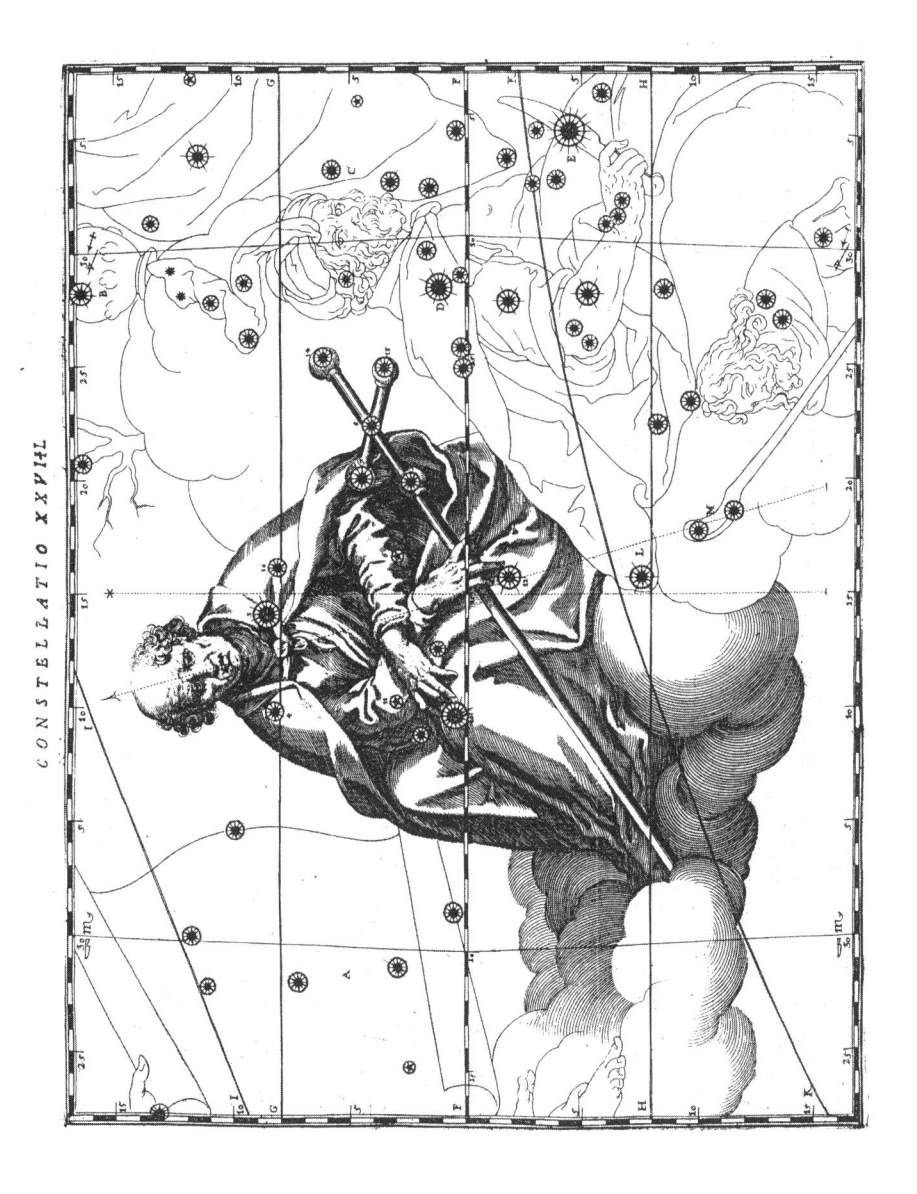

CONSTELLATIO XXXVIII

CONSTELLATIO XXIX.

CONSTELLATIO XXX.

CONSTELLATIO XXXI.

CONSTELLATIO XXXII.

CONSTELLATIO XXXIII.

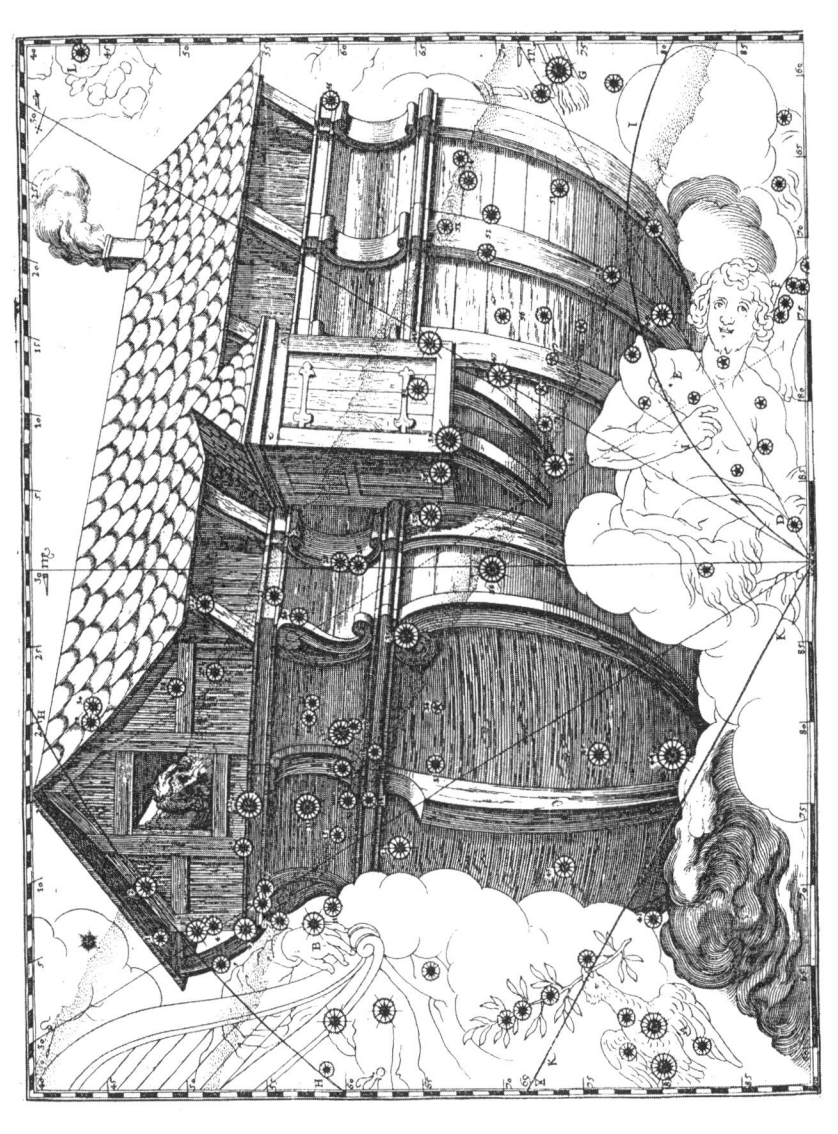

CONSTELLATIO XL.

— 59 —

REINER JAAKSON

WILDERNESS AS SACRED PLACE

ABSTRACT. Wilderness and the desert have been powerful motifs in Christianity. The ancient Jews living in villages saw the surrounding desert as a hostile wilderness. Althought it was threatening physically, wilderness was seen by the early Christians as also being promising spiritually. The desert was valued as a place where personal faith could be tested and be reinforced. In the monastic tradition wilderness became a place of refuge from worldly temptations and during tumultuous times remote monasteries became sacred islands of Christianity and civilization. The Biblical portrayal of wilderness as a sun drenched, hot desert was reinterpreted in Christian Europe, at least north of the Mediterranean, as a dark and impenetrable forest. The terms wilderness and desert were no longer necessarily synonymous and wilderness conquered. Wilderness today is appreciated even more as a sacred creation of God in need of protection. In contemporary society it is the cities, with their culture of materialism and consumerism, that have become the spiritual wastelands. The few remaining areas of wilderness in nature are sacred places where God's creation has not yet been ravaged by humans.

Pure space is an abstraction that has meaning only in its geographic dimensions and mathematical locational coordinates. The coordinates help to fix where we are and to define the direction of movement. As soon as we attribute meanings to space, such as "a vast open space", space ceases to be a physical abstraction and now begins to become an extension of ourselves. Once it has values attributed to it, space becomes place. Place has specific meaning, it has human context and historical associations, and it may imply belonging and identity. For example, "home" has multiple meanings. "Home" signifies not only a fixed location in space (where it is) but more importantly also a place that has emotional value for us (what it is). Home and residence are not necessarily synonymous. Residence is a physical shelter whereas in addition home is also an emotional shelter. Heidegger (1959) defines homelessness not as a lack of residence but as a disappearance of places that have emotional value for us and he proposes that homelessness is becoming a world fate. To Relph (1976), the contemporary world is characterised by placelessness, which he defines as a weakening of the distinctiveness of identity of places. Place may still have meaning but meaning has been standardized by a Macdonaldisation and Disneyfication of global culture. Technology has created uniformity, standardization, and impermanence. Placelessness has become a modern metaphor for human alienation.

Sacred places are places that have spiritual and religious meaning for us. A church, synagogue, or mosque is a sacred place. A sacred place may be sacred as a result of historical associations at locations where significant religious events have taken place. The exact places where Jesus walked are sacred places for Christians. Sacred historical places become formally recognized by the community of co-adherents of a religion. Sacred places can also be micro-locations of religious meaning for a select few people who created a sacred place. A small shrine to the Virgin Mary in the front yard of a house may have a specific meaning to the family that lives in the house: the shrine may commemorate an important rite of passage in the family, such as a marriage, birth, or death. Through our actions such as erecting a shrine or attaching a cross to a tree in a forest we have created a place that is sacred to us and where that sacredness is demonstrated to others.

Sacred places are cultural universals: they have occurred always, in every part of the world although the form of outward display of faith through art and artifacts varies between societies. In contemporary secular society, faith in most cases has become more a personal, private matter, an *eigenwelt* of experience of private space in one's self-consciousness. Overt outward display of faith in the secular world tends to be commercialized, such as Christmas as a shopping season. But, there are exceptions. In some countries there is a folk tradition of creating physical symbols to display faith boldly and unashamedly. Lithuania is a country where the overwhelming majority of the population is Catholic, and this despite some fifty years of occupation by the Soviet Union. Lithuanian secular culture and Catholicism are almost inseparable: to be Lithuanian is to be Roman Catholic. Lithuania is similar to Poland, Malta, and Ireland, countries where consideration of culture and society sooner or later inevitably includes consideration of the Catholic church in the country. Yet Lithuania was one of the last areas of Europe to be Christianised, and it remained a pagan enclave well into the 14th century. Knowledge of locations where pagan worship had taken place has continued to the present day. Many of these places of former pagan worship have been symbolically "baptised" by means of vivid Christian imagery.

Deep in the Lithuanian forests, there are clearings with groves of very old trees with hundreds of crosses that have been mounted over the centuries. These groves are sacred places, typically located in remote wilderness. They speak in a very powerful way of the Lithuanian people: this is a place where our pagan ancestors once worshipped, and today we as Catholic Lithuanians redefine this place by mounting crosses here as symbols of our own baptism as Christians.

These sacred forest groves in Lithuanian wilderness are part of a wilderness tradition that dates to the world of the Old Testament. The wilderness motif in the Bible follows two main themes. First, wilderness as threatening and evil, the realm of Satan, contrasted with the city as the centre of religion, order, and civilization. Second, wilderness as a place of refuge and solitude where faith can flourish free of the secular city and its temptations for sin. In Biblical history and down through the centuries to the present day wilderness has been interpreted in this dual fashion: as something positive and attractive and as something negative and threatening. I use the term "city" as a shorthand to refer to secular society, the built environment, technology, materialism, and consumer culture. Obviously, secular society exists also outside cities, in small communities and agricultural and other rural areas, but arguably it is the city that best exemplifies the penultimate technology, governance, and institutions of a society.

Wilderness is imbued with symbolisms and personal meanings which make the term wilderness difficult to define (Nash, 1982). The following constitute a selection of but three of the many diverse ways in which the term wilderness has been used in the Bible: (1) as a place of refuge: "Then Moses led Israel onward from the Red Sea, and they went into the wilderness of Shur..." (Exodus 15: 22); (2) as a hostile place of dangerous animals: "...the great and terrible wilderness, with its fiery serpents and scorpions..." (Deuteronomy 8:15); and (3) as the boundary between unpopulated desert and settled, cultivated land: "From there they set out, and encamped on the other side of the Arnon, which is in the wilderness that extends from the boundary of the Amorites..." (Numbers 21:13). The Bible includes what is essentially a geography of wilderness and human settlement. In the ancient world, the city was a compact physical entity, clearly demarcated from cultivated farmland, which in its turn was separated from the surrounding desert. The Hebrew word for wilderness (*midbar*) designated uncultivated or unsown land as contrasted with cultivated land. Uncultivated land was mostly desert, and the words desert and wilderness are used essentially interchangeably in the Bible. The desert threatened human physical survival with droughts and storms. However, the threat was more than physical. Desert and wilderness became synonymous as symbols of both physical desolation as well as testing of faith. Adam and Eve were expelled from Eden into the "cursed ground" of the desert of thorns and thistles. Jesus was tempted for forty days by the devil in the wilderness of Jordan. The desert epitomised the fall from the garden and the longing for a second Eden when God would restore Paradise: "I will make the wilderness a pool of water, and the dry land springs of water." (Isaiah 41:18).

Wilderness has also been portrayed in the Bible as a place of redemption from sin, where faith could be rediscovered and strengthened. God called Abraham and the Jews from civilization into the wilderness where Abraham was to found a nation for his people. "Wild nature is not here ...an implacable foe to be conquered but a spiritual oasis where God can be known directly, where humankind in some sense returns to Eden" (Oelschlaeger, 1991). To the ancient Hebrews, the boundary between civilization (the cities) and wilderness (the desert) was demarcated by a clear physical boundary. But the boundary was more than physical. Wilderness signified not only a physical desert but also a spiritual desert which separated those living in God's grace, free of sin, and those living in sin. That is, wilderness as both a physical state of nature as well as a human state of mind and soul. As much as the desert was a physical threat to survival, the Israelites found in the desert an escape from bondage and a place of redemption. Wilderness served as a place of refuge, somewhere to escape to for contemplation away from the sins and secularism of the cities. The harsh physical punishment of wilderness became a means to test faith. The desert wilderness both signified sin and promised redemption from sin.

Since the days of the early Christians, wilderness retreats have served as havens of simplicity and worship. "I am living in the wilderness wherein the Lord dwelt" (St. Basil the Great). Paradise has been perceived as a place we may discover after death and, for the living, as a form of private ecstatic being that can be known only to and by the individual. Thus outer paradise could, by extension, be defined as a place on earth that has attributes which facilitate the achievement of an inner state of paradise. People who have visited wilderness locations report that they have experienced a state of being that is very different from ordinary, everyday experience. Words or phrases used to describe this state includes: awe, awareness, mystery, humility, sense of presence of God. Wilderness offers us solitude, a state only rarely available in a society which puts stress on materialism, consumption and technology. St. Jerome (c. 342-420) advocated the notion of a strong interrelationship between desert, wilderness, and paradise. He contrasted the built environment and nature by pointing out that "(But) to me a town is a prison and a solitude, paradise." To the desert fathers wilderness was a place of solitude and by extension also a form of paradise. The Carmelites in Spain sought spiritual reinforcement by means of visits to retreats called deserts where solitude renewed their strength for charitable works back in the cities. Similarly today the availability of wilderness areas where we may find solitude gives us an opportunity for a reprieve from the commercialism and materialism of the secular city and, by recharging our spiritual batteries, strengthening our ability to resist being devoured by the city.

Is the wilderness and desert motif, especially in how it is revealed in monasticism, specifically Catholic or is the motif evident, perhaps in amended form, also in Protestantism? Williams (1962, page 65) suggests that Protestantism does not reveal wilderness or desert motifs in a strong way, and perhaps in no way:

> The Protestant Reformers were in no mood to flee into the wilderness, and were sober minded about Paradise. They were concerned only with the Fall therefrom and man's inveterate sin. They pilloried monasticism and for the most part had little sympathy with mysticism. (The) arena of Protestant combat with evil forces was the burgher's walled town, not the monk's enclosed garden in the wilderness.

While the wilderness and desert motif was largely absent in mainstream Protestantism it was not entirely absent in the Radical Reformation and persecuted sects such as the Mennonites and the Hutterites. These and other marginalized sects, which were hounded from city to city and from country to country, found spiritual solace in references in Scriptures to *desertum* and they found physical solace by fleeing to remote and inaccessible areas of wilderness. But the wilderness they sought was a European wilderness characterised not by the blinding sun, dryness, and scorched earth of the deserts of the ancient lands of the Bible but by the dark and impenetrable forests of temperate Europe north of the Mediterranean Sea. The European experience of forest wilderness was transplanted by Protestant colonizers to North America while in the Spanish New World colonies, some of which included arid regions, geography facilitated a continuation of the wilderness-as-desert motif. In New England the Puritans viewed wilderness as both a haven which offered protection from religious persecution but also as a demonic world that threatened the survival of body and soul. While the Puritans were clearing wilderness and building settlements, cultivating a Christian garden in a pagan wilderness, the Spanish and Portuguese conquistadors in Central and South America were more interested in conquest, gold, and discovery of El Dorado.

Wilderness as a physical entity frequently has been placed simplistically in a polarized position, as one of two opposites. A geography which polarises wilderness and city into opposing dualities ignores the nuances of transitions between city and wilderness. The Chinese geographer Yi-Fu Tuan (1974) refers to this transition zone as the rural "middle landscape" of villages and farms which are neither city nor wilderness. The late 18th and early 19th century Jeffersonian ideal viewed both the city and wilderness as profane, and the middle landscape of rural settlements as Edenic and as threatened by the city from one side and by wilderness from the other. The late 19th century vision extended the Jeffersonian ideal of the Edenic to also include wilderness. In addition to the dual Biblical images of wilderness-as-desert versus city-as-civilization and wilderness-as-refuge versus city-as-sinful, we have in the late 19th and early 20th centuries the emergence of an image of wilderness as pristine nature threatened by commerce and industry and hence in need of legal protection. It is the modern metropolis and a society of materialism, consumerism, and greed that have become a spiritual wasteland. Technology, industry and trade have become global in scale, creating in its wake a global culture. The predominant cosmology today is one of consumerism, and the city of commerce and industry has become a metaphor for the profane.

It is the profane city that has become a wilderness of spirit and it is nature's wilderness that has become a sacred place. The city as a human creation of built structures and marvels of technology adheres to a human dimension of time. What humans build will not be everlasting. Wilderness on the other hand has existed since creation. Wilderness consists of ecological processes that are forever ongoing, adhering to a dimension of time without a beginning and without an end: a dimension of time that is incomprehensible to humans. In wilderness humans can begin to imagine, although never fully comprehend, eternity. Here, humans can achieve

> ...a redirection of human attention from mundane affairs toward a world beyond - a time that is not yet but will be, a time where the soul exists forevermore. For Christianity is oriented toward the future. Its purpose and value can only be judged in re-

lation to eternity. "We have no abiding city, but we seek that which is to come." (Hebrews 13:14.– Russell 1981, p. 64)

From the earliest pioneer days in North America wilderness had served as a world "out there" which contrasted with and challenged settlements and civilization as the world "here". With the spread of settlement, wilderness ceased to be separated from civilization by a continuous frontier which demarcated wilderness on one side and urban settlements and cultivated land on the other. The spatial roles were reversed. In the beginning wilderness encircled human settlements but with increased growth and development human settlements encircled wilderness. Wilderness was no longer threatening but threatened. The expansion of settlement in North America quickly introduced a new understanding of wilderness as threatened and as worthy of being saved and protected. Wilderness, which had influenced national character and had become part of the North American heritage, was now valued in a new way and conservationists and nature essayists such as David Thoreau, Ralph Waldo Emerson, John Burrough, and John Muir advocated saving wilderness. To Ong (1959) this positive view of wilderness eliminates the negative desert metaphor by making wasteland the equivalent of desert while retaining the dialectic between desert and wilderness in the redemptive vision of the world since an initial experience of desert as wasteland is a prerequisite for appreciating it as wilderness.

With Bacon, Descartes, and Newton nature became desacrilized. The Newtonian mechanical view of nature dominates even today and has become entrenched in the scientific method. To the followers of Bacon, Descartes, and Newton, although nature is a creation of God it is not divine, nor is there a continuity between humans and the rest of the natural world. Humans have a soul and are in the image of God, but stand apart - aloof - from the rest of the natural world which, although made by God, does not contain God. The scientific method posits that through rational thought humans can discover the laws of nature, in order to better control nature. This Newtonian mechanical view of nature is very different from the medieval view prior to the Renaissance and the Enlightenment. St. Augustine believed that everything in nature has its place in Creation and glorifies the Creator, and that the Fall affected humans only, not nature. These competing views of the natural world present a dilemma for how we should treat wilderness today. If wilderness is to be saved it demands a concerted human effort to do so; wilderness will not survive if it is left unprotected. One way to protect wilderness is through natural resource management where rational decisions are based on ecology and the scientific method. For example, ecology demonstrates that wilderness helps to maintain biological diversity by protecting species of plants and animals from extinction. But arguments for the intrinsic worth of wilderness and the need to protect it can be based only in part on science. There is a rivalling stronger argument for wilderness protection which posits that every living species of plant and animal on earth is a creation of God and that each extinction of a species eradicates forever that manifestations of God's work. Religion and science argue in harmony here.

The United States government declared formally in 1890 that the frontier was closed and coincidentally the same year Yosemite Valley was preserved as a national wilderness park to protect it from logging and mining. A view of a paradisiac wilderness that is threatened by human settlement, instead of being a threat to human settlement, was something quite new. In the last hundred years the motive for the protection of wilderness has evolved from an emphasis to protect wilderness for its own sake, to an emphasis today to protect wilderness for the value that it has to us. In wilderness we come face to face with nature in its purest form devoid of anything manmade. This purity of nature may serve as a mirror to help us to reflect on the purity of our soul. By means of this witnessing of the magnificence of God's creation, wilderness facilitates a reawakening and strengthening of faith.

Wilderness as something that is threatened by human settlement is a product of the modern world, but the notion that wilderness can save the modern world from spiritual impoverishment is Biblical. As the last place on earth unaffected by the direct impacts of humans, wilderness presents to us God's creations of nature in pure form. If we lose wilderness we lose not only biological and physical natural resources but also a sacred place that facilitates spiritual self-discovery and renewal. This ancient role of wilderness as a test of faith and an opportunity for renewal of faith has acquired unique poignancy in the contemporary world. Wilderness now helps to save society by presenting to us God's creations of nature in a pristine form where we may find serenity and rejuvenation. Wilderness is still harsh on our physical survival but paradoxically this harshness has value because it humbles us into an awareness of our mortality and it has the power to reinforce our faith in God. Today, wilderness as a spiritual desert is to be found not in nature but in the secular world of commercialism, consumerism, and materialism. We have built cities of technological wonder and physical comfort, which at the same time are spiritual wastelands. We can build cities and other physical edifices to proclaim our trust in technology but we cannot create wilderness, although most certainly we can - and too frequently have - destroyed wilderness. Wilderness is God's creation and His gift to us. As a testimony of His love for us, God has given us wilderness as a sacred place where His presence is near. We as humans have a duty to save wilderness in nature as a testimonial of our love of God.

WORKS CITED

Nash, R. "Wilderness and the American Mind." New Haven: Yale UP, 1982.
Oelschlaeger, M. "The Idea of Wilderness." New Haven: Yale UP, 1991.
Ong, W.S. SJ "Personalism and Wilderness." *Kenyon Review* 21 (1959): 297-304.
Russell, J.L. "Time in Christian Thought." In J.T. Fraser (ed.). *The Voices of Time*. Amherst, Ma: U of Massachusetts P, 1981
Tuan, Yi-Fu. "Topophilia: a Study of Environmental Perception, Attitudes, and Values." Englewood Cliffs, NJ: Prentice Hall, 1974.
Williams, G. H. (1962) "Wilderness and Paradise in Christian Thought." New York: Harper and Brothers, 1962.

RANDALL A. ROSENFELD

SANTA CATERINA DA BOLOGNA (1413-1463), HER VIOLETA, AND A LATE-MEDIEVAL CONTEMPLATIVE PRACTICE

ABSTRACT. There are few saints for whom music was entirely absent from the spiritual part of their earthly careers. The involvement of most in the music of their familiar liturgies was so ordinary as to receive little comment from hagiographers. Most saints' active participation was purely vocal. Some, though, also used instruments other than the voice. Divers early medieval Irish saints used hand bells, and St. Dunstan is reputed to have commissioned an organ for Malmesbury abbey. Remains of medieval instruments are, however, scanty, and among those bits and pieces are few that can be ascribed to the manufacture, or ownership, of a saint. The vielle of the Poor Clare mystic, scribe, and author, S. Caterina of Bologna (1413-1463), is an exception. It, and a bow, are well preserved among her relics. The relatively good documentation for S. Caterina presents an opportunity as good as it is exceptional to examine a particular saint and her musical instrument within a particular culture. The evidence for the state of the instrument, and S. Caterina's ownership, is assessed, as well as the instrument's organological context. Analogues to S. Caterina's use of her vielle indicate that there was a learned tradition of using bowed chordophones in late-medieval contemplative practice.

> *[...] this trifling work, made with Divine assistance by me, the least little dog barking under the table* [Mt. 15, 27; Mk. 7, 28] *of the excellent and most fastidious servants and brides of the immaculate lamb, Christ Jesus, the sisters of the monastery of the Corpus Domini in Ferrara...*[1]

I wish to thank Joe Goering, Francesco Guardiani, and Giulio Silano for creating the most congenial conditions for the presentation of this paper, Manuela Scarci for ably presiding, and the luthier Philip Davis for early discussion of some organological features. Particular thanks go to Andrea Budgey, for discussing some of the points in this paper, providing the realisations of the musical examples, and performing them at the conference. All translations and drawings are mine. Neither Santa Caterina, or any of my friends, can be held responsible for errors in what follows.
The following abbreviations are used throughout:

Saints and the Sacred - A St. Michael's College Symposium
Joseph Goering, Francesco Guardiani, Giulio Silano eds. Ottawa: Legas, 2001

So Santa Caterina da Bologna (1413-1463) delineates a self-portrait with affective words drawn from the ancient well of abundant claustral humility. The work in which she sets her diminutive canine metaphor, *The Seven Spiritual Weapons*, became the most popular of her writings after her death. This is deservedly so, for the early modern judgement is sound; the work can still be read with profit; and the benefits confered are more than mere historical insight. Before the novice can learn to gird on any of the spiritual weapons, she and her sisters are summoned in spirit with an image of communal musical performance; that is, a sung dance (*carole*), a secular image here turned to sacred use, as was the *Song of Songs* in its exegetical traditions.[2] After the arms are presented to the

---

AA.SS.: *Acta sanctorum... martii tomus secundus...*, 'new edition' ed. Jean Carnandet (Paris and Rome, 1865), IX martii

Bibl. sanct.: *Bibliotheca sanctorum*, ed. F. Caraffa et al., 13 vols. (Rome, 1961?-1970)

Grove Art: *The Dictionary of Art*, ed. Jane Turner, 34 volumes (London, 1996)

Grove Instrument: *The New Grove Dictionary of Musical Instruments*, ed. Stanley Sadie, 3 vols. (London, 19841)

Grove Music: *The New Grove Dictionary of Music and Musicians*, ed. Stanley Sadie, 20 volumes (London, 1980; this is actually the sixth edition of the work)

Ill. Bembo, 'Vie italienne': 'Une vie italienne de sainte Catherine de Bologne', ed. F. van Ortroy and R. Lechat, in *Analecta Bollandiana* XLI (1923), 386-416

JAMS: *Journal of the American Musicological Society*

Lockwood, Ferrara: Lewis Lockwood, *Music in Renaissance Ferrara 1400-1505: the Creation of a Musical Centre in the Fifteenth Century*, Oxford Monographs on Music (Oxford, 1984)

Memorials of St. Dunstan: *Memorials of Saint Dunstan, Archbishop of Canterbury...*, ed. William Stubbs, Rerum britannicarum medii aevi scriptores, or Chronicles and Memorials of Great Britain and Ireland During the Middle Ages (Rolls Series) (London, 1874)

Sette armi: Santa Caterina Vegri, *Le sette armi spirituali*, ed. Cecilia Foletti, Medioevo e umanesimo, ed. R. Avesani et al., vol. 56 (Padua, 1985)

Tiella, 1974: Marco Tiella, *La <<violeta>> di s. Caterina de' Vigri (sec. XV) nel convento del Corpus Domini, Bologna*, Nuova metodologia quaderni di organologia, vol. 3 (Florence, 1974)

Tiella, 1975: *ibid.*, 'The Violeta of S. Caterina de' Vigri', in *The Galpin Society Journal* XXVIII (April, 1975), 60-70, pls. IV, XIII-XIV

Tinctoris, *De inventione*: Karl Weinmann, *Johannes Tinctoris (1445-1511), und sein unbekannter Traktat 'De inventione et usu musice': Historish-kritische Untersuchung*, ed. Wilhelm Fischer (Tutzing, 1961)

[1] *...questa picoleta opera facta con lo divino aiuto per mi, minema chagnola latrante soto la menssa delle excelente e dillichatissime serve e spoxe de lo immaculato angnello Cristo Iesù, sore del monasterio del Corpo de Cristo in Ferrara...*; *Sette armi*, p. 115.

[2] *...per amore del qualle con iubilo de core crido dicendo inverso le sue dillecatissime serve e spoxe: "Ciaschaduna amante che ama lo Segnare/ vegna alla danza cantando d'amore/ vegna danzando tucta infiammata/ solo dessiderando cului che l'à creata/ e dal pericoloxo statto mundano l'à sperata,/ ponendola nel nobilissimo claustro della sancta religione..."* (*...for love of Him, with praise in faithful heart, speaking in verse to those His most fastidious handmaids and brides: 'Each lover who loves the Lord,/ Comes to the*

novice, a wholly sacred image of communal musical performance is held out to her; to chant psalms in choir, in the expectation of meriting to sing in the presence of God.[3] These images accord well with the music of conventional sanctity we tacitly set, carelessly rehearse, and impatiently publish: true saints sing, real instruments are unclean. Yet this modern view of late-medieval musical propriety is delightfully confounded by Santa Caterina's personal use of music in her private devotions, as recorded and transmitted by others after she left to 'sing sweetly in the presence of her God'. It is the principal subject of this paper.

I begin with the briefest reference to saints and instruments, provide an outline of Santa Caterina's life, discuss her musical experience and describe her vielle, and place her bowed relic in its organological setting. I end by presenting Santa Caterina's vielle playing, not as a peculiarity, out of tune with her time, but rather as part of a tradition of late-medieval contemplative practice.

There are few saints for whom music was entirely absent from the spiritual part of their earthly careers. Their involvement in the musics of their familiar liturgies was so ordinary as to receive little comment from hagiographers. Most saints' active participation was purely vocal. Some, however, used instruments other than the voice variously within, and without, the formal liturgies. Among the preserved relics of early medieval Irish saints are handbells.[4] Of Anglo-Saxon saints, St. Dunstan is said

---

dance singing of love,/ Comes dancing all inflammed,/ Only desiring the one who created them,/ And to be set apart from the parlous state of the world,/ Placed in the most noble seclusion of Holy Religion...'); Sette armi, p. 115. Some of the medieval background to the tradition is sketched in E. Ann Matter, *The Voice of My Beloved: the Song of Songs in Western Medieval Christianity*, Middle Ages Series (Philadelphia, 1990); the field is vast, however.

[3] *...speranza, la quale a mi parlando per sua cortexia disse che veramente in cielo porò montare... / e nel cospeto del Dio mio dolcemente cantarò/ se in coro humilemente salmezarò...* (...Hope, who, speaking to me in her courtliness, said that truly I will be able to ascend into heaven..., and in the presence of my God I will sing sweetly,/ If I will sing psalms humbly in choir...); *Sette armi*, p. 161.

[4] Perhaps the most evocative of these relics is the handbell ascribed by tradition to St. Patrick; see Raghnall Ó Floinn, 'Clog Iarainn Phádraig agus a Scrín', in *Seoda na hÉireann: Ealaín Éireannach 3000 R.Ch.-1500 A.D.*, ed. Michael Ryan (Dublin, 1985), pp. 167-169, 192, cat. nos. 79 a-b. The date range proposed for the bell, saec. VI-saec.VIII (*i.e.*, from a half-century after Patrick's death, to centuries later), suggests the difficulties in determining the relationship of a saint to a bell. Indications of the use of the bells can be found in many *vitae, e.g.*, 'Betha Máedóc Ferna II' (Second Life of Máedóc of Ferns), in *Bethada Náem nÉrenn/ Lives of Irish Saints...*, ed. and trs. Charles Plummer, 2 vols. (Oxford, 1922), I, pp. 190-290 (text), II, pp. 184-281 (translation). These include warning off brigands (I, p. 211, II, p. 205), cursing enemies (I, pp. 236-237, II, pp. 229-230), use in prayer (I, p. 245, II, p. 238: perhaps used only to punctuate certain liturgical movements, or to mark certain

to have been an expert player of the *tympán*, *cithara*, and other instruments.[5] There are traditions that he gave musical implements to abbeys, such as the organ which was at Malmesbury.[6] Remains of medieval in-

---

words, such as *nomina sacra*), and signalling the hours for communal prayer (I, p. 245, II, p. 238: this last may not be a handbell). A bell from Temleport, County Cavan, and now at the Public Library in Armagh, is said to have been St. Máedóc's (*Clog Maedóic*). Charles Plummer, in his edition of *Vitae sanctorum Hiberniae*...(Oxford, 1910), vol. I, pp. clxxvi-clxxvii, lists other *loci* attesting to additional uses for bells. Many of these are miraculous. A typology of early Irish handbells is found in Cormac Bourke, 'Early Irish Hand-Bells', in *Journal of the Royal Society of Antiquaries of Ireland* 110 (1980), 52-66 (St. Máedóc's bell is cat. no. 4, pp. 61, 65). Richard Sharpe, in his recent translation of Adomnán of Iona, *Life of St. Columba* (Harmondsworth, 1995), citing Bourke at p. 269, note 82, states that the handbells were clapper-less. Unfortunately, this conforms neither with Bourke's direct statements, nor with the archaeological evidence presented.

[5] *Iterum cum videret dominum regem saecularibus curis fatigatum, psallebat in timpano sive in cithara, sive alio quolibet musici generis instrumento; quo facto tam regis quam omnium corda principum exhilarabat* (*Again, when he* [i.e., Dunstan] *saw that the lord king* [i.e., Áthelstan] *was worn down by worldly concerns, he used to play upon the tympán or on the cythara, or on some other musical instrument. His playing used to bring joy to the heart of the king* [cf. I Reg. 16, 23], *as much as it gladened the hearts of the thanes*); 'Vita sancti Dunstani auctore Osberno', in *Memorials of St. Dunstan*, pp. 79-80. More striking is the story of St. Dunstan's *cythara*, when he didn't directly play it: *Qui assumpta in manibus cithara, ad domum tendit religiosae, citharam in pariete suspendit, opus ad quod venerat diligenter instituit. Cumque manum operi, cor autem atque labia Deo praepararet, apparuit in domo gloria Domini, quae illum jocunda suavitate reficiebat, caeteros vero insolita admiratione exterritos reddebat. Nam cithara illius quam affixam parieti fuisse diximus, ita ut erat, pendens in paxillo, absque ullo moventis dumtaxat hominis impulsu, consuetam omnibus hujus antiphonae meldoiam acutissima simul ac discretissima modulatione personuit: "Gaudent in coelis animae sanctorum..."... At ille mundissimo mundissimi cordis intuitu coelestem illum musicum intendens, admoneri se intelligit, ut vias duriores arripiat, ut Christi vestigia propius sequatur... audivimus olim rudentem asinam verba edidisse; citharam vero sine humano impulsu sensualiter cecinisse nunquam audivimus* (*Dunstan, taking the cythara in his hands, went to the house of that religious woman. Upon arriving he hung his cythara upon the wall, and then, with due attention, set upon the work for which he had come* [i.e., to execute a prepatory drawing for a stole to be embroidered in gold thread]. *As he readied his hand for work, setting his heart and lips to praise God, the glory of the Lord* [evidently an *aspectus Dei*] *appeared in the house, which reinvigorated Dunstan with its pleasing sweetness, as declared to those who were terrified at the unaccustomed wonder. Then his cythara, which, as we said, was attatched to the wall (and so it was, hanging on a peg), played without any human intervention whatsoever, so that all could hear the usual melody of the following antiphon, together with a very high and most distinct modulation: "Gaudent in coelis animae sanctorum..."... Dunstan, listening to that heavenly music with the purest contemplation of a most pure heart, understood the admonition that he should take the harder paths, so that he might follow in Christ's footsteps* [I Pet. 2, 21]... *Although we have heard that a braying ass once uttered words* [Num. 22, 28-30], *we have certainly never heard a cythara play secular music on its own*[!]...; 'Vita sancti Dunstani auctore Osberno', in *Memorials of St. Dunstan*, p. 80. It is not now accepted that St. Dunstan wrote the antiphon *Gaudent in caelis*; see David Hiley, *Western Plainchant: a Handbook* (Oxford, 1995), p. 581.

[6] According to William of Malmesbury, among St. Dunstan's gifts to the abbey was an organ *Mirae magnitudinis signa, non quidem, ut nostra fert aetas, dulci sed incondito sono strepentia, organa quae concentu suo in festivitatibus laetitiam populo excitarent, in quorum circuitu hoc distichon*

struments are, however, scarce,⁷ and among those bits and pieces are few that can be ascribed to the manufacture, ownership, or gift, of a saint. Not a case fragment, pipe, or slide of a 'Dunstan' organ survives, nor does peg, or tuning key of *tympán*, or *cythara* stand sealed in a shrine. The best chance for the association of a material object with a holy woman, or man, to endure is for such an object to be preserved as a relic. Survival in a museum case, although it means survival for the instrument, also often means that the object became entombed there through, as it were, a weak link in a chain of provenance; often that chain is irretrievably broken. Santa Caterina's vielle survives in a relic case, and, never having passed through the hands of the antiquities trade,⁸ its provenance is both long, and respectable. It is, indeed, an unusual survival. What do we know of its owner?

Caterina Vigri was born (1413) in Bologna into a family of the Ferrarese patriciate.⁹ There is a tradition that her father was trained as a

---

litteris aeneis affixit: Organa do sancto praesul Dunstanus Adhelmo [sic.]/ *Perdat hic aeternum qui vult hinc tollere regnum* (*Signs of astonishing benificence, not, indeed, such as our age can produce, a noise with a sweet but disordered sound, an organ such as can excite the joy of the people when it is played on feasts. Around the border of this instrument the following distich appears, attatched in letters of bronze: I, Dunstan the bishop, give this organ to saint Aldhelm;/ Let he who wishes to remove it from here lose the eternal kingdom*); 'Vita sancti Dunstani auctore Willelmo malmesberiensi', in *Memorials of St. Dunstan*, pp. 301-302; also Jean Perrot, *The Organ from Its Invention in the Hellenistic Period to the End of the Thirteenth Century*, tr. Norma Deane (Oxford, 1971), pp. 223-224; Peter Williams, *A New History of the Organ, from the Greeks to the Present Day* (Bloomington and London, 1980), p. 38; ibid., *The Organ in Western Culture, 750-1250*, Cambridge Studies in Medieval and Renaissance Music, ed. Iain Fenlon *et al.* (Cambridge, 1993), pp. 199-200, 202, 230-231 *et seq.* (Perrot's translations of ancient sources are generaly much more reliable than those provided by Williams). St. Dunstan is also said to have given bells; see Hiley, as in note 5 *supra*.

⁷Although now somewhat incomplete due to the continual accumulation of archaeological debris, a good idea of the range of surviving objects (and their disconcertingly partial state) can be had from Frederick Crane, *Extant Medieval Musical Instruments: a Provisional Catalogue by Types* (Iowa City, 1972). Instruments we would associate with 'high art' are in the minority; of those, only the harps (cat. nos. 341.1-3, 342.1-2, pp. 17-18), and the Wartburg gittern (cat. no. 323.2, p. 15: called a 'mandora or lute' by Crane) come close to Santa Caterina's vielle (cat. no. 331.7, p. 17) in their states of preservation.

⁸A study of a recent, and dramatic case of the dangers to accurate, attested, and usable provenance created by the antiquities trade at all levels is Ian Mathieson Stead, *The Salisbury Hoard*, forward by Lord Renfrew of Kaimsthorn (Stroud, 1998). Nor is the remarkable, and strangely unedifying example of Sotheby's ever to be overlooked.

⁹A modern account, mostly reasonable, is in Foletti's introduction to *Sette armi*. Capsule accounts are Jacques Heerinckx, 'Catherine de Bologne', in *Dictionnaire de spiritualité, ascétique, et mystique, doctrine, et histoire*, ed. Charles Baumgartner *et al.*, t. II (Paris, 1953), cols. 288-290; Gian Domenico Gordini, 'Caterina da Bologna', in *Bibl. sanct.*, vol. III, cols. 980-982; S. Spanò, 'Caterina Vigri', in *Dizionario biografico degli italiani*, ed. Alberto M. Ghisalberti *et al.*, vol. 22 (Rome, 1979), pp. 381-383. The level of disharmony among these accounts is strik-

lawyer, but that he chose to serve a greater family, the d'Este of Ferrara, as a diplomatic retainer.[10] She spent her early years as a lady in waiting, and companion to Margherita, daughter of Niccolò III of Ferrara. It was probably at that time that Caterina acquired her facility with Latin, and her literary education. At around the age of fourteen (perhaps thirteen, perhaps fifteen), she chose to enter religion, joining a house in Ferrara for pious women, a house which likely owed much to the *devotio moderna*.[11] Sometime within the next five years Caterina and many of her sisters became Poor Clares at the *Corpus Domini* in Ferrara. Between entering religion, and embracing the Rule of St. Francis, Santa Caterina was tried by temptations orchestrated by the Enemy. It was after this period that she wrote her treatise on *The Seven Spiritual Weapons* (1438; it was never published in her lifetime), and the virtuosic Latin metrical rosary on the 'life, death, and resurrection of the Lord, and the mysteries of the life of Christ and the Virgin' (1445).[12] In 1456 she was sent to Bologna, the city of her birth, to be the first abbess of the new *Corpus Domini*, a daughter house to that of the same name in Ferrara. The surviving paintings and manuscripts attributable to her hand, including her breviary, were apparently produced while she directed the house in Bologna.[13] More significantly, at this period she enjoyed mystical visions of Christ, the Virgin, St. Francis, St. Thomas Becket, and other saints.

---

ing. Spanò (p. 381) wishes Santa Caterina to be born *nel capoluogo emiliano* (=Ferrara), yet the *vita* by Dionysio Paleotti, the first given in *AA.SS.*, clearly states *nata est Bononiae* (p. 36).

[10] *Sette armi*, pp. 36, 38. Foletti (p. 38) cites Grassetti, *Vita di S. Caterina de Bologna*, to the effect that Santa Caterina's father was a professor of law at Padua about the time she was born. I cannot find this in the Latin version; rather, Grassetti merely states that Santa Caterina's father obtained a degree in both laws at Bologna (...*et juris utriusque lauream adeptus Bononiae*; G. Grassetti, 'Vita II beatae Catharinae bononiensis', in *AA.SS.*, p. 47).

[11] *Sette armi*, pp. 46-47. In a comment after this paper was delivered, an audience member made the intriguing suggestion that the introduction, or the spread of the *devotio moderna* in Italy may be connected in some way or other to the presence of prominent musicians from the Low Countries in various Italian cities and courts. This is an attractive suggestion, and would repay study.

[12] Caterina de' Vigri, *Rosarium: poema del XV secolo*, ed. and tr. Gilberto Sgarbi, with a 'theological essay' by Enzo Lodi (Bologna, 1997). The description, quoting Grassetti, is on p. ix.

[13] These works have been treated most recently in Jeryldene M. Wood, 'Breaking the Silence: the Poor Clares and the Visual Arts in Fifteenth-Century Italy', in *Renaissance Quarterly* XLVIII, 2 (1995), 262-286, and *ibid.*, *Women, Art, and Spirituality: the Poor Clares of Early Modern Italy* (Cambridge, 1996). Wood has performed a useful service in attempting to place these works in their art-historical, institutional, spiritual, and intellectual contexts. Her presentations are, however, singularly unreliable, *e.g.*, 'Breaking the Silence', 273, note 24, cites Serena Spanò Martinelli, 'La biblioteca del "Corpus Domini" bolognese: l'incensueto spac-

For much of her time as a Poor Clare her health was not good. She died in 1463, after a serious illness, and a year's reprieve bought through the prayers of many. Obedient, solicitous, and exemplary in life, she proved incorruptable in death (fig. 1).[14] She still resides with her sisters of the *Corpus Domini* in Bologna, enthroned, serene, solicitous yet in her chapel-sized reliquary, the *Capella della Santa*.[15] And if she chose to arise, she would find her vielle within convenient reach.

We know naught of Santa Caterina's musical education. We can, however, infer the time and place she may have acquired the rudiments, and succeeded to a proficiency in performance: the period of her service at Ferrara, as a lady-in-waiting to Margherita d'Este. Caterina was between nine and eleven years of age when she was employed as the princess' companion, and between thirteen and fifteen years old when she left that earthly court to apprentice herself to religion. These were typically the years when aristocratic women in Northern Italy received their formation.[16] At first consideration, Ferrara would seem to be the perfect

---

cato di una cultura monastica femminile', in *La Bibliofilía: Rivista di storia del libro e di bibliografia* LXXXVIII, I (1986), 1-23, to state that the theological holdings of the library offer clear proof of Santa Caterina's 'intellectual and spiritual leadership'. The 1602 inventory Spanò Martinelli edits was not drafted as a catalogue of the library, and all the dated and datable books listed were acquired after Santa Caterina died; in fact, most were acquired long after.

[14]Foletti, in *Sette armi* (p. 3), remarks: ...*e i fatti prodigiosi che si verificarono dopo il disseppellimento del corpo, trovato incorrotto...* (...*and the marvellous facts which were verified after the disintering of the body, discovered to be incorrupt...*). The Bollandist editor of the *vitae* of Santa Caterina in the *AA.SS.* was much struck by the incorruptability of her remains when he visited the *Corpus Domini: Inter illustria Italicae pietatis monumenta...* [*est*] *incorruptum Virginis Catharinae corpus; quod Bononiae religiose accedentibus offertur spectabile, per crates vitreamque fenestram, in eo pariete, qui latus ecclesiae Domini Corpus dextrum separat ab interiori sacello, in quo ipsa viventi similis (nisi quod partium patentium color obfuscatus ad nigredinem vergat) mollisque adhuc et tractabilis considet, divina dumtaxet sustenta virtute, quod anno MDCLX illac transuentes nostris ipsimet oculis venerabundi aspeximus...* (*Among the famous monuments of Italian piety... is the incorrupt body of the virgin Caterina; this remarkable relic is shown to those who come devoutly to Bologna, through a lattice work and glass window let into that wall, which divides the right side of the church of the Corpus Domini from the inner chapel. Seated there, she seems like one who is alive (except that on the portions of her body which are not covered, a darkened colour has turned to black), with flesh which is still soft and yielding. Passing by that way in 1660, we saw with our very eyes the body of the venerable one, preserved solely by Divine power...*); *AA.SS.*, p. 35.

[15]Certainly a more commodius, decorative, and powerful space than the utilitarian cupboard in which Bentham whiles away most of his year in gloomy London.

[16]See Paul F. Grendler, *Schooling in Renaissance Italy: Literacy and Learning, 1300-1600*, The Johns Hopkins University Studies in Historical and Political Science, 107th series, vol. 1 (Baltimore and London, 1989), pp. 93, 96, 97 (most of the evidence presented is later than Santa Caterina's time). Grendler briefly and usefully surveys the prescribed content of female education according to the writings of theorists (pp. 87-89), *e.g.*, Leonardo Bruni (1370-1444) recommeneds the *studia humanitatis*, with the exceptions of *disputatio* and *con-*

place for Caterina to have acquired a first-class literary and musical culture; until, that is, one realizes that that court's literary, musical, and artistic pre-eminence occurred sometime after Santa Caterina had left.[17] During most of Niccolò III's reign Ferrara enjoyed a musically indifferent culture. This changed with fair rapidity under Niccolò's successor, Leonello, for it was under him that the fame of the outstanding singer, improvisor, and gittern virtuoso, Pietrobono, began to grow spectacular.[18] It is worth saying that, although Santa Caterina most probably became learned at the court of Ferrara (as stated earlier), there is no direct evidence that she did.[19] It is just possible that she acquired her good

---

tionem habere (p. 87). Grendler's statement that ...*a significant minority of girls studied the Latin humanities, usually with male houshold tutors* (p. 93), likely describes Margherita's and Caterina's instructor(s).

[17] The standard monograph on the musical culture of Ferrara under the d'Este is Lockwood, *Ferrara*, which at pp. 11-27 treats the cultural tenor of Niccolò III's rule. The political character of Niccolò III's rule is examined in Trevor Dean, *Land and Power in Late Medieval Ferrara: the Rule of the d'Este, 1350-1450*, Cambridge Studies in Medieval Life and Thought, Fourth Series, 7, (Cambridge, 1988), pp. 23-27, *et seq*.

[18] An improvement in intellectual life at court due to Leonello's influence is eveident even before he became marquis in 1441; Lockwood, *Ferrara*, pp. 34-40. For Pietrobono, see Lockwood, *Ferrara*, pp. 98-108, and *ibid.*, 'Pietrobono', in *Grove Music*, 14, p. 744. Pietrobono's time at Ferrara, though not his time at court, overlapped with Santa Caterina's. It is not known if they ever met, and indeed it seems unlikely after she entered religion. According to modern musicology, Josquin Desprès sojourn at court (1503) was the most important musical event in Ferrara's history. A long-lived contemporary might not necessarily agree; see Lockwood, *Ferrara*, p. 98.

[19] Many authors have taken the possibility that Santa Caterina was educated in high literary culture, and music, at the court, not as speculation, however likely, but as fact, *e.g.*, the authors listed in note 9 *supra*, with the exception of Foletti. The earliest *vita* of Santa Caterina seems to make no mention of her education; Ill. Bembo, 'Vie italienne' (presumably written shortly after Santa Caterina's death, this is the first of two *vitae* of the saint by her fellow nun, friend, and successor as abbess of the *Corpus Domini* of Ferrara). Nor is her education at the court of Ferrara mentioned in the *vita* by Dionysio Paleotti, 'Vita beatae Catharinae bononiensis', tr. Joannes Antonius Flaminius, in *AA.SS.*, pp. 36-45 (written in 1511, and translated from Italian into Latin in 1522). A much later source does state that Santa Caterina did receive a good literary education while she was at the court of Ferrara: *Ibi [Ferrariae] latinarum litterarum prosecuta est studium, quarum rudimentis coeperat Bononiae imbui: in eisque tantos brevi progressus habuit, ut non modo quoscumque libros latine compositos intelligeret: sed prout ferebat ocassio, scriberet ipsa, componeretque nonnulla eleganti emendatoque stylo, quae in hunc usque diem servantur* (There [at the court of Ferrara] *she pursued the study of Latin letters, the beginnings of which she had begun to acquire at Bologna. And she soon made such great progress that she not only understood any book written in Latin, but, as the occasion demanded, she herself would write. She composed some works in a refined and correct style, works which are preserved to this day*); G. Grassetti, 'Vita II beatae Catharinae bononiensis', in *AA.SS.*, p. 47 (published 1620, compiled from vernacular sources). It should be noted that Grassetti implies that she did not learn to play vielle there (see note 28 *infra*). In the half century following Santa Caterina's death it may not have

education within cloistered walls, after having left the court. Or perhaps her 'higher education' was gained in both places. Wherever, and whenever the learning was imparted, it was done to great effect.

Santa Caterina's writings provide some notion of her opinion of music. As indicated earlier, she is quite willing to use music in the figural language of spiritual direction, as in *The Seven Spiritual Weapons*.[20] There is nothing unusual in this; music has provided some of the stock language for spiritual and mystical writing since antiquity.[21] One could be forgiven for considering its cultivation a characteristic of mendicant spirituality, or at least a characteristic of some varieties of Franciscan affective writings.[22] And, with a little effort, Santa Caterina's opinion on the right attitude to performance can be discovered barely sheathed among *The Seven Spiritual Weapons*.

Two passages in particular instruct us. In one, the novice can read: *...He will summon us still to return an account of the talent* [Mt. 25, 14-28] *of good will granted to us to use in His praise, and for the salvation of our soul, and the souls of those near to us.*[23] In the other, the novice is told of the *...most holy doctor Saint Augustine, who said that it is impossible to take pleasure in present delights,*

---

seemed necessary to state that she had been educated at court, for that would have been understood by anyone who read that she had lived there as a companion to Margherita d'Este. Grassetti's *vita* may print what up till the early seventeenth century was an orally transmitted tradition current in the *Corpus Domini* about Santa Caterina's education, or he may be presenting an undocumented assumption, or invention, of his own devising. Grassetti did not hesitate to elaborate and change his materials; see note 28 *infra*.

[20]See notes 2 and 3 *supra*.

[21]Many examples could be advanced. The following instance is mild: *Erat autem David vir in canticis eruditis, qui harmoniam musicam non vulgari voluptate dilexerit eaque Deo suo, qui verus est Deus, mystica rei magnae figuratione servierit.Diversorum enim sonorum rationabilis moderatusque concentus concordi varietate compactam bene ordinatae civitatis insinuat unitatem* (David, moreover, was a man learned in song, such a one as delighted in harmonius music, not with common pleasure, but for his God, who is the One True God. David used a mystical figure to express a great thing: the rational and orderly agreement of different sounds in concordant diversity makes known the composed unity of a well-ordered city); *Sancti Aureliani Augustini episcopi De civitate Dei libri XXII*, ed. B. Dombart, vol. II (Leipzig, 1918³), lib. XVII, cap. XIV, p. 235.

[22]This can be traced to the beginnings of Franciscan literature, *e.g.*, Thomas de Celano, 'Vita secunda', in *Fontes franciscani*, ed. Enrico Menestò and Stefano Brufani *et al.*, (Assisi, 1995), cap. LXXXIX-XC, pp. 558-559; anon., *Compilatio assisiensis, ibid.*, cap. 38, p. 1511, cap. 66, pp. 1565-1567, cap. 83-85, pp. 1594-1603; anon., *Speculum perfectionis, ibid.*, cap. IX, pp. 2013-2016; anon., 'I fioretti di san Francesco', ed. P. B. Bughetti, notes by Feliciano Olgiati, in *Fonti francescane: scritti e biografie di san Francesco d'Assisi...*, ed. Ezio Franceschini *et al.* (Padua, 1982³: reprint of the 1926 Quaracchi edition, with notes of 1977), pp. 1592-1593 (end of 'Della seconda considerazione delle sacre sante istimate').

[23]*...al quale ce converà ancora rendere raxone del talento della buona voluntade a nui concesso per exercitarlo in laude de lui e a ssalute de l'anima nostra e di nostri prosimi; Sette armi*, p. 120.

in the expectation of enjoying future goods [Aug., *Enarratio in ps. CXXXVI*, 16]. *For that reason, most beloved sisters, be content not to have any pleasure or delight in this world...*[24] To anyone impaired by the 'art-for-art's-sake' murrain, Santa Caterina's words would, I suppose, seem anti-musical. That is not a mistake I would care to make. The first passage instructs that any skill which can be turned to praise had best be so used. This is a clear incitement to be musical. The second passage warns that if we direct our appetites solely to worldly pleasures, such as secular entertainments, we have effectively consigned ourselves to an uncomfortable playing position among the instruments depicted on the right wing of Bosch's *Garden of Earthly Delights* altarpiece. Musical activity must be directed to its proper use.[25] This is its justification. Santa Caterina's high opinion of music, and the importance she attatched to performance, become even clearer upon viewing her visions.

Musical imagery plays an important role in two of these mystical experiences. Neither survives in a direct account from the saint's hand, but they are recorded in her various *vitae*. The earliest statement of the visions is by her fellow nun and friend, the Blessed Illuminata Bembo.[26]

---

[24]...*dice el sacratissimo doctore santo Augustino che l'è impossibile a goldere i beni prexenti e li futuri. Adoncha, dilectisseme sorele, siate contente de non avere in questo mondo alcuno piacere né dilecto...*; *Sette armi*, p. 121.

[25]St. Dunstan is said to have expressed a similar opinion: *Et quamvis his omnibus artibus magnifice polleret, ejus tamen multitudinis quae musicam instruit, eam videlicet quae instrumentis agitatur, speciali quadam affectione vendicabat scientiam; sicut David psalterium sumens, citharam percutiens, modificans organa, cimbala tangens; sed non sicut hii quorum inertiam et luxuriosum otium propheticus noster increpat armentarius; "Qui dormitis", inquit, "in lectis eburneis, et lascivitis in stratis vestris; qui comeditis agnum de grege et vitulos de medio armenti; qui canitis ad vocem psalterii, sicut David. Putaverunt se vasa cantici habere, bibentes in phialis vinum"* (*And, although he* [i.e., St. Dunstan] *was wonderfully able in all these arts* [*philosophorum scientias*, etc.], *nevertheless, of that multitude of arts, that skill which furnished music, and by this he meant music performed on instruments, he used to defend with a certain proper argument. He would say 'play in the spirit in which David took up the psaltery, plucked the cythara, played measures on the organ, and struck the bells; but avoid the practices of those whose idleness and extravagant leisure our prophetical herdsman exclaimed against, when he declared "you who sleep on beds of ivory, lying lustfully in your bedclothes, and you who eat the lamb of the flock, and the calf from the middle of the herd, along with you who imbibe wine in wine bowls, thinking them vessels of song, and that you sing to the sound of the psaltery, like David"*[Am. 6, 4-6]'); 'Vita sancti Dunstani auctore Osberno', in *Memorials of St. Dunstan*, p. 78 (the final sentence has been rendered in the second person to aid in comprehension). If these views are not demonstrably Dunstan's, Osbern certainly thought they could be his. The evidence for the esteem in which instrumental practice was held by many who were well educated, well placed, and well respected, and the use of instruments in sacred contexts, has been assiduously overlooked in recent pages emanating from a peculiarly insular sect of musicologists, and their camp followers.

[26]Antonio Coccia, 'Bembo, Illuminata', in *Bibl. sanct.*, vol. II, cols. 1088-1089. Beata Illuminata also experienced visions, and was abbess of the *Corpus Domini* in Bologna after

There is a fair certainty that what the Blessed Illuminata wrote is what she heard from Santa Caterina herself.

In the centre of the garden were steps of precious stones, which he [i.e., a 'magnificent king'] mounted on up to a tribunal, or throne, of a king. This throne was engraved all over, and wonderfully worked, and covered with a countless multitude of little boys who were vested in small tunics coloured vermilion, each with a white stole. On their breasts, over the tunics, was a type of shield, which bore a small lamb, its coat purest white, most decoratively worked. Each boy wore at his neck a circlet of fine gold, and carried in his right hand a flowering palm of lilies and roses, white and vermilion, and in his left hand a musical instrument. All played, singing: "Gloria, laus, et honor, etc. [processional hymn for Palm Sunday]", with a clear voice and a most sweey melody. And, according to her [i.e., Santa Caterina], such was the sweetness and charm of that song and sound, that, experienced together with the beauty of those little ones, it seemed there was gathered together there all the joy and delight of this world, and that bleakness and sorrow together are as nothing in comparison.[27]

The 'magnificent king' is St. Francis, and the 'countless multitude of little boys' are the Holy Innocents (Ill. Bembo, 'Vie italiene', 413-414). In this glittering mystical setting, where those who were poor, downtrodden, or martyred in this world wear the symbols of their transformation, the music created by singers with instruments is sweet, charming, and delightful. It is the music of divine praise.

Another of Santa Caterina's visions proved more personally engaging, and exemplary:

Know, O daughters, that I withdrew for a time into a meadow of such wonderful beauty that there is no human language that could ever describe it. In the centre of the meadow was a throne worthy of an emperor, on which God sat in such wondrous and

---

Santa Caterina's death. Her account of Santa Caterina's visions in her first *vita*, Ill. Bembo, 'Vie italienne', is the ultimate written source of all later accounts.

[27] *In el mezo del zardino erano gradi de pietre preciose, sopra li quale se saliva ad uno tribunale overo sedia del re, tute intagliate, e lavorati mirabilemente, coperti de innumerabile multitudine de fanzulini, vestite de certi tonicele de colore vermiglio con stolle biancho. In mezo del pecto sopra le tonicele era a modo de uno scudeto, e in quelo uno agnelino candidissimo ornatissimamente lavorato. Al colo portavano uno circolino de fino oro; nella dextra una palma fiorita de zili e roxe, bianche e vermeglie; e in la sinistra uno stromente da sonare. Tuti sonando cantavano:<<Gloria, rlaus et honor>> etc. con voce chiara et dulcisima melodia. E secondo el parere de questa sore, tanto era la dolceza et suavità de questo canto e sono, e insiema la belleza de questi picolini, che essendo radunati sieme tute le alegreze et piacere de questo mondo, parireve una tristicia e dolore a respecto de quela;* Ill. Bembo, 'Vie italiene', 413.

ineffable dignity that my heart was nearly incapable of recording it. To his right was seated his beloved mother, on whose throne were placed saints Stephen and Laurence, and all about them was a multitude of angels. Before the Almighty was one [angel] *who played a small vielle. Playing by heart, he caused these words to resound, that is to say: "Et gloria eius in te videbitur* [Is. 60, 2]*". As I beheld this wonder, and heard that sound, my soul began to leave my body; yet God, who is sublime, immanent on that throne worthy of an emperor, held out His right arm, and said to me: "Daughter, attend well to these things which resound, which are what I say: 'Et gloria eius in te videbitur'* "*. She then said that He next revealed that He said to her what He wished to say: "Et gloria eius", etc. Thereafter, she had to have a small vielle for herself, which she played several times a day. When she did so, she seemed to disappear the way wax does in a fire* [Ps. 67, 3]*, for at one time she would sing the verse "Et gloria eius", etc., and at another she would stand with her face turned heavenwards, still as a mute.*[28]

---

[28] *E sapiati, figliole, che io me ritrovay per alquanto spacio in uno prato de tanta mirabile belleza che non è lingua humana che may lo potese exprimere. Nel mezo del quale era una sedia imperiale suso lo quale era Dio de tanta mirabile et indicibile dignità che lo core me mancha pur a ricordarmene. E a lato a luy alla sua mano drita era la sua dilecta mater, la sedia dela quale li suy, pomi l'uno era sancto Stepheno e l'altro sancto Lorentio, e de intorno a ley era multitudine de angeli; davanti alo Omnipotente era uno che sonava una violeta, lo sono del quale corde resonua queste parole, cioè: "Et gloria eius in te videbitur". E videndo io queste mirabile cose e udendo questo sono, l'anima comenzò a partirse dal corpo. Ma lo grande Idio, istando suso questa sedia, destese lo suo brazo drito e presime dicendome:<<Figliola, intende bene quelo che risona quelo sono che dice: "Et gloria eius in te videbitur">>. E qui dise che li aperise cioè che li dixe quelo che volleva dire "Et gloria eius", etc. E dise che como li ebe dicto questo, disparve dali ochi soy ogni cosa et fu subito meliorata et romase in tanto iubilo per più mesi spessissimo dicendo: "Et gloria eius", etc. E oltra li fu de besogno che se li atrovase una violeta et quela più volte lo zorno sonandola parea che tuta se deleguase como fa la cira al focho, ora cantando lo dicto verso "Et gloria eius in te videbitur", ora stava con la facia verso el cielo, stando como muta*, Ill. Bembo, 'Vie italiene', 401. The apparition of the divine instrumentalist occurs in earlier Franciscan literature. At the conclusion of the 'Second Consideration of the Holy Stigmata' (*ca.* 1370-1390), it is reported that when St. Francis was contemplating the state of life of the saints, he requested the grace to sample a little of that joy. An angel appeared, and played one bowstroke of melody, which was of such sweetness that had the angel played anymore, St. Francis' soul would have left his body; see 'I fioretti di san Francesco' (as in note 22 *supra*), pp. 1592-1593. The risk of divine music causing the soul to separate from the body occurs in another mystical experience, in which Santa Caterina hears an angelic choir sing the last *sanctus* of the *Sanctus* at mass; Dionysio Paleotti, 'Vita beatae Catharinae bononiensis', tr. Joannes Antonius Flaminius, in *AA.SS.*, p. 38. The Latin version of the *vita* by Paleotti follows quite closely the Blessed Illuminata's accounst of the vision with the vielle playing angel. Grassetti's telling, on the other hand, presents many differences amid a host of circumstantial detail not present in the earlier versions. Needless to say, this does not inspire confidence in Grassetti. According to him, Santa Caterina's partial recovery occurred after she had received the last rites, and the esctasy which insued produced in her that ...*skill of extraordinary vielle playing...* (...*mirabilis illa pulsandae... cytharae peritia...*). He further states that she had never received any training on the instrument (...*quod numquam didicerat...*), and implies that she only played the

Santa Caterina was clearly greatly affected by this mystical experience. It took place a year before her death, and marked that partial remission of her illness.[29] It is one of the most striking accounts from the late middle ages of the use of an instrument, and one of the least well known. It is the only instance for which we know the owner of an instrument, and something of her interior life; why she used her instrument, and something of how she used it; and for which we can know the instrument in more than its name.

The vielle is a small instrument, just under 49 cm. in length (fig. 2).[30] It is, indeed, always referred to as a 'small vielle', a *violeta* (or *lyra parva*), in the early sources.[31] The body, endpin, neck, and pegbox are continuous, that is, they are carved out of a single piece of wood (Tiella, 1974, p. 7; Tiella, 1975, 61). The body was hollowed-out, possibly with a gouge. There is no separate fingerboard, the neck is merely continued up to a height sufficient to serve as the surface for stopping the strings. A small space has been hollowed-out at the very top of the pegbox, perhaps to serve as a storage area (Tiella, 1975, 65). Hardwood is used, probably a variety of maple (Tiella, 1974, p. 7; Tiella, 1975, 61). The single-piece construction is quite robust, and, as far as can be determined, the walls of the body are strikingly thick, at about 6 mm. If a small devil were hit

---

instrument once (...*dimissa, quam numquam deinde tetigit, cythara*...)!; . Grassetti, 'Vita II beatae Catharinae bononiensis', in *AA.SS.*, p. 66. It is not clear why Grassetti made these changes. His replacing the *violeta* of the original sources with *cythara* probably reflects his desire to use a more classicizing vocabulary, made doubly prestigious and rectable by the occurrence of the term in biblical and patristic literarture. His usage may also reflect his unfamiliarity, or discomfort, with the type of instrument Santa Caterina played.

[29]Dionysio Paleotti, 'Vita beatae Catharinae bononiensis', tr. Joannes Antonius Flaminius, in *AA.SS.*, p. 40. Paleotti remarks that the prayers of the sisters were 'efficacious in dissuading God' from calling her at that time.

[30]Tiella, 1974, p. 6; Tiella, 1975, 60, 62-63 (the length given in the text, 49 cm., is slightly greater than that specified on the drawings, 48.8 cm.). Tiella's 1974 monograph is a more coherent and detailed presentation of the vielle than his 1975 article. The maker of the instrument is anonymous. It is just possible that Santa Caterina made the vielle, although there is no evidence, or tradition, to that effect. It is Tiella's opinion that the instrument is the work of a professional luthier; Tiella, 1974, p. 12; Tiella, 1975, 67. The first *vita* by the Blessed Illuminata offers no defintie opinion on this point, but the wording in Paleotti's *vita* strongly implies that Santa Caterina did not make her vielle: *Adeo quidem ut necessarium fuerit, ut lyram illic parvam sorores invenirent...* (*So, indeed, it became necessary that the sisters should find a small vielle...*); Dionysio Paleotti, 'Vita beatae Catharinae bononiensis', tr. Joannes Antonius Flaminius, in *AA.SS.*, p. 40.

[31]See notes 28 and 30 *supra*. One of the changes imposed by Grassetti on the narrative of Santa Caterina's life is to make the *violeta* a full-sized instrument, a *cythara*. The terminology of the early *vitae* is instructive, for, applied to Santa Caterina's surviving instrument, it provides a concrete idea of what some educated Italians considered a 'small' vielle.

with this instrument, it would certainly remember it. There are two bellies, both flat. The upper, about 3mm. thick, is, curiously, also out of hardwood, possibly maple, and the lower belly is a softwood, either spruce or fir.[32] There is no soundpost, and there may never have been one, and a single bar is glued under the upper belly (Tiella, 1975, 61, by implication). The bridge, pegs, tailpiece, and nut, are of bone. The top profile of the bridge is quite flat, perhaps indicating that more than one string was played at a time. The instrument apparently shows no signs of ever having been fitted with more, or less, than four strings (Tiella, 1974, pp. 8-9). The pitches Santa Caterina preferred for the open strings are not now known. Late-medieval evidence would suggest tuning in fifths.[33] It is possible that the strings were tuned in double courses,[34] or that the top string was a melody string, and the other three functioned as drones (fingered, or not).

A bow also survives with the instrument (fig. 2) (Tiella, 1975, 68-69). The material of which it is made has yet to be identified in the literature. The stick is apparently round, and slightly longer (51 cm.) than the vielle. The bow has a fixed frog, and there seems to be provision for fewer hairs than on a modern bow.[35]

Placing details of morphology aside, the general aspect of Santa Caterina's little vielle will strike the reader who attends performances of medieval music as, in a word, odd. It does not look like the instruments, speculative reconstructions of 'rebecs' and 'vielles' ('medieval fiddles'), used in present day performances of medieval music. Santa Caterina's vielle, indeed, almost appears to be a cross, or hybrid, between our categories of 'rebec', a tear-drop shaped instrument with vaulted back and usually three strings, and 'vielle', an instrument with an oval to rectangular outline (sometimes waisted), flat back and belly, and four or five

---

[32] Tiella, 1974, p. 7; Tiella, 1975, 74. The earlier discussion is better. Tiella speculates that this part may not be original.

[33] *...per... diapentem...*; Tinctoris, *De inventione*, lib. IV, p. 42. If the bridge were absolutely flat, and the four strings were meant to be played simultaneously, a tuning of four single courses in fifths would present a problem. Even set up as a three course instrument, with one double string, and two single string courses (see note 34 *infra*), there would be an uncomfortable ninth between the bottom and top open strings.

[34] *...sive quinque... sic et per unisonos temperate: inequaliter...* (*...or five strings, arranged in double courses, though unequally* [*i.e.*, with five strings, there will be two courses of double strings, and one course consisting of a single string]...); Tinctoris, *De inventione*, lib. IV, p. 42. Tinctoris' *...per geminam diapentem...* would seem to rule out a re-entrant tuning; *ibid.*

[35] *Ibid.* The bow is not fitted with its original hair, for there is a seventeenth-century record of rehairing; Tiella, 1974, p. 15; *ibid.*, 1975, 68.

strings.[36] Copies of her instrument are not widely used, if at all, for performing fifteenth-century music, even that of Northern Italy, yet hers is the only vielle which seems to survive in a reasonably complete state.[37] There is clearly something wrong, either with Santa Caterina's bowed relic, or with us. I fear the latter is the case.

This issue is not difficult to decide. If Santa Caterina's vielle has no close analogues, then if original, it cannot be taken as normative for any wide tradition of vielle making. Its significance for organology, and the modern recreation of medieval music, is then nil; it would only be important in her story. It could, in that case, be a forgery, a false relic.

The most active period for the imaginative confection of 'ancient instruments' was the nineteenth century, for that is when the great collections, national and private, were being assembled.[38] No place was a better hunting ground for historic instruments than Italy. Italian craftsmen were long used to making the past vivid with whatever concrete features would confirm connoisseurs in their judgements. Among the firms supplying finely-crafted 'antique' instruments, that headed by Leopoldo Franciolini stood out, both for the size of its trade, and for the fact that Franciolini was successfully prosecuted for commercial fraud in 1910.[39] Among the imaginatively conceived and ill-attested creations of Franciolini, however, none so far uncovered have the particular features of Santa Caterina's vielle; its two bellies on different levels, the complex contours of its back, or its design of rose.[40] Slightly disquieting, to me at

---

[36]Tiella, much concerned with placing Santa Caterina's vielle on a strictly constructed line of organological development (1974, p. 10), floates the hypothesis that an earlier, saec. XV^1 'form' (rebec?) was altered into a *viola da brazzo* 'form' saec. XV^2 (1974, pp. 13-14; 1975, 67-68). Tiella wisely retreats from this notion, only to fall into the trap of labelling Santa Caterina's vielle a 'transitional instrument'. Teleology has no place here. Santa Caterina, and her contemporaries, would have been much surprized to learn they were playing on 'transitional' instruments. Who, after all, lives in a 'transitional' period, making 'transitional' music?

[37]Novgorod examples from the central middle ages, and English examples from the wreck of the Mary Rose (saec. XVI^1), are much less well preserved.

[38]John Barnes and Charles Beare, 'Forgery', in *Grove Instrument*, 1, pp. 789-790. This is not to say that there was not a manufacture of 'retrospective' instruments, and instruments with labels claiming false pedigrees, in the seventeenth and eighteenth centuries. Few of these, however, were fantastic in quite the way the nineteenth-century forgeries could be.

[39]Edwin M. Rippin, *The Instrument Catalogues of Leopoldo Franciolini*, Music Indexes and Bibliographies, ed. George R. Hill (Hackensack, 1974); *ibid.*, 'Franciolini, Leopoldo', in *Grove Instrument*, 1, p. 794. Franciolini paid his fine, and his work continued.

[40]See Ripin, *Catalogues* (as in note 39 *supra*), particularly plates on pp. 43, 46. Tiella points out that there are no suspicious features in the construction of the saint's vielle, either in materials, or techniques; see Tiella, 1974, pp. 11-12; *ibid.*, 1975, 65-66. Margaret Anne

any rate, is the number of strings on the saint's vielle. A treatise from the end of the fifteenth century specifies three, or five strings, and many fifteenth-century representations show three-stringed 'rebecs', and five-stringed 'vielles'.[41] As stated earlier, forgers tend, consciously or not, to update the models they employ to conform to the tastes of their times.[42] A copy of one of Fra Angelico's angels from the *Linaiuoli* altarpiece, by a nineteenth-century follower of the beatified Domincan, clearly shows this. The rebec of Fra Angelico's angel has three strings (fig. 3), that held by the angel in the copy has four (figs. 4 a-b), the number of strings usual on nineteenth-century violins. My disquiet, however, can be dispelled by recalling my qualifiers; the 'three and five formula' is just a tendency; the number of strings was not rigidly standardized. The small vielle in a well-known genre piece by Lorenzo Costa seems to show four strings (fig. 5).[43]

Perhaps the best indication Santa Caterina's vielle is not a forgery resides in its provenance. If her vielle were a manuscript, its localization would be taken as nearly a sure thing. There has been no break in ownership. References to maintenance of the bow occur in the late seventeenth century.[44] And, if one accepts the evidence of the *vitae*, the recorded provenance of the vielle stretches back nearly to the saint's day.

The instrument, then, is not a forgery. Are there any analogues?

Two paintings by Bartolomeo Mantagna show instruments whose form bears some resemblance to Santa Caterina's vielle (figs. 6-7), yet they are, in truth, not that different from what we now exclusively label

---

Downie, in her superb *The Rebec: an Orthographic and Iconographic Study*, Ph.D. dissertation, West Virginia University (1981), vol. I, pp. 295, 525, accepts Santa Caterina's vielle as authentic. She discusses Franciolini's versions of the past in vol. I, pp. 296-307.

[41]*Enimvero: sive tres ei sint chorde simplices ut in pluribus: per geminam diapentem: sive quinque (ut in aliquibus) sic et per unisonos temperate: inequaliter* (For the vielle may have three single string courses, arranged in double fifths [e.g., G-d-a] (as on most fiddles), or it may have five strings (as on others), arranged as two double courses, with one single string course [e.g., giving the same range as the fiddle with three strings]); Tinctoris, *De inventione*, lib. IV, p. 42.

[42]E.g., the relentless *décolletage* favoured by the Spanish Forger, and the stiffly saccharin features of his faces, reveal nineteenth-century expectations and tastes more than they do those of the fifteenth and sixteenth centuries; see William Voelkle, assisted by Roger S. Wieck, *The Spanish Forger* (New York, 1978) (more pieces attributable to his atelier have since been found, and some of those may be forgeries of forgeries).

[43]Jill Dunkerton, Susan Foister, Dillian Gordon, and Nicholas Penny, *Giotto to Dürer: Early Renaissance Painting in The National Gallery* (London, 1991), 'The Concert', cat. no. 50, pp. 342-343 (NG 2486), painted in Bologna, *ca.* 1485-1490; Maria Cristina Chiusa, 'Lorenzo (di Ottavio) Costa', *Grove Art*, 8, pp. 3-4 (Chiusa dates the altarpiece to 1492). Costa was trained at Ferrara.

[44]See note 35 *supra*.

'rebecs'.[45] The instrument whose back is visible in Fra Angelico's 'Coronation of the Virgin' altarpiece from S. Domenico in Fiesole (fig. 8), has a form that suggests some features of Santa Caterina's vielle.[46] Greater in significance than some more or less similar features these instrumentrs share, is the variety they show. Santa Caterina's vielle was no oddity; it was part of a tradition of bowed instruments that allowed considerable formal variation. The evidence of her instrument deserves to be taken seriously, supported as it is by contemporary and slightly later depictions, as those depicted instruments are validated by the existence of her vielle.[47] If we are serious about recovering what we can of the tools of earlier performance practice, then Santa Caterina can instruct us through her vielle. I look forward to hearing of a modest miracle effected through this bowed relic.

Mention of performance practice brings us back to contemplative practice. Are there any analogues to Santa Caterina's use of a vielle in contemplation?

---

[45]Bartolomeo Mantagna, 'Madonna and Child, enthroned with angel musicians, and SS. John the Baptist, Bartolomeo, Augustine, and Sebastian', Vicenza, Museo Civico (formerly in the church of S. Bartolomeo, Vicenza), ca. 1485, and the 'Madonna and Child, enthroned with angel musicians, and SS. John the Baptist, and Jerome', Pavia, Museo della Certosa, ca. 1490; see Leonello Puppi, *Bartolomeo Mantagna*, pref. by Sergio Bettini, Profili 2 (Venice, 1962), pp. 136-137, figs. 37-38 (Vicenza), and pp. 121-122, figs. 57-58 (Pavia); Marco Tanzi, 'Vicenza', in *Il Quattrocento: La pittura nel Veneto, tomo secondo*, ed. Mauro Lucco (Milan, 1990), p. 610, fig. 729 (Vicenza), and p. 614, fig. 737 (Pavia); Francis L. Richardson, 'Bartolomeo Mantagna', *Grove Art*, vol. 21, pp. 904-906. Features to compare between Santa Caterina's vielle and these instruments are: i) the two bellies in different planes; and ii), the fact that the lower belly is narrower than the upper belly.

[46]John T. Spike, *Fra Angelico* (New York, London, Paris, 1996), p. 118, ca. 1450-1453 (Paris, Musée de Louvre, inv. 314, no. 1290); William Hood, 'Angelico, Fra', in *Grove Art*, 2, pp. 30-40 (Hood assigns a date ca. 1430-1435). The contours of the back of this instrument are simpler than those of Santa Caterina's vielle, but the shape is, like hers, not what is usually encountered in modern reproductions. The back of the Fra Angelico instrument suggests that the front, if not comprising two bellies in different planes, does share with Santa Caterina's instrument the feature of a marked 'step' between the narrower section towards the endpin and the section closer to the neck. It is worth observing that more variation is to be found in Fra Angelico's depictions of bowed strings than in those of his contemporaries, and immediate successors.

[47]Mary Remnant is to be lauded for noting the existence of Santa Caterina's vielle in both her article 'Fiddle', in *Grove Music*, 6, p. 529, and in her monograph, *English Bowed Instruments from Anglo-Saxon to Tudor Times*, Oxford Monographs on Music (Oxford, 1986), pp. 2, 29. Her statement, however, that this instrument is anomalous, and not in any way to be taken as representative of 'average fiddles' (p. 29) just won't do, for Santa Caterina's vielle is, at present, the *only* decently preserved of medieval fiddles.

Johannes Tinctoris (*ca.* 1435-1511?) was possibly the chief musical theorist of his day, and he was a more than able composer.[48] Like Santa Caterina's father, and like the composer Guillaume Dufay, his highest university qualification was as a lawyer.[49] In a passage from an epistolary treatise version (published 1481-1483) of his now fragmentary *On the Discovery and Practice of Music*, a passage with which some scholars seem uncomfortable,[50] Tinctoris states:

These two instruments, the rebec and the vielle, have an intmate significance for me. I say an intimate significance, for it is these two instruments among the rest which raise my soul to a pious disposition [Aug., *Conf.* 10. 33. 50]; *every vielle and rebec passionately inflames my heart to the contemplation of celestial joys. Beacuse of this, I wish that they would be reserved more for sacred purposes, and the private solace of the soul, than be occasionaly used at public feasts, and associated with common things.*[51]

Tinctoris spent much of his working life at the Neapolitan court, which is where he was when the version of the treatise cited was published. About twenty years after Santa Caterina contemplatively used her vielle, Tinctoris reports in print his own similar use (-did he have visions

---

[48] Heinrich Hüschen, "Tinctoris, Johannes', in *Die Musik in Geschichte und Gegenwart: Allgemeine Enzyklopädie der Muzik*, ed. Friedrich Blume (Kassel, 1966), Bd. 13, cols. 418-425; *ibid.*, 'Tinctoris, Johannes', in *Grove Music*, 18, pp. 837-840; Ronald Woodley, 'Iohannes Tinctoris: a Review of the Documentary Biographical Evidence', in *JAMS* XXXIV, 2 (1981), 217-248.

[49] Dufay earned a *baccalarius in decretis*, probably from Bologna; see E. Trumble, 'Autobiographical Implications in Dufay's Song-Motet *Juvenis qui puellam*', in *Revue Belge de musicologie/ Belgisch tijdschrift voor Muziekwetenschap* 42 (1988), 31-82, particularly at 41-45; David Fallows, in his *Dufay*, The Master Musicians (London and Melbourne, 1987²), p. 35, and note 21 on pp. 281-282, favours Rome as the place where Dufay most likely earned his degree. It is not certain were Tinctoris earned his law degree(s?), possibly at Orleans, but he styled himself variously as *in legibus licentiatus*, as *jurisconsultus*, and as *iurisperitus*, among other titles; see Woodley (232), as in note 48 *supra*.

[50] Although the passage is mentioned, there seems a reluctance to discuss it, *e.g.*, Christopher Page, 'Reading and Reminiscence: Tinctoris on the Beauty of Music', *JAMS* XLIX, 1 (1996), 11-14, who reproduces and translates the passage, but does not discuss what it implies for the *learned*, and sacred recreational use of these instruments.

[51] *Hec itaque duo instrumenta mea sunt. Mea inquam: hoc est quibus inter cetera: animus meus ad affectum pietatis assurgit: quaeque ad contemplationem gaudiorum supernorum: ardentissime cor meum inflammant. Quo mallem ea potius ad res sacras: et secreta animi solamina semper reservari: quam ad res prophanas et publica festa interdum applicari*; Tinctoris, *De inventione*, p. 46. For the genre of what survives, and its possible relation to what has been lost, see Ronald Woodley, 'The Printing and Scope of Tinctoris's Fragmentary Treatise *De inventione et usu musice*', in *Early Music History: Studies in Medieval and Early Modern Music*, ed. Iain Fenlon, 5 (1985), 239-268.

as well?). The conclusion is inescapable: highly educated people, spiritually motivated people, used bowed stringed instruments in their pursuit of the holy. Or at least they did in Italy in the second half of the fifteenth century. If one is willing to include the story of St. Francis' vision of the vielle playing angel from *The Second Consideration on the Holy Stigmata*, then one can argue more temporal depth for the practice.[52] I certainly would.

Barring the discovery of notated accounts, we will never know how Santa Caterina set *Et gloria eius in te videbitur*, and how she performed it. That, however, is no reason not to try a conjectural reconstruction.

Et gloria eius in te videbitur is described as a verse in Santa Caterina's vision. In the Roman liturgy it is the verse to the short responsory for Nones on Sundays in Advent, *Super te Ierusalem*.[53] The setting is largely syllabic. The vielle was probably silent during the intonation. It most likely formed part of the 'choir', so to speak, joining the saint's voice after the intonation. While it is possible that the vielle merely provided a drone, or played in unison with Santa Caterina's voice, I do not find these possibilities particularly compelling. It is much more likely that Santa Caterina embellished the plainchant settings with the type of polyphony found in Franciscan *laude* manuscripts of the first half of the fifteenth century.[54] The first conjectural realization offered here is a simple note-against-note syllabic setting (musical example 1); the second conjectural setting is more rhythmically elaborate (musical example 2). There is, indeed, no reason why Santa Caterina would not have set the chant differently every time she used it.

---

[52]See note 28 *supra*.

[53]The 'modern' Roman liturgy is historically connected to the development of the Franciscan liturgy in many respects; see S. J. P. van Dijk and Joan Hazelden Walker, *The Origins of the Modern Roman Liturgy: the Liturgy of the Papal Court and the Franciscan Order in the Thirteenth Century* (Westminster, 1960). Santa Caterina's breviary is, unfortunately, not notated.

[54]Venice, Biblioteca Nazionale Marciana, MS Ital. Cl. IX, 145, *ca.* 1450, Veneto, fols. 110 *bis*-111*r* (*Laudiamo Yhesu*), and 114*v*-115*r* (*Vergine benedetta*), provide the models for the simpler setting, and fols. 91*v*-92*r* (*Pange lingua*), the model for the more complicated setting; see Elisabeth Diederichs, *Die Anfänge der mehrstimmigen Lauda vom Ende des 14. bis zur Mitte des 15. Jahrhunderts*, Münchner Veroffentlichungen zur Musikgeschichte Bd. 41, ed. Theodor Göllner (Tutzing, 1986), pp. 161-163, 201-202, 215-217 (commentary on *Laudiamo Yhesu*), 218-219 (commentary on *Virgene benedeta*), 219-221 (commentary on *Pange lingua*), 396-398 (diplomatic transcriptions). The transcription and settings presented here are by Andrea Budgey. Voice, or vielle, could have performed either part.

Fig. 1 Santa Caterina da Bologna, after Niccolò dell'Arca (attributed), saec. XV^2, terracotta?, Modena, Galleria Estense, detail

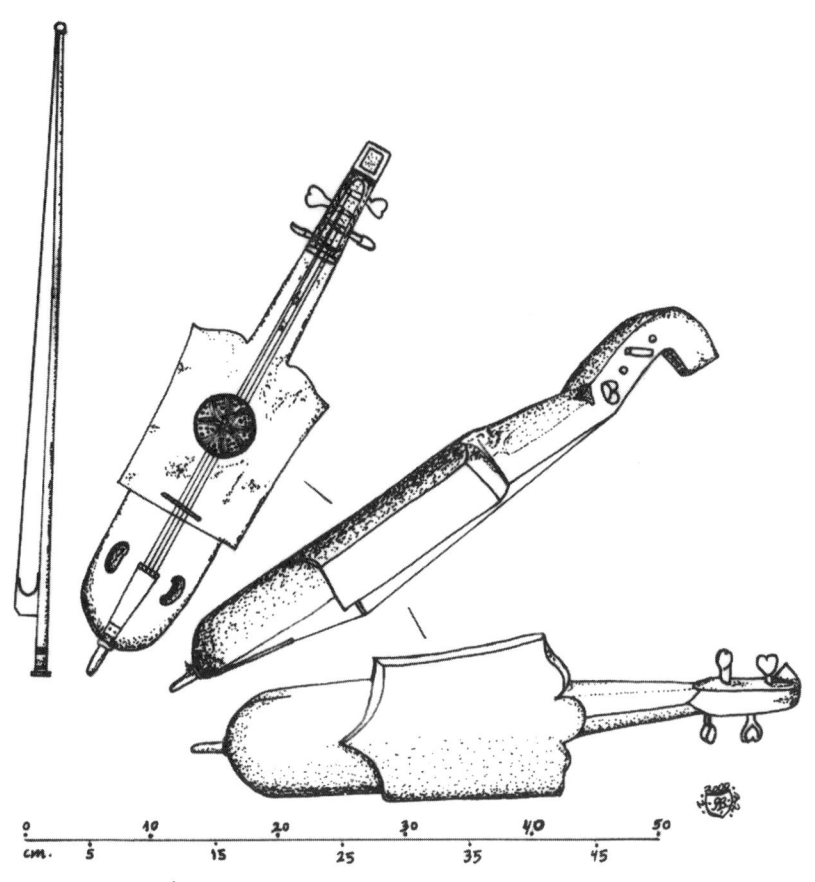

Fig. 2 Santa Caterina da Bologna's *violeta*, anonymous, saec. XV[1]?, various woods and bone, Bologna, *Corpus Domini*, redrawn after Tiella, 1975

Fig. 3   After Fra Angelico, rebec from image of angel musician on the *Linaiuoli* altarpiece, 1433-1436, Florence, Museo San Marco

Fig. 4 a   Follower of Fra Angelico, angel musician after the *Linaiuoli* altarpiece, saec. XIX, Toronto, private collection *(reproduced with permission)*

Fig. 4 b   detail of fig. 4 a

Fig. 5   After Lorenzo Costa, vielle in 'The Concert', painted in Bologna, ca. 1485-1490, London, The National Gallery (NG 2486)

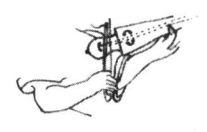

Fig. 6   After Bartolomeo Mantagna, rebec in 'Madonna and Child enthroned with angel musicians, and SS. John the Baptist, Bartolomeo, Augustine, and Sebastian', ca. 1485, Vicenza, Museo Civico (formerly in the church of S. Bartolomeo, Vicenza)

Fig. 7   After Bartolomeo Mantagna, rebec in 'Madonna and Child enthroned with angel musicians, and SS. John the Baptist, and Jerome', ca. 1490, Pavia, Museo della Certosa

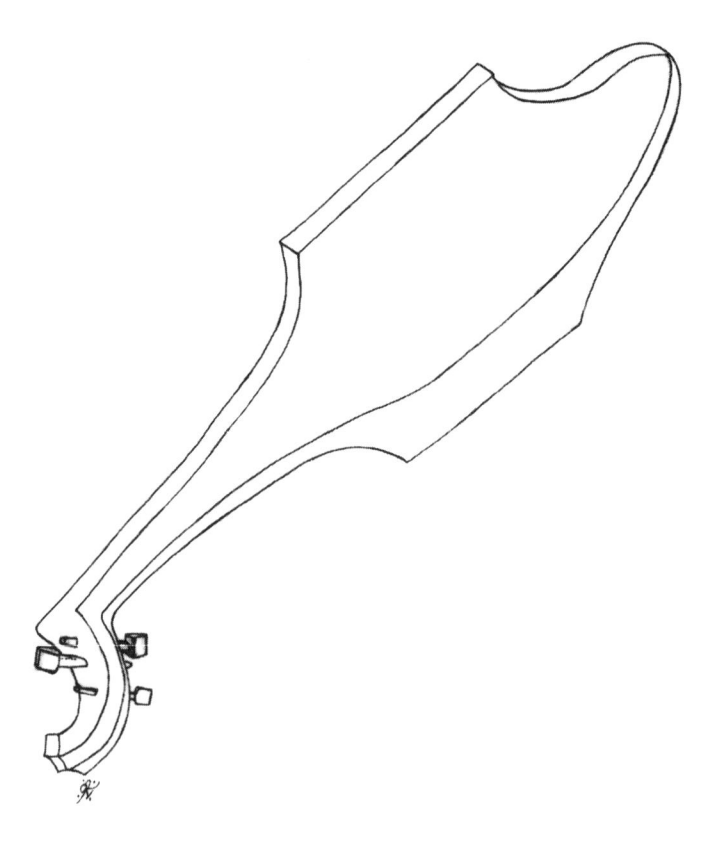

Fig. 8　After Fra Angelico, vielle in the 'Coronation of the Virgin' altarpiece, *ca.* 1450-1453, Paris, Musée de Louvre (inv. 314, no. 129; formerly in S. Domenico in Fiesole)

SANTA CATERINA DA BOLOGNA (1413-1463)

Music example 1

Short responsory (Nones) – Sundays in Advent

℞. Su- per te, ie- ru- sa- lem, ✱ o- ri- e- tur do- mi- nus.

℣. et glo- ri- a e- ius in te vi- de- bi- tur.

Dox. Glo- ri- a pa- tri, et fi- li- o, et spi- ri- tu- i san- cto.

return to ℞.

Second part after Venice, Bibl Marciana, MS Ital. Cl. IX, 145, fols. 110-111ʳ, 114ᵛ-115ʳ

©Andrea Budgey

Music example 2

Short responsory (Nones) – Sundays in Advent

℞. Super te, ierusalem, ✻ orietur dominus.

℣. Et gloria eius in te videbitur.

Dox. Gloria patri et filio et spiritui sancto.

Return to ℞.

Second part after Venice, Bibl. Marciana, MS Ital. Cl. IX, 145, fols. 91ᵛ-92ʳ
(x = alteration of chant)

© Andrea Budgey

SERGIY KUZMENKO

THE LIFE OF ST. ANDREW THE FOOL AND CULT OF HOLY FOOLS IN BYZANCE

ABSTRACT. Two main hagiographic sources about Byzantine holy fools are the Life of Symeon the Fool of Emessa (mid sixth century) and the Life of Andrew the Fool of Constantinople. In my paper I will make a brief comparative analysis of the two Vitae, and will determine the difference in the notion of holy folly as expressed in both sources. In my opinion, Vita Sancti Andrei Sali uttered a reconsidered attitude towards the madness feigned for religious purpose, and made a bold emphasis on the predominance of reason in apparently foolish behaviour of the salos (holy fool). The Life of Andrew the Fool of Constantinople appears to be a compromising apology of holy folly in the late-seventh century – the time of controversial discussion on accounts of fools and official prohibition of this extreme type of asceticism.

The goal of this paper is to analyze the *Life of St. Andrew the Fool* as a source about holy folly, and reveal some new aspects in the attitude towards this religious phenomenon by comparing the Life to earlier narratives about holy folly.

As a very general definition one may say that holy folly is feigning madness for religious purposes. One of its main objectives is to conceal the saint's own virtue, hiding it under the guise of apparently foolish or even aggressive behaviour. The second typical feature of the holy folly is a metaphorical communication of the fool with the surrounding society. The notion of holy folly and the attitude towards it was changing during the ages. Having become extremely popular during fifth-sixth century, the figure of holy fool gained a negative reputation later, until it completely disappears from the scene.

The *Life of Andrew the Fool* is the biggest and the latest narrative about holy fool in the Byzantine hagiography. Its hero Andrew the Fool is said to live in 5th century and be a contemporary with the author himself, although some chronological incongruities reveal that that the vita was written considerably later. According to L. Rydén the Life was written in the sixth decade of the 10th century;[1] this view was argued by C. Mango who suggested its date of composition falls into late 7th century.[2]

Now let us consider some important aspects of holy folly and trace their representation in *The Life of St. Andrew the Fool*.

Originally, feigning madness is found in the monastic communities of the Upper Egypt. These first records of simulated folly are related to some anchorites of the Egyptian deserts who pretended to be mad in order to escape the vain glory of the world. Such motivation can be found in the paterikon legends about Egyptian monks abba Moses,[3] abba Symeon,[4] and abba Ammon[5] all of whom had lived in the fourth century. The actions of these desert fathers can be explained as the desire to remain an anchorite even when the world came to see them in their seclusion: having no further place to hide, they hid in madness, thus becoming distanced from those who were close to them.[6] The connection between holy folly and monasticism is very noticeable in the early hagiography:[7] many examples of simulated folly and strange behaviour of the saint either took place in or after leaving a monastic community. The marvelous example is found in *The Life of Symeon of Emessa* (who lived in the 6th century): for thirty years he has been a monk, practicing solitude in the desert, after which, having gained spiritual perfection the left his place to mock the world.

The *Life of St. Andrew the Fool* is totally different in this respect: Andrew had never been a monk or belonged to a monastic community. This innovation is not accidental: the freedom of the fool was confronting with the discipline of the monastic order.[8] As a consequence, simula-

---

[1] L. Rydén, "The Date of Life of Andreas Salos," *Dumbarton Oaks Papers* 32 (1978), 153; id. *The Life of St. Andrew the Fool*, Uppsala, 1995, vol.1, 41-57.

[2] C. Mango, "The Life of Saint Andrew the Fool Reconsidered," *Rivista di Studi Bizantini e Slavi* 2 (1982): 297-313.

[3] *The Sayings of the Desert Fathers: The Alphabetical Collection*, translated by Benedicta Ward (Kalamazoo, MI: Cistercian Publications, 1984), 140.

[4] *The Sayings*, 224-5.

[5] Ibid., 27.

[6] Antoine Guillaumont, "La folie simulée, une forme d'anachorèse," in id, *Études sur la spiritualité de l'Orient chrétien*, Spiritualité orientale, no. 66 (Bégrolles-en-Mauges, France: Abbay de Bellefontaine, 1996), 125-7.

[7] S. Ivanov, *Vizantijskoje jurodstvo (Holy Folly in Byzance)*, Moscow: Mezhdunarodnyje otnoshenija, 1994, 35-53.

[8] Ibid., 53-62

tion of madness was banned at monasteries (692),[9] and *The Life of St. Andrew* conformed with this attitude.

The desire to withdraw from the world was not the only motive to assume the mask of folly. The early hagiography depicted other Christian heroes - individual ascetics unknown to the rest of the world. [10] These "secret saints" did not belong to a particular social or religious group, they might live in monastic communities or be laymen, some of them were even married, but what they had in common - concealed sanctity - later became a leading motif in the vitae of holy fools, which, though, also underwent some modifications. While in the early hagiography, a "secret saint" is very coherent in his desire to remain unknown and is revealed either by a careful observation[11] or through a vision,[12] sometimes posthumously, in the case of a "complete" holy fool there is always a confidential friend who later appears as a "témion bien informé" to the hagiographer.[13] There are two such persons in *The Life of St. Symeon* (his ascetic fellow John and the pious deacon John), similarly, there are two confidential friends in *The Life of St. Andrew* (young man Epiphanios and the author himself). However, unlike *The Life of Symeon*, the role played by informants is considerably more active in *The Life of Saint Andrew*. Epiphanios is not less central to the narrative than Andrew himself; reading the vita one receives an impression that the folly of Andrew to a greater extent serves the purpose of proper religious education of the young man who is identified by the author as the future patriarch of Constantinople.

The most significant example of the concealing sanctity through simulated madness in the early sources is found in *The Lausiac History* in a narrative about a woman who was working in the monastery's refectory exercising her ascetic skills by pretending to be mad.[14] Although in this narrative the reader sees an example of "harmless folly,"[15] further leg-

---

[9] Ibid., 77; J. B. Mansi, ed., *Sanctorum Conciliorum nova et amplissima collectio*, vol. 11, P., 1901.

[10] Krueger, *Symeon the Holy Fool: Leontus's Life and the Late Antique City*. Transformation of the Classical Heritage, no. 25. (Berkley: University of California Press, 1996), 57-71; Ivanov, *Vizantijskoje jurodstvo*, 33-4, 36-42.

[11] John Moschos. *The Spiritual Meadow (Pratum Spirituale)*, translated by John Wortley (Kalamazoo, MI: Cistercian Publications, 1992), 92.

[12] LH, 98

[13] H. Delehaye, *Les passions des martyrss et les genres littéraires*, repr. Brussels, 1966, 182f; LSAF, vol.1, 28.

[14] LH, 98-100. This episode from LH is quoted almost in all studies about holy folly, since it is the first time when the technical term denoting holy fool (σαλός) is employed.

[15] Ivanov, *Vizantijskoje jurodstvo*, 37.

ends developing the same motif depict the behaviour of the secret female saint as provocative.[16]

Provocation, as a favorite method of mocking the world, later becomes a "norm" of the holy fool's behaviour.[17] The behaviour of Symeon the Fool is highly provocative: first time he appears in Emessa dragging a dead dog on a rope behind him, then he puts out candles during liturgy by throwing nuts into them, gives away goods of a merchant, washes himself in the women's bath, gorges with sausages in the Holy Thursday, defecates in public, makes a belt of sausages and anoints people with mustard, etc. Even his death under a bundle of twigs was a confusion for citizens of Emessa who concluded: "Behold, his death is another idiocy."[18] Unlike Symeon, Andrew is more moderated in his provocative behaviour. As a rule, there is always strong reason for his wild actions, e.g., he slaps a poor man to give him charity. Sometimes he also plays fool just for the sake of a "decent" public opinion (e.g., pretending to be drunk and pushing people), but never goes wild or becomes as close to the blasphemy as Symeon does.

The crucial virtue of the holy fool is freedom from passion - *apatheia*,[19] which also links the holy fool to the early monastic tradition. This term denoting a higher grade of spiritual perfection is frequently found in such major sources on the monastic life as *The Lausiac History* and *The Spiritual Ladder*. A monk who possesses *apatheia* can withdraw cold and heat, fight hunger and thirst, and stay vigil for weeks. As an extreme case, the saint is freed from body to such a great extent, that he even doesn't feel shame when his naked body is exposed. In theological sense, this saintly shamelessness may be regarded as restoration of the original paradisiacal state, when the first man was not ashamed of it's own nature.[20] A brilliant example of connection between nude and *apatheia* is found in *The Lausiac History*, where abba Serapion[21] tries the *apatheia* of a female recluse, offering her to take off her clothes and walk naked through the middle of the city. As the recluse denied his proposal motivating her answer that such a gesture would scandalize people, the saint replies: "See then, no longer be proud of yourself as more pious

---

[16] Ibid., 41-2.
[17] Ibid., 47-9.
[18] VSF, 102; translation after Krueger, 169.
[19] v. P. Miquel, *Lexique du désert*, Abbaye de Bellefontaine, 1986, 113-134; Rydén, "The Holy Fool." In *The Byzantine Saint*, ed. Sergei Hackel, 106-13. London: Fellowship of St. Alban and St. Sergius, 1981.
[20] About "shamelessness of the righteous" see Ivanov, *Vizantijskoje jurodstvo*, 22-4, 41.
[21] LH, 109-16.

than all others and dead to the world, for I am more dead than you and show by my act that I am dead to the world; for impassively and without shame I do this thing".[22] In the church history of Evagrius is found the following fragment (referring probably to Symeon of Emessa):

> There are only few, but nevertheless they do exist, who became impassive (ἀπαθεῖς) due to their virtue and who returned to the world in the place of troubles. Pretending to be troubled by the evil spirit, they trample the vain glory. [...] They often go to bath where they often meet with women and wash themselves together with them. They gained such control over passions that they became masters of their natural instincts, and do not respond to the call of their sex neither by sight nor by touch nor by the blaze of desire.[23]

Such an eccentric behaviour of ascetic, also found in *The Life of Symeon*, but not in *The Life of Andrew*. The nakedness as a metaphor of poverty is preserved in *The Life of Andrew*, but has lost its provocative feature, and his impassivity never conflicts with social convention. Even the term *apatheia* is not used in *The Life of Andrew*.[24]

For the early monastic hagiography the withdrawal from the world and departure to the desert is associated with the war against the Satan. When Christianity became the official religion of the Roman Empire, the warriors for Christ left for the wilderness to destroy the last refuge of the unclean spirits, which fled away ashamed by victory of Christianity. When the desert was conquered in its turn, the ascetic realized that the real abode of devil was the world. That is why monk leaves the desert and goes into the city, appearing there as a "wandering monk"[25] or holy fool. Not only the place but the very strategy of this combat was changed for a holy fool: he does not wait for the enemy's assaults, sitting at the same place, but wanders in the world chasing the enemy not only spiritually, but in real space and time. This is the vocation of holy fool: to be there where the need for the saint is particularly high.

---

[22] Transl. after W. K. L. Clarke, ed. & tr., *The Lausiac History of Palladius*, London, 1818, 132.
[23] VSE, 34.
[24] This is also due to the fact that this term received a negative connotation in connection with origenistic controversy; v. A.Guillaumont, *Les "Kephalaia gnostica" d'Évagre le Pontique et l'histoire de l'Origénisme chez les Grecs et chez les Syriens*.
[25] Palmer, Andrew N. "Semper Vagus: The Anatomy of a Mobile Monk." In *Studia Patristica* no. 17, vol. 2 (Papers of the 1983 Oxford Patristic Conference), ed. Elisabeth A. Livingstone. Kalamazoo, MI: Cistercian Publications, 1989: 255-60.

For Symeon the combat with devil is not just a private contest, his mission is to help others. After thirty years of desert life he said to his ascetic companion:

> What more benefit do we derive, brother, from passing time in this desert? But if you hear me, get up, let us depart; let us save others. For as we are, we do not benefit anyone except ourselves, and have not brought anyone to salvation,[26]

Changing traditional ascetic life the sake of salvation of other is also found in the early monastic hagiography,[27] however, unlike his predecessors, Symeon's efforts are directed not to the salvation of a particular person, but of the whole society:

> While the saint was there (in Emessa), he cried out against many because of the Holy Spirit and reproached thieves and fornicators. Some he faulted, crying that they had not taken communion often, and others he reproached for perjury, so that through his inventiveness he nearly put an end to sinning in the whole city.[28]

To be able to perform such a task, Symeon had to gain spiritual perfection becoming fool. This is why the description of Symeon's foolishness is preceded by long introduction revealing his monastic life. Nevertheless, holy fool remained a controversial figure bringing the scandal and confusion for the society. His actions are still too drastic and appalling and his freedom of choice is too independent in assuming the mask of folly to become a long-living hagiographic character. That is why for Andrew folly is not a free choice but an order of the Heavenly King, who wants to defeat the devil through his servant Andrew. There is no initiative in Andrew; "things happen to him,"[29] and is not concerned about salvation of the other, except for his intimate friend Epiphanios who, however possesses his own spiritual insight.

Conclusion:

The Life of St. Andrew the Fool indirectly reflected many controversies regarding holy folly by eliminating some "difficult" parts of it. Whether or not it was done on purpose and what was the primary intention of the author, we do not know precisely. Our understanding of this "roman hagiographique"[30] in a great extent depends on our knowledge when

---

[26] Krueger, 148.
[27] Ivanov, "A Saint in a Whore-house." *Byzantinoslavica* 56 (1995, 2): 439-46.
[28] Krueger, 165.
[29] LSAF, 32.
[30] Mango, 297.

and under which conditions it was written. Although it seems difficult to answer *what* was the intention of the author, a reconsidered attitude towards the holy folly was manifested, and this new paradigm of the holy fool's behaviour influenced further development of holy folly in late mediaeval Russia.

ABBREVIATIONS

LH   Butler, Dom Cuthbert, ed. *The Lausiac History of Palladius: The Greek Text Edited with Introduction and Notes.* Cambridge: University Press, 1904 (reprint 1967).

LSAF   Rydén, Lennart, ed. *The Life of St Andrew The Fool.* 2 Vols. Uppsala, Sweden: Uppsala, 1995.

VSF   Festugière, A.J., and L. Rydén, eds. *La vie de Syméon le Fou et Vie de Jean de Chypre.* Paris: Librarie Orientaliste Paul Geuthner, 1974.

PETER COFFMAN

EADBURG OF REPTON AND SOUTHWELL MINSTER: NORMAN SHRINE-CHURCH FOR A SAXON SAINT?

ABSTRACT. Of the several Anglo-Saxon Saints named Eadburg, the one generally referred to as Eadburg of Repton is perhaps the most enigmatic. She may have been an Abbess of Repton around the year 700, and she is recorded in The Resting Places of the Saints as resting in the Minster at Southwell. She vanishes from subsequent recorded history, and it is generally assumed that her cult was suppressed by the Normans after the conquest. The fabric of the Anglo-NormanMinster at Southwell, however, may suggest otherwise. The Norman church is essentially intact from the crossing westward, and its east end can be reconstructed archaeologically. One of the most striking aspects of Norman Southwell is the number of design features that are apparently derived not from Norman models, but from pre-conquest Anglo-Saxon ones. It is not obvious why the Normans, having re-built Southwell as part of a systematic demolition of Anglo-Saxon culture, should build a new church that reminds one of its Saxon predecessor. One compelling reason, however, may have been the continuing presence of the shrine of the Anglo-Saxon Saint Eadburg, and this paper will explore the circumstantial evidence for that argument.

Little is known about the St. Eadburg whom history associates with the Anglo-Saxon Minster at Southwell, Nottinghamshire. She is believed to have been Abbess of Repton around the year 700. She was a friend to Saint Guthlac, to whom she sent the unusual gifts of a coffin and funeral shroud.[1] *On the Resting Places of the Saints* records that she was buried in Southwell Minster, near the River Trent. No record of her cult or shrine dates from after the Norman Conquest of 1066, and it is generally assumed that her cult was suppressed by the Normans. However, while no written documents reveal the post-conquest fate of Eadburg, one highly informative "document" is still largely intact – the Anglo-

---

[1] See W.E. Hodgson, "Southwell", *Memorials of Old Nottinghamshire*, Everard L. Guilford, Ed. (London, 1912), pp. 239-269.

Norman fabric of Southwell Minster itself. The purpose of this paper is to examine that fabric, and its historical context, for evidence that the cult of St. Eadburg did indeed survive the Norman Conquest.

There have been at least four major building campaigns at Southwell.[2] Of the Anglo-Saxon church, which had probably been completed by the middle of the tenth-century, little can be said for certain except that it existed.[3] A document of 956 records that the manor of Southwell, along with surrounding lands, was given by King Eadwig to Oskytel, the Archbishop of York.[4] The manor is likely to have contained a church, which, after it moved into the Archbishop's sphere of influence, seems to have been embellished and may have been enlarged in the succeeding 110 years.[5]

Following the Norman Conquest of 1066, virtually every major Anglo-Saxon church in the country was demolished and re-built, in what must rank as one of the most comprehensive and systematic examples ever recorded of the subjugation of one culture by another.[6] Documentation indicates that the Norman building at Southwell was begun during or very shortly before the reign of Archbishop Thomas II, between 1109 and 1114.[7] Everything west of the east face of the crossing, right up to and including the façade, is part of Thomas' church.[8]

---

[2] For the architectural history of Southwell Minster, see G.M. Livett, *Southwell Minster*, (1883); Arthur Dimock, "*The Cathedral Church of Southwell* (London, 1898); A. Hamilton Thompson, "The Cathedral Church of the Blessed Virgin Mary, Southwell, *Transactions of the Thoroton Society*, 15 (1911); Norman Summers, *A Prospect of Southwell* (London, 1974); Jennifer S. Alexander, Ed., *Southwell and Nottinghamshire: Medieval Art, Architecture and Industry*, The British Archaeological Association Conference Transactions XXI (1998).

[3] For the architectural context of Anglo-Saxon Southwell, see Alfred Clapham, English Romanesque Architecture Before the Conquest (Oxford, 1930); H.M. and J. Taylor, Anglo-Saxon Architecture (Cambridge, 1965-1978); Eric Fernie, The Architecture of the Anglo-Saxons (London, 1983).

[4] The ultimate source for this is the *Great White Book of York*, in which a 14th century copy of the 10th century document is preserved. See also Arthur Dimock, p.3-4; Summers, p. 18-19.

[5] See Thompson, p. 15-16.

[6] For another case study in Norman cultural imperialism, see Eric Fernie, *An Architectural History of Norwich Cathedral* (Oxford, 1993). For a more general analysis of the effect of the Norman Conquest, see Fernie, "The Effect of the Conquest on Norman Architectural Patronage", *Anglo-Norman Studies 9* (1986).

[7] The source for this is the *White Book of Southwell*, a collection of largely 14th century copies of earlier documents, which records a reference to the re-building of Southwell Minster during the reign of Archbishop Thomas II of York (reigned 1109-1114). See also Summers, p. 30-33; Arthur Dimock, p. 7; Thompson, 16-17.

[8] For a plan of Anglo-Norman Southwell, see Alfred Clapham, *English Romanesque Architecture: After the Conquest* (Oxford, 1930).

The Romanesque church had scarcely been complete for half a century before the east end was torn down, around 1234, and replaced by a larger, Early English Gothic one by Order of Archbishop Walter de Grey.[9] Finally, around the year 1290, Archbishop John le Romaine commissioned the building of the Minster's chapter house, thereby providing medieval Europe with one of its greatest artistic jewels.[10]

With respect to the continuing veneration of St. Eadburg after the Norman Conquest, it is the first two campaigns that concern us here: the Saxon campaign or campaigns, about which practically nothing is known, and the Norman one, which is, relatively speaking, well-documented and still largely intact. The *Victoria History of the County of Nottinghamshire* sums up both the conventional wisdom on the status of Saxon saints in Norman England, and its unsatisfactory application to St. Eadburg: "We know that the Norman prelates who followed the Conquest possessed but scant respect for the native saints of the land, but it is not easy to account for the disappearance of a shrine which clearly was an object of frequent pilgrimage in the early 11th century."[11] Recently, David Rollason has cast serious doubt on the notion that Norman-appointed prelates made any systematic effort to suppress the cults of Saxon saints at all.[12] True, Lanfranc did question the sanctity of some Saxon saints, but Rollason argues that this was more in the spirit of intellectual inquiry than cultural snobbishness. Moreover, Rollason points out that a saint's relics were not only among a church's greatest spiritual asset, but a crucial tool in the defense of traditionally held lands, possessions and privileges.[13]

Moreover, the political context of the Norman Conquest suggests another reason why the veneration of Saxon Saints would not be suppressed. While the Conquest is most frequently interpreted today as a huge cleaver which comes down in the middle of English medieval his-

---

[9] The patron of the Early English choir was Archbishop Walter de Gray, whose indulgences issued in 1234 for those contributing to the work at Southwell are recorded in the *White Book of Southwell*. See also Summers, p. 37.

[10] According to the *White Book of Southwell*, Archbishop John le Romaine used fines levied against prebends to finance the chapter house; see also Summers, p. 39-40. For further discussion of the chapter house and its extraordinary sculpture, see Nikolaus Pevsner, *The Leaves of Southwell* (London/New York, 1945); and Jean Givens, "The *Leaves of Southwell* Revisited", *Southwell and Nottinghamshire: Medieval Art, Architecture, and Industry*, The British Archaeological Association Conference Transactions XXI, (1998).

[11] William Page, Ed., *Victoria History of the County of Nottinghamshire* (London, 1906).

[12] David Rollason, *Saints and Relics in Anglo-Saxon England* (Oxford, 1989).

[13] For a discussion of how the cult of saints in Anglo-Saxon England was linked to monastic rights and privileges, see Rollason, p. 196-214.

tory, the Bayeux Tapestry, which is the major "official" Norman version of events, presents a different point of view. According to the Normans, William was Edward the Confessor's chosen successor, and Harold had recognized this by swearing an oath of loyalty – an oath which he broke when he claimed the crown on Edward's death. The Tapestry shows Harold both swearing that oath and paying the appropriate price at the Battle of Hastings for breaking it. The Norman Conquest, then, was not an interruption of English history, but the proper fulfillment of it. Saxon saints, far from posing a threat to the Norman rulers, actually attest to their dynastic legitimacy – especially since the new Norman king had been appointed by the last Saxon saint, Edward the Confessor.

These arguments suggest why Eadburg's cult *should* have continued uninterrupted after the Conquest, but do not provide any evidence that it *did*. Written history is completely silent on the subject, but built history has a bit more to say. Specifically, about three-quarters of the Norman Minster remain intact, and the remainder can be reliably reconstructed through a combination of above and below-ground archaeology.[14] And one of the most striking features of the Norman building is its resemblance not only to Norman architectural models, but Anglo-Saxon ones.

To put things in perspective, it must be said that no one living in Southwell around 1109, when the Norman Minster was begun, would have confused the behemoth that was rising in their village with a Saxon church. Several features strongly affirm the presence of the conquerors. For example, the twin-towered façade was all but unknown in Saxon England, but became the norm after the Conquest, inspired by Norman models such as St-Etienne at Caen – itself a foundation of William the Conqueror. Ironically, this French church is among the most influential buildings in the history of English architecture, and its presence is felt inside Southwell as well as outside. The Minster's three-story elevation with its nave arcade, deep and lofty gallery, and clerestory with wall-passage is clearly derived from Normandy (although not as precisely copied as such earlier examples as Norwich, Peterborough and Ely).

Another architectural characteristic which the Normans imported to England might be better characterized as a state of mind, which is manifested architecturally. John Bilson, writing in the early 20th century, was

---

[14] For reconstructions of the Romanesque fabric, see Peter Coffman, "The Romanesque East End of Southwell Minster", *Southwell and Nottinghamshire: Medieval Art, Architecture, and Industry*, The British Archaeological Association Conference Transactions XXI (1998); —, "The Romanesque Rib Vaults of Southwell Minster", *Transactions of the Thoroton Society*, vol. 98 (1994).

the first to observe what he termed the "logic" of Norman architecture.[15] That is, Norman architecture exhibits a certain inner rationality which gives it an undeniable sense of architectonic reasonableness. An example of this is the articulation of the nave gallery at St-Etienne: each shaft possesses its own capital which carries its own order of the arch above. The fragments of Anglo-Saxon architecture which survive suggest that this was foreign to the Saxons' way of thinking and designing. For example, The church tower at Earls Barton shows Saxon exuberance at its best, but shows little regard for the architectonic rigor of Norman design. At the post-conquest church at Southwell, the Norman state of mine has clearly taken hold, as the design of the Minster's nave gallery shows.

In these ways, the Norman patrons of the 12th-century Minster asserted their presence and power in the way one would expect of a conqueror. Other design features, however, seem deliberately to affirm continuity with the Saxon past; an affirmation so out of character with the steamrollering nature of the Norman Conquest that it requires some explanation – such as the continued veneration of a local Anglo-Saxon saint.

The most obvious and striking Saxon feature of Norman Southwell is the plan, specifically the design of the east end. Examples of the "classic" apsidal eastern terminations of great Norman churches can still be seen at St-Nicolas, Caen and the Abbey church of Lessay. As mentioned earlier, the eastern arm of Norman Southwell was replaced in the 13th century by a Gothic choir, but its original plan is known from excavations carried out in 1852 and 1857.[16] What the excavations show is a rectilinear eastern termination, completely without precedent in Normandy. It was, however, standard practice in Saxon England. Geographically, the nearest example to Southwell would have been the Saxon church at East Bridgford, now known only from excavations un-

---

[15] John Bilson, "The Beginnings of Gothic Architecture", *Journal of the Royal Institute of British Architects*, vi (1899), 289-326.

[16] For reports on the excavations, see James Dimock, "Architectural History of the Church of the Blessed Mary the Virgin, of Southwell", *Journal of the British Archaeological Association*, vol. VIII (1853), pp. 265-303; also "Lincoln Diocesan Architectural Society Thirty-Fourth Report", *Associated Architectural Societies Reports and Papers*, 14 (1877), vi. John Bilson, apparently unaware of the 1877 report, questioned the evidence for a square east end in a letter; see W.E. Hodgson, *The Life of Thomas II* (Nottingham 1909), p. 86. The present author, however, supports the findings of the LDAS (Coffman, 1998).

dertaken at the beginning of the 20th century.[17] An extant Midlands example of a square Saxon east end can still be seen, albeit with some obvious subsequent fiddling with the fenestration, at Repton – the town where Eadburg had been Abbess.

Details apart from the planning suggest further Anglo-Saxon echoes. One of the more puzzling features of Norman Southwell is the round, porthole-like clerestory windows. Once again, this is a feature with no precise Norman model. The closest approximation would be at the church of Notre-Dame sur l'eau, at Domfront, where round windows appear in the eastern walls of the transepts, just above the roofline of the apsidal transept chapels. A similar arrangement can occasionally be seen in Anglo-Norman architecture, particularly in the north, as Stuart Harrison has demonstrated in his reconstructions of Rievaulx and Kirkstall.[18] These windows, however, appear at the terminal wall of a nave, choir, or transept, and not in an axial sequence at clerestory level as at Southwell. One place where they do occur in such a sequence, however, is the Church of St. James in Avebury, Wiltshire, where the round Anglo-Saxon windows at clerestory level are still visible in the heavily reworked fabric.

Further decorative details of Southwell's Norman church may be reflections of its Saxon heritage, although the question is at present a rather controversial one. The problem is rooted in the work of James Dimock, who, in 1853, published an article on Southwell Minster in the *Journal of the British Archaeological Association*, in which he included a diagram of several bits of masonry which he had found used as rubble core inside the Norman fabric.[19] They included fragments of ornament generally assumed to have been introduced to England after the Norman conquest, such as chevron, beakhead, and billet. The tantalizing question is, where did these bits come from? Dimock concluded, not unreasonably, that since bits found inside the core of a building usually precede, chronologically, the building in which they are entombed, these must be from of the Anglo-Saxon Minster. It is not unusual for fragments of a demolished building to be used as infill in the one replacing it; the prob-

---

[17] See C. Keyser, "The Norman Architecture of Nottinghamshire," *British Archaeological Association Journal*, XIII (1907).

[18] See Peter Fergusson and Stuart Harrison, "The Rievaulx Abbey Chapter House", *The Antiquaries Journal*, volume LXXIV (1944), p. 211-255; and Stuart Harrison, "Kirkstall Abbey: The 12th-Century Tracery and Rose Window", *Yorkshire Monasticism: Archaeology, Art and Architecture, from the 7th to 16th Centuries*, (London, 1995).

[19] James Dimock, 1853.

lem is that these fragments don't conform at all to our accepted notions of what Saxon buildings looked like.

As examples such as Earls Barton and Barton on Humber show, we do know that Anglo-Saxon builders were fond of ornament. But precisely what range of forms that ornament took is hard to say, since only a tiny fraction of Saxon buildings still stand, and not a single major Anglo-Saxon cathedral or abbey church has survived. Trying to reconstruct the appearance of major Saxon buildings is a bit like trying to put together a 1000-piece jigsaw puzzle, with 999 pieces missing and the remaining one badly defaced. Nevertheless, most architectural historians dismiss out of hand Dimock's claim that these fragments could have come from the Anglo-Saxon Minster. It is not hard to see why. At first blush, all of Dimock's fragments look as though they could be Norman. Anyone who speaks the visual language of Anglo-Norman ornament, however, will recognize that the familiar decorative vocabulary is spoken here with a highly idiosyncratic accent. A comparison of some of Dimock's drawings with comparable ornament in the still-standing, and unquestionably Norman, nave and transepts is instructive.

In the case of the billet ornament, Dimock points out that, while the motif is unmistakable, the precise profile is utterly unlike that of any of the billet ornament in the standing Anglo-Norman fabric. Similarly, the stringy, tubular chevron that Dimock found is very different from the standard toothy zigzag so common in Anglo-Norman buildings. The beakhead which he uncovered is far simpler than that associated with the Norman work in the standing north porch and west door, and typologically seems earlier.

All this led Dimock to conclude that these fragments were not from any Norman building at Southwell, but from its Saxon predecessor. The problem is that, if Dimock is correct, then virtually every decorative feature that so dominates our impression of Southwell's Norman Minster is in fact a re-invention of an Anglo-Saxon motif – a fact which would require a radical reassessment both of Anglo-Saxon architecture and its relationship to architecture after the Conquest. Rather than face such a re-assessment, it is far simpler to dismiss Dimock's claim out of hand – a dismissal made immeasurably easier by the loss of the primary evidence. Dimock placed these bits in the passageway between the choir and chapter house in 1853 for "safe" keeping; needless to say, by 1883, G.M. Livett reported that they had disappeared without a trace: "...not one... now remains to tell its tale. How or when they were removed no one at present seems to know".[20] With only this drawing for evidence, it is very tempting to conclude that these are Norman fragments which Dimock has somehow misrepresented and ineptly mistaken for Saxon.

This explanation, however, is not without its own difficulties. If Dimock's bits are from a Norman building, then what are they doing encased within the fabric of what is, as far as we know, the earliest Norman building in the area? Moreover, why does their design not match any existing Norman ornament in the Minster? The latter argument, of course, is greatly weakened by the unavailability of the fragments; we are very reluctant to take a Victorian antiquarian's word for anything. Maybe, if we could lay eyes on these stones, we would find that they in fact look perfectly Norman; maybe Dimock's illustrator just got it wrong.

For all we know, these fragments may now be stopping open the doors of garden sheds all over Nottinghamshire. As luck would have it, however, one needle in that large haystack remains locatable. Among the many pieces of stone arranged in the Provost's garden adjacent to the Minster at Southwell is one that should raise the eyebrows of anyone interested in the history of Anglo-Saxon and Anglo-Norman architectural ornament. It is Dimock's billet; now rather weathered but unmistakably matching his illustration of 1853.

What is the ultimate source not only of this billet, but of Dimock's other fragments, the illustrations of which we must now accept as accurate? Are they fragments of an undetermined Norman building, boasting designs unique in Anglo-Norman ornament? Or are they Anglo-Saxon fragments, which served as models for the ornamentation of a Norman building which continued to enshrine its venerable Anglo-Saxon saint, Eadburg? There is no proof either way, but the question, at the very least, needs to be re-opened.

Finally, it should be observed that, had the veneration of Eadburg continued uninterrupted after the Conquest, this would hardly be a unique situation. In spite of the popular notion that Saxon saints were despised by the Normans, Norman England has no shortage of examples of Saxon saints whose cults not only continued but were enhanced after the conquest.

For example at Malmesbury, Saint Aldhelm's relics were translated with great pomp from the cloister to the high altar of the new Norman church. The so-called Malmesbury Chasse, now in the Art Gallery of

---

[20] Grenvile Mairis Livett, *An Account of the Collegiate and Cathedral Church of Southwell* (Southwell, 1883), p.52.

Ontario, is thought to have contained a relic of Aldhelm's predecessor Maidulph, another pre-conquest saint who continued to be venerated at Malmesbury.[21]

At Winchester, Saint Swithun's relics were translated from the Saxon to the Norman Cathedral in 1093. His shrine remained the most popular pilgrimage destination in Norman England, only surpassed after the martyrdom of Thomas Becket in Canterbury Cathedral in 1170.

North of the River Trent, and closer to Southwell, Saxon saints also continued to prosper. At the previously mentioned Repton, St. Wyston remained a popular subject of veneration. St. John of Beverley, an 8th century Bishop of York, continued to be venerated at the church he founded until the Reformation. His body is believed to repose still beneath the nave floor of the current Gothic building.

By far the most famous, and popular, Saxon saint in the north was Cuthbert of Durham.[22] There is also no better documented case of a Saxon saint's being understood by the Normans as not only holy, but of immense value to the new regime. The housing of Cuthbert's shrine was the occasion for the building of one of the grandest Romanesque churches in Europe; a building which still astonishes with its monumentality and technical audacity. The interior of Durham boasts the earliest datable rib-vaults in the medieval world. Various theories have been put forward to explain their presence here, but the most compelling current theory has been put forward by Malcolm Thurlby. According to Thurlby, Durham's ribs represent an inflation of the baldaccino over St. Peter's tomb in Old St. Peter's to a monumental scale, thereby making the entire church building into a sacred canopy over the shrine of Cuthbert.[23] Thus, one of the most important innovations in the whole

---

[21] On the history of Malmesbury Abbey, see Thomas Perkins, *The Abbey Churches of Bath and Malmesbury: and the Church of Saint Laurence, Bradford-on-Avon* (London, 1901); Richard H. Luce, *The History of the Abbey and Town of Malmesbury* (Chippenham, 1979). On St. Aldhelm, see M.R. James, *Two Ancient English Scholars, St. Aldhelm & William of Malmesbury* (Glasgow, 1931). On the Malmesbury Chasse, see Marie-Madeleine Gauthier, *Émaux méridionaux: Catalogue international de l'oeuvre de Limoges.* Vol. I, *L'Époque romane* (Paris, 1987).

[22] The literature on the cult of Cuthbert is extensive. Of particular interest here is Barbara Abou-el-Haj, "The Audiences for the Medieval Cult of Saints", *Gesta* 30 (1991) 3-15; Rollason, 215-239.

[23] See Malcolm Thurlby, "The Roles of the Patron and the Master mason in the First Design of the Romanesque Cathedral in Durham", in *Anglo-Norman Durham 1093-1193*, pp. 161-184; Eds. David Rollason, Margaret Harvey, Michael Prestwich (Woodbridge, 1994). For further recent discussion of Durham's ribs, see Michael J. Jackson, Ed., *Engineering a Cathedral* (London, 1993).

history of medieval architecture originates with a Norman patron's wish to honour an Anglo-Saxon saint. The translation of Cuthbert's relics into the Norman Cathedral in 1104, during which his body was found to be both incorrupt and perfectly supple, produced a deluge of tears among prelates and lay observers alike.[24] If the fact of Cuthbert's nationality had ever caused anyone any anxiety, it had certainly disappeared by then.

This list is by no means comprehensive, but is only brief sampling of the Anglo-Saxon saints who enjoyed continuous veneration after the Conquest. As David Rollason has explained, "the relics of English saints were not symbols of resistance [to the Conquest] but treasures to be guarded... in [the church's] eyes, the saints themselves were chiefly useful in defending their lands, possessions and privileges against the depredations which the turbulence of the conquest had engendered."[25]

To this illustrious list of Saxon saints in Norman churches, it seems reasonable to add the name of Eadburg. Full proof will probably never be forthcoming, as the documentation which could settle the question once and for all simply does not exist. The building itself, however, is an irrefutable document — albeit one prone to many different interpretations. At the very least, Norman Southwell is a building with numerous Anglo-Saxon echoes; echoes which we may assume were imbued with meaning to the people who chose to put them there. And, if one accepts Dimock's evidence, the Minster becomes an elegant Norman lady dressed up in Saxon jewelry, in deference to her venerable local saint.

Acknowledgements

I would like to thank the vergers of Southwell Minster, especially Mr. Richard Legg, for kindly allowing me unlimited access to all parts of the Minster and its gardens. I have also benefited from assistance on numerous aspects of my research on Southwell and Eadburg from Professor Malcolm Thurlby and Professor David Hill. I am grateful to Professor Joseph Goering, Professor Francesco Guardiani, Professor Dominico Pietro-Paulo and Professor Giulio Silano for organizing an excellent conference; and to Mr. Randall Rosenfeld for helping me take part in it.

---

[24] Abou-el-Haj, p. 4-7.
[25] Rollason p. 222.

List Of Illustrations

Fig. 1 – The surviving Anglo-Norman fabric of Southwell Minster, from the north-west. Photo by Peter Coffman.

Fig. 2 – Reconstruction of Southwell Minster from the south-east, as it would have appeared around the end of the 12th century, showing the rectilinear east and round clerestory windows. Illustration by Anthony Harrison.

Fig. 3 – Southwell Minster, nave interior to the east, completed ca. 1170. Photo by Peter Coffman

Fig. 4 – Norman "logic" in the nave of S.-Etienne, Caen. Photo by Peter Coffman.

Fig. 5 – Anglo-Saxon exuberance at Earls Barton, ca. 1000. Photo by Peter Coffman.

Fig. 6 – Fragments found by James Dimock in the core of the Norman fabric, 1853. Reproduced courtesy of the President and Council of the British Archaeological Association.

Fig. 7 – Double billet: the sole survivor of Dimock's fragments, currently in the Provost's garden. Photo by Peter Coffman.

Fig. 1. *The surviving Anglo-Norman fabric of Southwell Minster, from the north-west. (Photo by Peter Coffman).*

Fig. 2 – *Reconstruction of Southwell Minster from the south-east, as it would have appeared around the end of the 12th century, showing the rectilinear east and round clerestory windows. (Illustration by Anthony Harrison).*

Fig. 3 – *Southwell Minster, nave interior to the east, completed ca. 1170.*
(Photo by Peter Coffman).

Fig. 4 – Norman "logic" in the nave of S.-Etienne, Caen. (Photo by Peter Coffman).

Fig. 5 – *Anglo-Saxon exuberance at Earls Barton, ca. 1000. (Photo by Peter Coffman).*

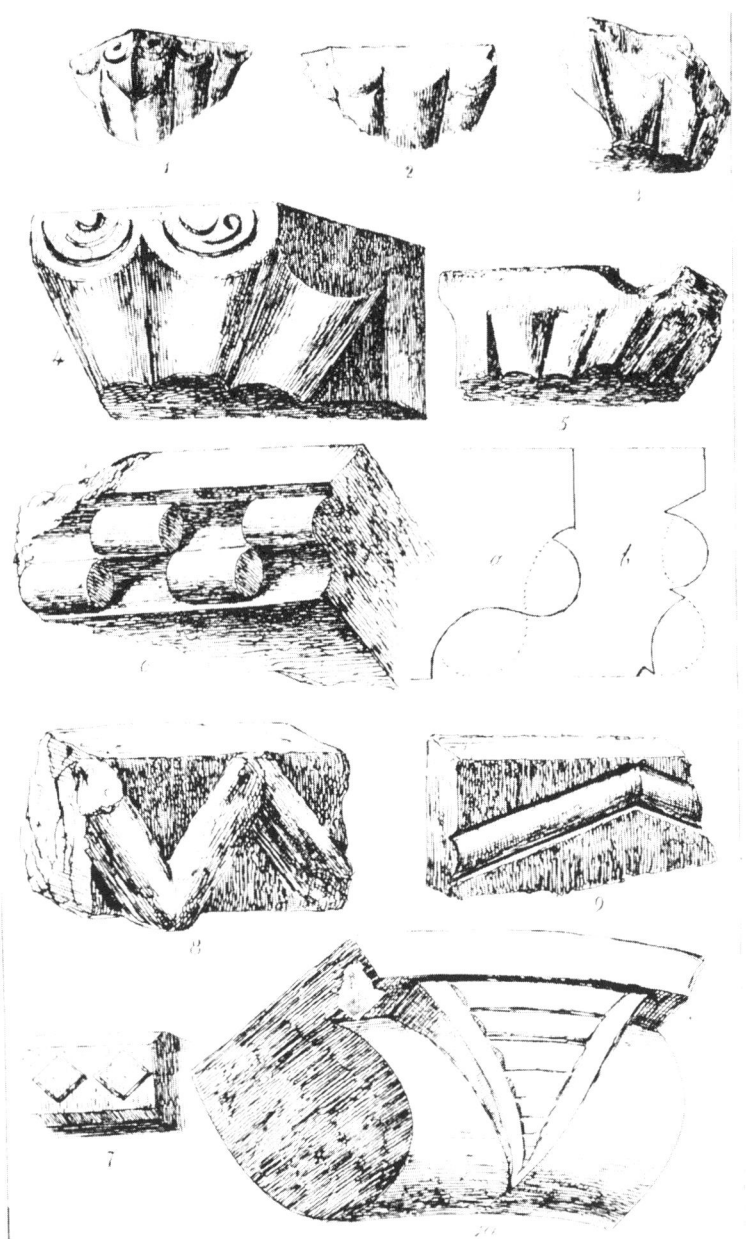

Fig. 6 – *Fragments found by James Dimock in the core of the Norman fabric, 1853.*
(Reproduced courtesy of the President and Council of the British Archaeological Association).

Fig. 7 – *Double billet: the sole survivor of Dimock's fragments, currently in the Provost's garden. (Photo by Peter Coffman).*

ERIC GRAFF

HOLIER THAN THOU, OR HOW THE BETTERS GET THE GOODS: AN EARLY BRIDGETTINE PIONEER'S LETTER HOME

ABSTRACT. This paper will discuss the letter of Katillus, an early Bridgettine brother in England, to the Confessor General of Vadstena in Sweden. The letter concerns the establishment of the first Bridgettine monastery in England, which is to be done by converting a hospital for the poor into a house for the brothers and sisters of St. Bridget's order. My paper will uncover some new details about the spread of St. Bridget's *cultus* into England and focus especially on the argument contained in this letter, namely that the appropriation of goods reserved for the poor is justified because 'divine worship is to be increased'. In order to circumvent the canonical prohibitions against such appropriation, Katillus constructs an elaborate rationale based upon assessing the relative holiness of various religious groups. Although this planned conversion was never accomplished (the Bridgettine house of Syon was founded on a new site in 1415), in the formulation of the plan we may see, behind the calm exterior of institutional religious practice, a 'hostile' takeover in the making. Katillus' case for violating a canon of the Church relies as much on the worldly estimation of sanctity as on the need of a young devotional movement to find room for expansion.

My subject today is the letter of Katillus Thornberni to Ericus Johannis, the Confessor General at Vadstena, the Bridgettine motherhouse in Sweden. Katillus was one of the so-called Bridgettine 'pioneers' who came to England charged with making arrangements for the founding of the first English monastery of St. Bridget's order.[1] His letter now rests in the Uppsala University Library in Sweden.[2] One of the library's cata-

---

[1] For a discussion of the international growth of the order over time, which, however, passes lightly over the fifteenth century, see "The Growth and Expansion of the Order" by Sr. Patricia, O.SS.S., pp. 27-48 in James Hogg, ed. *Studies in St. Birgitta and the Brigittine Order*, 2 vols. Salzburg: Institut für Anglistik und Amerikanistik, 1993.
[2] The manuscript is kept by itself under the designation Uppsala University Papersbrev 1410-1420.

loguers, Dr. Monica Hedlund, suggested that I edit this short, but damaged document, which provides a candid glimpse of the administrative efforts leading to the eventual founding of Syon Monastery in 1415.[3] Now that I have edited the text, the letter poses more questions than ever. For example, the letter is dated on St. Olaf's day, July 29th, but in what year was it written? What was the impetus for the proposal contained in this letter in the first place? Why did this proposal fail in the end? Finally, how did our humble Katillus come to make the startling argument that because his order was especially holy, it had the right to evict the poor and to seize the goods reserved for their use? I believe the solution to these problems ultimately depends upon an accurate answer to the question of the letter's date. However, in order to deal with the document at all, we must supply some context for the discussion, so that we can judge the actions of our pioneering scribe, Katillus, who is not yet present at the story's beginning.

Lord Henry Fitzhugh, soon to be our benevolent benefactor, comes from York to Sweden in the Fall of 1406 with a royal delegation; he is charged with overseeing the marriage of Philippa, King Henry IV's daughter, to Eric of Pomerania, King of Sweden, Denmark and Norway. Yet Fitzhugh goes further than that: the *Diarium Vadstenense*, the annal of the Bridgettine community, records his announcement on November 28th of that year that he intends to sponsor the building of the first Bridgettine house in England.[4] In fact, Fitzhugh asks for two brothers to be sent under his protection to York and gives letters granting property to them, at Cherry Hinton, upon their arrival. Impressed with Fitzhugh's offer, the Bridgettines send one delegate, Brother Hemmingus, who travels to England and prepares to import the kernal of a new monastery, but two problems arise to forestall the plan. Hemmingus dies during his return trip, and the royal opinion in England turns against establishing the Bridgettines in this manner. As a solution to the first problem, the community at Vadstena elects two brothers to go to England and pursue the matter; Johannes Petri and (at last, 'our man in York')

---

[3] I must thank Dr. Hedlund for her suggestion and for her contagious interest in the career of Katillus Thornberni, as well as Stephan Borgehammar and George Rigg, both of whom generously answered my many questions regarding the letter's transcription. I hope that the full edition, including a diplomatic transcription of the manuscript and translation, will be shortly forthcoming.

[4] Gejrot, Claes, ed. *Diarium Vadstenense: The Memorial Book of Vadstena Abbey*. Stockholm: Almqvist and Wiksell, 1988. In the *Diarium*, Fitzhugh is referred to as Henry 'Rawinzwatt' (for his manor Ravensworth); his visit is recorded in item 147 in the chronology.

Katillus Thornberni.⁵ In order to solve the second problem, Johannes and Katillus will have to find a way both to appease the English king's concerns over alien priories and to honor the generosity of their patron Lord Fitzhugh. In addition, they must provide the means to support a double house of Bridgettine sisters and brothers.

Let us consider this last task first. When St. Bridget of Sweden asked for papal sanction to "plant a new vineyard" according to the dictates of Christ, she blended the monastic rules of the Benedictines and Cistercians and the less rigorous Augustinian rule in order to define a new community of men and women living a cloistered life under the rule of the holy Savior.⁶ It was no novelty that both sexes could live a monastic life in the same institution; the Gilbertines had been doing that in England since the 1140s. Yet the prescribed size and diversity of the fully constituted Bridgettine house set severe demands before Johannes and Katillus, who had to plan for the financial and material sustainment of the monastery. When they arrived in England in the Spring of 1408, they must have been shown the property at Cherry Hinton. Perhaps they were even housed there for a time. But they would have known that the grounds were not suitable for the conventual living of men and women; the division of space and utilities is a prime concern for dual communities. In short, Johannes and Katillus were forced before all else to consider the size and revenues of their proposed establishment.

As they realized that the manor given by Lord Fitzhugh was unfit for their purposes, they began to develop alternate plans. We cannot know whether this bruised the ego of their sponsor. No doubt Fitzhugh, who was close to the king in administrative matters, also became aware of the legal problems with mortmain legislation that arose in this affair.⁷ He had intended to hand over property to the Bridgettines and endow it in perpetuity. Had such an endowment passed directly to the newly chartered religious community, the feudal identity of the land and its rents would have been transferred to Swedish subjects, then amortized as

---

⁵ For Hemmingus, see *Diarium Vadstenense* # 155; for the election of Johannes and Katillus, see # 161.

⁶ Ingvar Fogelqvist discusses the mixed character of the Rule of the Savior in his article, "The New Vineyard: St. Birgitta of Sweden's *Regula Salvatoris* and the Monastic Tradition" in Alf Härdelin, ed., *In Quest of the Kingdom: Ten Papers on Medieval Monastic Spirituality*. Stockholm: Almqvist & Wiksell International, 1991.

⁷ Ernst Kantorowicz provides a good general discussion of these problems in his book *The King's Two Bodies*. Princeton: Princeton University Press, 1957; pp. 164-192. Short of settling the Bridgettines at Cherry Hinton, Fitzhugh may have been content to see his gift of land form part of the new community's endowment.

Church property. The same problem had existed with many English religious houses after the Norman Conquest. Technically, their administrative allegiance lay with the large monastic foundations in France. Indirectly, these 'alien priories' might even represent the interest of the French king. When Edward I promulgated the Statute of Mortmain, *De viris religiosis*, in 1279, he wanted to curtail the reservation of English lands for religious (and therefore untaxable) use, especially when such lands were beholden to the directives of a foreign mother-house. As we will see, Katillus offers the beginning of a solution to this sticky problem in his letter, which carries an entirely new, and highly suspect, proposal for the monastery's creation.

The letter opens with a series of flattering comparisons between its recipient Lord Ericus Johannis, Vadstena's Confessor General, and the guardians of paradise, a mirror of virtues, even a light on the candelabra showing the way for those coming to God. These blandishments are not too extravagant for the time. The reference to paradise may reflect Lord Eric's recent role in establishing the monastery of Paradise, a new Bridgettine house in Italy.[8] Twice in the introduction, Katillus mentions the biblical Sion, which leads me to believe that the name for their new community had already been chosen. Then the letter turns mysteriously to the subject of proper order in religious preferments, but we'll return to this subject in a few moments, turning as abruptly from it as does Katillus:

> But now I leave this matter, writing to you about the progress which the illustrious prince, the King of England and the lord Henry Fitzhugh have made and are making in arranging the foundation of our monastery in England, and where they propose to build it, as will be clear below in the underwritten articles proceeding in order.[9]

From this point on, the letter becomes an itemized agenda and justification for the revised plan; namely, to convert the hospital of St. Nicholas outside of Walmgate Bar, York into the new monastery. This is a fine idea, but at first glance is patently illegal. St. Nicholas' hospital was a royal foundation annexed to the parish of Saint Nicholas, and its goods were stipulated for the use of the sick or poor.[10] One of the oldest tenets

---

[8] For references to Ericus Johannis in the *Diarium Vadstenense*, see items 119, 258, 264, 347 and 577 in the chronology.

[9] Translations from the letter, of course, are my own.

[10] For a detailed account of the Hospital of St. Nicholas outside Walmgate Bar, see: David Knowles and R. Neville Hadcock, *Medieval Religious Houses, England and*

in canon law is the prohibition against alienating or converting goods reserved specifically for the poor. But Katillus demonstrates his familiarity with legal sources. Number one:

> ...it should be understood that this hospital can indeed be transformed because a place of secular clerics can be changed informally into a place for religious, and a religious place conversely into a secular place in the case of a deficiency of those religious persons (if they are not to be found there). Also this hospital was founded for the infirm, as is clear in its letters of confirmation, and such ones are not found or sustained there at present nor <have been> for a long time since. And these <judgments> are clearly established by those <cases> that are read and noted: 'Extra', Concerning holy buildings[11] ... and Concerning religious houses[12].... . So in the sight of the law it can be done and is expressly permitted.

Katillus has cleverly emphasized the dedication to the infirm, rather than to the poor, and has introduced the familiar argument that the hospital was understaffed. So far, he lays out just the precedents for conversion between secular and religious institutions.

The poor, nevertheless, prey on Katillus' mind. Number Two:

> ... in the view of conscience these things may be done, since the laws say it is allowed: 'Extra', Concerning religious houses. Although it appears in similar cases that goods collected for the use of the poor should not be appropriated to another use without the authority of the apostolic see (even if that use into which it will have been converted is known by all to be more pius than the previous use), nevertheless, in our case they can be appropriated with apostolic authority ... , and it is more deserving so to convert, because divine worship is to be increased, which here happens as much in number as in quality of persons.

Here Katillus gives, complete with footnotes, his rationalization for countervening the usual canons, but his argument is noticeably thin. Having just cited two canons in which exceptions were made to the usual order, he declares that the law expressly allows this sort of conversion. On this basis, he recommends that the conscience may be set at ease over the matter. Next he adds the assumption that regulars, those like himself who live according to a strict rule, contribute more to divine worship than seculars, who observe a more casual regimen. Most impor-

---

Wales (Longman 1971), pp. 338, 409; also Victoria County Histories, *Yorkshire*, iii, 346-349 and Dugdale's *Monasticon Anglicanum*, vi, part 2, pp. 709-711.

[11] Friedberg, Émil, ed. *Corpus Iuris Canonici*, vol. 2. Leipzig, 1881: book 3, title 48, chapter 5, column 653.

[12] Friedberg, Émil, ed *Corpus Iuris Canonici*, vol. 2. Leipzig, 1881: book 3, title 36, chapter 5, column 603.

tantly, perhaps, he has shown that with papal approval all things are possible.

The letter continues with item number three, in which Katillus advises that King Henry IV should write to the pope for a licence to transfer the property. Items four and five, written on the bottom of the letter's recto side, suffer badly from damage to the manuscript, but appear to call for two sisters and two brothers to be sent from Sweden and charged with taking possession of the new house. The following item, at the top of the verso side, is much clearer, at least to look at. Number six:

> ...that these persons so licensed by the permission of our lord king should come to England and arrive as his lieges.

The difficulty here is that Katillus seems to be speaking of England's king as his own. It is possible that our protagonist, a Dane by birth, a Swede by profession, may already have pledged English fealty. At any rate, he indicates that the arriving cohort of Swedish Bridgettines will take English citizenship before claiming their lands. In this way, the new house does not retain the character of an alien priory. Indeed, Katillus will define the process of possession in order avoid any hint of foreign influence. Item seven calls for the king to witness the election of one of the delegate nuns as abbess or prioress. In item eight, the king then confers the hospital with its rights and privileges (according to the form designated by the pope) on the new abbess in 'pure perpetual alms'. Finally, Katillus proposes that the diocesan of York, the archbishop's chief financial officer, "apply both his consent and authority in all matters" having to do with the Bridgettines and their monastery. In other words, the English Bridgettines will receive their property not from Fitzhugh but from the English king and will submit themselves voluntarily to the organizational scrutiny of the English diocesan at York. Were it not for these concessions, the entire undertaking might seem more like a hostile takeover than like the peaceful growth of a pius order. By submitting themselves to the native authority, the Bridgettines are able to suggest that the hospital of St. Nicholas be converted as subjects asking only for the king's discretion in choosing between two royal establishments.

At this point, Katillus is on a roll. He has introduced the canonical precedents for his unusual plan of action and allayed royal concerns about foreign houses. He has briefly noted the hospital's suitability for conversion and now attacks its current administration:

> But since it is grievously reported in modern time that one master and six women (not the least bit sick) are found there, and thence the monies received

(against the prohibitions of the canons) are converted into other extraneous uses, therefore your aforementioned son, **wishing to provide for the salvation of these abusers** and to turn the goods of this hospital to better uses — namely into the building and sustainment of a monastery of the Order of the holy Savior by Saint Birgitta of the country of Sweden from a new foundation and approved by the apostolic see, since it is said to be apt for this and well disposed both in its goods and possessions — should strive and purpose together with others conferring about this new endeavor.

So it appears that all along Katillus has been trying to save the abusers from themselves, for they have already violated the canon against appropriation by mismanaging the hospital's funds. He goes on to state the intended number of Bridgettines who will occupy the same site: 60 women and 25 men, all recluses. This explains his earlier boast that divine worship will benefit both in number and quality. Certainly with six residents and one curator the hospital was nearly empty. Its residents, moreover, practised the Augustinian rule very casually; there was very little communal prayer, and practically no singing of the hours. In a fully constituted Bridgettine house, the abbess and nuns are served by 13 priest brothers who administer confession and celebrate masses, and by 4 deacons and 8 other men.[13] One of the priests acts as a confessor general. The usual daily offices are sung by the brothers, while the sisters observe the Office of the Virgin. Undoubtedly Katillus was convinced about the virtue of this plan, and he was not the first to assert the superiority of regular over secular religious lifestyles. So even if his rationale bends the rules of strict and compassionate interpretation of Church law, we may safely avoid viewing his efforts as cynical. Although we see in this letter an argument directly contrary to the spirit and the letter of the canons, we also recognize that Katillus appeals to a prior concern — prior from the point of view of the salvation of souls — the maintenance of the worship of God.

So much for the rationale contained in the document; but under what circumstances did Katillus make these arguments, and why was this proposal abandoned in the end? As I have already indicated, pinpointing the date of the letter is crucial both to establishing these motives and to speculating about the proposal's failure; so now we must consider the year in which this proposal was sent to Vadstena. Its current shelfmark (Uppsala University Library Papersbrev 1410-1420) offers a rough estimate as to the letter's date. Since we know that Katillus was in England

---

[13] Eklund, Sten, ed. *Sancta Birgitta: Opera Minora I, Regula Salvatoris*. Stockholm: Almqvist & Wiksell, 1975: chapter 13, pp. 119-120.

between 1408 and 1421, his letter could theoretically date from any of the seven years between 1408 and 1415, when King Henry V laid the cornerstone at Syon. Monica Hedlund, in her article on Katillus and his books, hazards the guess that the letter was written early in this period, but hers is still the only reply to the question.[14] Without the aid of explicit evidence to help situate this letter in its context —there is no acknowledgement of Lord Eric's having received the letter, no other mention of it in the existing diary of Katillus or in the diary of Vadstena — we are left to supply the information from the document itself and from what we can discover about its proposal.

We can begin by delving into the records of St. Nicholas' hospital. Along with its parochial church, it had by 1408 become a likely candidate for serious reform. It had been in trouble since at least May of 1400, when the king issued a writ protecting one of his royal agents, who was responsible for assessing the aliened rents of the hospital, from legal procedings against him.[15] In November of 1408, John Newton, Treasurer of York, was commissioned "to visit the hospital and survey the defects and do all things concerning the visitation and reformation of the premises; as the king's kinsman Thomas, archbishop of Canterbury, the chancellor, to whom the visitation of the king's hospitals pertains, is too busy."[16] Curiously, the king's pursuit of Newton's report stalled until 1 November 1410, when the king ordered the resumption of another legal case involving St. Nicholas' church and its newly appointed warden Robert Wolden.[17] We have no sure indication that Fitzhugh saw Newton's report, but we do know that the two men were acquainted. It seems unlikely to me that Fitzhugh would not have taken an interest in a dilapidated property so well-endowed for the Bridgettine needs (St. Nicholas' was a relatively large place already equipped to house men and women). Furthermore, Katillus may have been working directly from a copy of Newton's report. The next mention of St. Nicholas in the Patent Rolls, in January of 1416, quotes from the 1408 report. We may speculate that several phrases which appear both in the 1416 order and in Katillus' letter (e.g., the form of the remembrance of the king's ancestors and of the hospital's mission as well as the emphasis on the increase or decrease of divine worship), result from a common

---

[14] Hedlund, Monica. "Katillus Thornberni, A Syon Pioneer and His Books." *Birgittiana* 1 (1993), pp. 67-87: see esp. pp. 68-69 and note 3 for discussion of this letter.
[15] *Calendar of Close Rolls*, Henry IV, iiii, p. 187.
[16] *Calendar of Patent Rolls*, Henry IV, iiii, p. 65.
[17] *Calendar of Close Rolls*, Henry IV, iiii, p. 132.

dependence upon Newton's findings, which he likely sent to the king early in 1409. Apparently, Katillus was writing with the aid of Newton's papers in addition to the hospital's charter and the *Liber extra*.

Yet this reconstruction gets us just half way home. Katillus himself renders up the most telling clues about the time of his writing. Let's return, then, to the opening of the letter, from which we turned so quickly before. Immediately after the greeting, Katillus makes a series of puzzling remarks:

> ... from the day on which he was anointed, when Saul was changed into a king, **suddenly there followed 'this change of God's right hand'**. On this account, I presume to say that you <Lord Eric> care for the gates of Sion above all the tabernacles of Jacob. ... Indeed it is right and just that those who have been proven for a long time in good living and regularly tested with virtuous exercizes should be preferred to others in the distinction of governing; and seniors in a higher rank and office should be favored instead of novices, lest the head be turned into the tail and once more the tail of Juno's bird will be marked with the eyes of Argus.[18] Since it would be most wrong and absurd that the inexperienced should be preferred to the masters, the young to the old, rude men to distinguished ones (**and so the cleft stone would not be healed and the lord's David would not be honored** ...), therefore even you should not wonder that I write these things to you..., since the flock forgets its food at the sound of the harp.

In this pastiche of biblical and Ovidian reference, Katillus discloses his generalized concern for hierarchical order and for the appreciation of devout experience. What could he mean by all this business about Saul, and 'the lord's David', and the cleft stone? We have seen already that he holds firmly to notions of graded sanctity in matters of worldly affairs, but since, at the opening of the letter, he does not attach his comments to anything concrete, we can only wonder what caused him such anxiety. The answer, of course, does not seem surprising once we have found it. Katillus was writing during a summer that must have been filled with uneasiness for the devout; the same summer when the unity of the Church, not to mention a myriad of financial and administrative initiatives, hung in the balance. Since March of 1409, the Council of Pisa had been negotiating an end to the Great Schism. News of the deposition of the two contending popes and the election of Pope Alexander V spread quickly from Italy. The Cardinals informed King Henry IV by dispatch on 26 June, 1409. If the plan to convert St. Nicholas' had been hatched by Fitzhugh and Newton, then Katillus would have been waiting to hear

---

[18] Cf. Ovid, *Met.* 1, 625-723

the outcome of the council before he sent his proposal. By 29 July 1409, he could be fairly sure that the papacy would be open to hearing the King's petition, and so he sent the letter for Lord Eric's approval. The anointing of Saul, the honor of the Lord's David, the cleft stone; all these allude to the announcement of the papal election in 1409.

We might expect, then, that the Bridgettines would have lived happily ever after at the old St. Nicholas grounds. Instead, they were installed at Twickenham in 1415 and moved to more spacious accommodation at Isleworth in 1432.[19] I'm sorry to say that I don't know precisely why the plan to convert St. Nicholas' hospital failed. King Henry IV's petition to the pope regarding the plan exists in manuscript, but has never been edited.[20] It is easy to imagine that either Lord Eric or the pope might have declined to continue the process, but neither of them have left a record of their assent or refusal. The young king's role in the foundation of Syon Abbey has been discussed at length by Neil Beckett, but Henry V's program for a collection of royal religious houses at Sheen, if it had been formulated at all by 1409, was in abeyance at least while his father's illness lingered. We know only that he took up the work at Sheen almost as soon as he received the crown.[21]

Consequently, I am left to explain the value of this historical dead end to our discussion of sanctity. We need not, I think, accuse Katillus or his sponsers of callousness in their disregard of the ailing hospital and its residents. If my reconstruction of the genesis of this plan is accurate, Fitzhugh and Newton were merely trying to find a better use for goods that had been poorly managed before. As the treasurer of the archdiocese of York, Newton himself would exercise supervision of the new community through the office of the diocesan. It was left for Katillus to support the proposal with legal and moral arguments, which he did despite his apparent hesitation over the matter of the poor. He supplied for his superiors at Vadstena all the necessary notes and reasons, relying finally on the commonplace assumption that spiritual betters (here defined in relation to regular versus secular life) had a claim to whatever goods stood at the Church's disposal.

---

[19] For Syon's charter and foundation, see: David Knowles and R. Neville Hadcock, *Medieval Religious Houses, England and Wales* (Longman 1971), p. 202; also Victoria County Histories, *Middlesex*, iii, 97-100 and Dugdale's *Monasticon Anglicanum*, vi, part 2, p. 542.

[20] British Library Add. MS 24062, fol. 150.

[21] Beckett, Neil. "St. Bridget, Henry V and Syon Abbey" in James Hogg, ed. *Studies in St. Birgitta and the Brigittine Order*, 2 vols. Salzburg: Institute für Anglistik und Amerikanistik, 1993.

The natural predilection for order (arranged according to perfection) had been articulated by Thomas Aquinas more than two hundred years before,[22] and both clerics and laymen had depended on it as a principle of structure in society for much longer than that. Nearly as prevalent as our theory of gravity was the idea of the spiritual order, in which more perfect men and women should lead and instruct the less faithful, drawing them upward as it were by the attraction of their holiness. Closer to the time of Katillus, visionaries like St. Brigett reinvigorated efforts by the Church to pursue idealized Christianity in this world. We still depend upon mystics like St. Bridgett to teach us how Christians in the Middle Ages saw their perfect faith. Of course, we still rely on Aquinas to define the rationale of a holy society. But we need, no less than the guidance of these august figures, the experience of someone like Katillus, not just to give us a personality with whom we can sympathize, but to remind us that notions of sanctity can lead even the proven disciple into dubious affairs.

---

[22] See, for example, the treatment of Questio 184 in *Summa Theologiae* II, ii.

CHRISTOPHE POTWOROSKI

THE THEOLOGIAN AND THE "LITTLE WAY"

ABSTRACT. The recent declaration of Saint Thérèse of Lisieux as Doctor of the Church has focussed attention on her doctrinal importance for all faithful. This paper raises the question of her significance as a point of reference for theology and theological reflection.

On October 19, 1977, Pope John Paul II declared Sainte Thérèse de Lisieux to be a Doctor of the Church. In the homily accompanying this act, he explained the significance of this ecclesial gesture. "Indeed, when the magisterium proclaims someone Doctor of the Church, it intends a signal to all the faithful, and in a special way to those giving in the Church the fundamental service of predication or following the delicate task of theological research or teaching, that the doctrine professed and proclaimed by a certain person can be a **point of reference**, not only because it conforms to revealed truth, but also because it throws a new light on the mysteries of faith, a deeper understanding of the mystery of Christ."[1]

My aim in this paper is to inquire into the way in which saints in the Catholic Church, and more particularly Doctors of the Church, are "signals" to the faithful. More specifically, I am interested in the implications of the little way as a "point of reference" for those involved in "theological research or teaching." In an age where the very foundations upon which theological reflection is built are questioned, such a point of

---

[1] *Homily*, n. 3, in *L'Osservatore Romano*, Edizione quotidiana 20-21 ottobre 1997. For a recent and popular presentation of the subject, see Bernard McGinn, *The Doctors of the Church: Thirty-Three Men and Women who Shaped Christianity* (New York: Crossroad, 1999).

Saints and the Sacred - A St. Michael's College Symposium
Joseph Goering, Francesco Guardiani, Giulio Silano eds. Ottawa: Legas, 2001

reference would indeed be welcome. What is the path offered for theology to follow?

The indications are already there. In a reference to the writings of Vatican II, John Paul noted that, with the assistance of the Holy Spirit, the Church continually grows in the understanding of the deposit of faith. Moreover, this process of growth is made up of various strands and contributing elements. The growth comes not only from the study and research grounded in contemplation to which theologians are called, not only from the magisterium to which is given the charism of truth, but also by that "profound understanding of things spiritual" which is given by the life and the experience, with the riches of the gifts of the Holy Spirit, of those who let themselves be guided by the Spirit of God namely the saints (cf. *Dei Verbum*, 8). The Dogmatic Constitution on the Church, *Lumen Gentium*, teaches that in the saints it is "God himself who speaks" (n. 50).

The questions thus becomes more specific. How can theologians benefit from the life and experience of the saints? By seeing the lives and experience of saints as part of the mission of the Holy Spirit in our age precisely for the benefit of the Church. The saints contribute to our understanding of the Gospel. Each saint is given, in this perspective, a particular mission to throw light on one forgotten or neglected aspect of revelation. This is how the Swiss theologian Hans Urs von Balthasar put it: "The Spirit meets the burning questions of the age with an utterance that is the key-word, the answer to the riddle. Never in the form of an abstract statement (that being something that it is man's business to draw up); almost always in the form of a new, concrete supernatural mission: the creation of a new saint whose life is a presentation to his own age of the message that heaven is sending to it, a man who is, here and now, the right and relevant interpretation of the Gospel, who is given to this particular age as its way of approach to the perennial truth of Christ. How else can life be expounded except by living? The saints are tradition at its most living, tradition as the word is meant whenever Scripture speaks of the unfolding of the riches of Christ, and the application to history of the norm which is Christ. Their missions are so exactly the answer from above to the question from below that their immediate effect is often one of unintelligibility; they are the signs to be contradicted in the name of every kind of right-thinking--until the proof of their power is brought forth. Saint Bernard and Saint Francis, Saint Ignatius and Saint Teresa were all of them proofs of that order; they were like volcanoes pouring forth molten fire from the depths of Revelation; they were irrefutable proof, all horizontal tradition notwithstanding, of the vertical presence of the living Kyrios here, now, and today."[2]

The question of her significance is thus meant not only in terms of personal life and destiny of the theologian, but as it pertains to the very method and unfolding of theology as a discipline. That very distinction between personal life and intellectual discipline already suggests a problematic area in need of serious correction. One of the first benefits of the renewed interest in saints on the part of theology is the closer relations between spirituality and theology, not only as an interest in a cognate discipline, but as a growing awareness that truth is not only something to be understood and known, but also loved. In this light, the title of John Paul's Apostolic Letter on this occasion is significant: *Divini amoris scientia*.

The role of saints in the history of the Church, and in the history of theology too, continually speaks against the divorce between heart and intellect, between spirituality and theology.

The theologian might be tempted to use a variety of approaches when reading Sainte Thérèse: psychological, sociological, spiritual, or theological. Before all other readings, an emphasis on the objectivity of the mission suggests itself against all forms of sentimentalism. Sainte Thérèse herself abhorred any form of "sugary" or "syrupy" spirituality.

The mission of Sainte Thérèse is basically that of "spiritual childhood", this is her "little way". As Doctor of the Church, this means not only that her life and experience are authentic interpretation of the Gospel, based on the unity of word and life that is at the heart of all Christian existence, throwing a new light on neglected truths, but that this life and experience is expressed in a teaching which is astonishingly clear. Thus, she has not only a theological mission, but also a doctrinal mission.[3]

This doctrine of the "little way" can be described first in a negative way (what it is not) and then in a positive way (what it is).

The "little way" is first of all the rejection of all forms of moralism. It is a deconstruction of sorts aimed at the notion of Christian living based

---

[2] Hans Urs von Balthasar, *Theology of History* (San Francisco: Ignatius Press, 1994), 109-10.

[3] Cf. Hans Urs von Balthasar, *Two Sisters in the Spirit: Thérèse de Lisieux and Elisabeth of the Trinity* (San Francisco: Ignatius Press, 1992) 233. Although the original version of this study on Thérèse appeared in 1950, and many spiritual, historical and theological studies have appeared since, Balthasar's monograph remains extremely useful, particularly in recognizing the value of her doctrinal mission for theology. In this way, it anticipates John Paul II's declaration.

on duty. It is a rejection of legalism, and the view of holiness as some sort of heroism. Finally it is the rejection of the notion of human freedom as autonomy. In all of these cases, Sainte Thérèse's approach is that of a warrior (she often compares her mission to that of Joan of Arc), and her opponent is all forms of Pharisaism. Hans Urs von Balthasar says: "Her battle is to wipe out the hard core of Pharisaism that persists in the midst of Christianity; that human will-to-power disguised in the mantle of religion that drives one to assert one's own greatness instead of acknowledging that God alone is great."[4]

For Sainte Thérèse, perfection is not the goal of holiness, in fact she speaks of the "temptation of perfection": "Sanctity does not consist in performing such and such acts; it means being ready at heart to become small and humble in the arms of God, acknowledging our own weakness and trusting in his fatherly goodness to the point of audacity."[5] Again: "Jesus does not demand great deeds but only gratitude and self-surrender."[6]

Progress does not come through the acquisition of skills or knowledge, but through losing everything; it does not mean climbing but descending.[7] Sainte Thérèse was responsible for the novices in the convent at one time, and in this context she recalls the visit of one novice who said to her: "When I think of everything I still have to acquire!" Sainte Thérèse answers: "You mean to lose! Jesus takes it upon himself to fill your soul in the measure that you rid it of its imperfections. I see that you have taken the wrong road; you will never arrive at the end of your journey. You are wanting to climb a great mountain, and the good God is trying to make you descend it; he is waiting for you at the bottom in the fertile valley of humility."[8]

Instead of counting and measuring one's progress in order to advance in perfection, a form of spiritual capitalism or accounting, Sainte Thérèse relies on poverty: "I cannot rely upon anything, not on one single work of mine, for security...But this poverty is a real light and grace for me. I thought of how I could not pay God for even one the faults I had committed in the whole of my life, and that precisely this could by

---

[4] *Two Sisters* 241.

[5] *St. Thérèse of Lisieux: Her Last Conversations*, translated by John Clarke (Washington, DC: Institute of Carmelite Studies, 1977) 129 n.

[6] *Story of a Soul: The Autobiography of St. Thérèse of Lisieux*, translated by John Clarke (Washington DC: Institute of Carmelite Studies), 188.

[7] Cf. Balthasar *Two Sisters*, 245.

[8] In Ida F. Görres, *The Hidden Face: A Study of St. Thérèse of Lisieux* (New York: Pantheon, 1955), 338.

my richness and strength If I wished. And so I prayed, O my God, I beg you yourself to pay the debt I have contracted towards the soul in Purgatory, but do it as God, so that it will be infinitely more successful than if I said my Offices for the Dead. And I took great comfort in the thoughts expressed by Saint John of the Cross in his canticle: 'Pay all the debts.' I have always related this to love. I feel that one can never repay this grace...it is a source of such peace to be utterly poor, to count on nothing but God."[9]

Thus, because she attaches such importance to poverty, Sainte Thérèse is highly suspicious of all forms of asceticism and penance. Early in her religious life, she had "a strong inclination to works of penance." "I had taken too much pleasure in them and so the good God let me realize that the strictest penances can be mingled with natural satisfaction."[10] This relates to the traditional catholic notion of merit, which Sainte Thérèse does not exclude. When asked if she wants to acquire merits, she answers: "Yes, but not for myself. For souls, and for the needs of the whole Church..."[11] "Merit does not arise from performing great deeds or giving much but in receiving and loving."[12] Even in suffering or in martyrdom, the point is not the record of suffering, the achievement, but the intensity of love. Every penance that increases true love is good; any penance that narrows and preoccupies the soul is harmful.[13] "Certainly every penance is laudable and meritorious if one is convinced that the good God requires it of one. Even if one errs in doing it, [God] is touched by the intention. But I could never bind myself to anything if it became a constant preoccupation...; as our mother Saint Teresa says: God is not concerned with a heap of trifles, as we too easily believe; and we should never let anything narrow our souls."[14] Love is the measure of every penance and every action: "Love is the one thing at which we should aim, consequently we should always prefer that deed into which we can crush most love, whether it is 'harder' or 'easier'; it is better to do something that is in itself indifferent than something 'worthwhile' in itself if we can do the first more lovingly than the second."[15] And again: "Out of love, I will suffer and, out of love, rejoice."[16]

---

[9] *Last Conversations*, 137.
[10] In *Hidden Face*, 296-97.
[11] *Last Conversations*, 153.
[12] *General Correspondence*, translated by John Clarke (Washington DC: Institute of Carmelite Studies, 1982-1988), 2:794-95.
[13] Cf. Balthasar *Two Sisters*, 249-50.
[14] In *Hidden Face*, 302-3.
[15] In *Hidden Face*, 303.

We find in Sainte Thérèse the demolition of an ethic of works and duty, in order to allow the miracle of divine grace to illuminate the life of every Christian. Rather than calculating the measure of her progress toward perfection, she realizes that God himself does not calculate as it is against his innermost essence which is love. Grace is not limited by calculations or reckoning. She comes up with a wonderful image to describe this situation: "Alas, I have always noticed, in comparing myself with the saints, the same difference between them and myself as we see between a mountain whose summit is lost in the clouds and an obscure little grain of sand trampled underfoot by passers-by...It is impossible for me to grow great...But we live in an age of inventions: today there is no need to go to the trouble of climbing stairs; among rich people, an elevator has replaced the stairs. I also wished to discover an elevator to take me up to Jesus; because I am too little to climb the steep stairway of perfection."[17]

The need for an elevator simply reveals the complete dependence which "expects everything": "To be little means recognizing one's nothingness, expecting everything from the good God, *as a little child expects from its Father*...Even among the poor, a child is given everything it needs so long as it is little; but as soon as it grows up, its father will no longer feed it and says, 'Work now, you can look after yourself.' Well now, it is because I did not want to hear those words that I have not wanted to grow up, because I feel incapable of *earning my living, the eternal living of heaven.*"[18]

This is the realism at the heart of Sainte Thérèse's little way, the heart of her mission. Instead of counting on the merit of her works, she yields to the power of divine grace. Unlike the "great" saints who enter heaven by the merit of great and heroic works, the "eagles", Sainte Thérèse remains "little", a "small bird", who wants to enter heaven by trick, "a trick of love that will give me entry, me and other poor sinners."[19] What is this trick? "It is quite simple. Hold nothing back. Distribute your goods as soon as you get them...If, at the moment of death, I were to present my little coins to have them estimated at their true worth, our Lord would not fail to discover dross in them that I should certainly go and deposit in Purgatory. Are we not told that, although the great saints

---

[16] *Story of a Soul*, 196.
[17] *Story of a Soul*, 207-8.
[18] *Saint Thérèse of Lisieux, the Little Flower of Jesus*, revised translation of *Histoire d'une âme* by Thomas Taylor (New York: P.J. Kennedy, 1926), 295.
[19] *Saint Thérèse of Lisieux, the Little Flower of Jesus*, 294-95.

appear before Gods's judgment seat with their hands full of merits, yet they sometimes go to that place of expiation because no justice is without blemish in the eyes of the Lord?"[20] And then comes her notion of God's justice: "When I think of the good God's statement: 'I shall come soon and bring my reward with me, repaying everyone according to his works,' then I say to myself that he will find himself very embarrassed with me, because I have no works! So he will not be able to repay me according to my works. Very well, then, I trust that he will repay me according to his works."[21] "In the evening of this life I shall appear before you empty-handed, for I do not ask you, Lord, to count my works. All our justices have stains in your sight. So I want to be clad in your own *Justice* and receive from your *Love* the possession of *yourself*. I want no other *Throne* or other *Crown* than *you*, O my *Beloved*."[22]

From a positive perspective, the "little way" can be described as surrender or consent to the love of Christ. Clearly, there is more to the "little way" than denouncing creeping Pharisaism. It is a *way*, drawing the whole person into the service of Christ. Sainte Thérèse wants to empty her soul of all her own perfection in order to create for the love of God within her. As Balthasar says, "what matters is not her love or even her love for God; all that matters now is that God wishes to be loved and must be loved...God is the beggar of love. It means that love of man is transformed into the *pure service* of God's love, and this service extinguishes the last remnants of self-seeking in human love, in Christian love even. Faith, hope and charity become what Christ wills them to be: a living representation of the Father, which means the pure service of the Father's will."[23]

The basis of the "little way", then, is a series of renunciations in order to allow for the power of divine love, a surrender, even a darkness, so that the glory of divine love may be manifest.

"I need to forget the earth; here below, everything wearies me, everything is an effort, I find only one joy, to suffer for Jesus...But this *unfelt* joy is above every joy...I hit upon the secret of suffering in peace. The word *peace* does not mean *joy*, at least not *felt* joy; to suffer in peace, it is enough to will whatever Jesus wills."[24] This suffering in peace is always with a purpose, always before a presence: "To give pleasure to Jesus."

---

[20] *Saint Thérèse of Lisieux, the Little Flower of Jesus*, 310.
[21] *Last Conversations*, 43.
[22] *Story of a Soul*, 277.
[23] *Two Sisters*, 270, 272.
[24] *General Correspondence*, 1:546.

There is even a renunciation of any fruit of one's offering: "I cannot bring myself to say 'Dear God, this one is for the Church; this other, dear God, is for France', and so on. The good God knows already what use he will make of my little merits; I have given him everything to do as he pleases, and in any case it would make me tired to be saying at every moment, 'Give this to Peter and that to Paul.' I do it quite automatically when a Sister asks me for some special purpose, but after that I never think of it. When I am praying for my missionary brothers, I do not offer up my sufferings. I say simply, 'Dear God, give them everything I wish for myself.'"[25] She also says: "Please understand that to love Jesus, to *be* his *victim of love*, the weaker one is, without desires or virtues, the more apt one is for the operations of that consuming and transforming Love."[26]

Just as the goal of perfection is abandoned, so too is any notion of progress along that way. Every means of measurement is left behind, as the only measure rests with God: "Then Jesus took me by the hand and brought by into a subterranean way, where it is neither hot nor cold, where the sun does not shine and rain and wind do not come; a tunnel where I see nothing but a brightness half-veiled...My Spouse says nothing to me nor do I say anything to him either save *I love him* more than *myself*, and, in the depth of my heart, I feel that this is true, for I am more his than my own!...I do not see that we are advancing toward the mountain that is our goal, because our journey is under the earth...I shall consent, if it is his will, to walk all my life in the dark road upon which I am, provided that one day I arrive at the goal of the mountain of love but I think it will not be here below."[27]

This renunciation of progress and of one's own measure clearly means that we will fall, that we will be unfaithful, that we will live in distraction. But even here, this does not fall outside the "little way." In a situation reminiscent of St. Augustine's *felix culpa*, Sainte Thérèse rejoices in her faults because they give her the chance to see the mercy of God [Not that these are not serious faults, but rather faults that do not offend God]: How fortunate I am to see my imperfection, to need God's mercy so greatly at the hour of my death."[28] Or again: "Whenever I have been guilty of a fault that causes me sorrow, then I know that this sadness is a result of my infidelity. But I do not let it rest at that...I say to the good

---

[25] *Last Conversations*, 133.
[26] *General Correspondence*, 2:999.
[27] *General Correspondence*, 1:651-52, 667.
[28] *Last Conversations*, 116.

God, 'I know that I have deserved this feeling of sorrow, nevertheless, let me offer it to you as a trial bestowed on me by your love. It grieves me that I have done it, but I am glad to have this suffering to offer to you.'"[29] "The remembrance of my faults humbles me and prevents me from relying upon my own strength, which is only weakness; it just tells me more and more of God's mercy and love."[30]

The "little way" is the way of spiritual childhood. Sainte Thérèse speaks and lives as a child, at home with God. "Personally I find perfection quite easy to practice because I have realized that all one has to do is *take Jesus by the heart*. Consider a small child who has displeased his mother by flying into a rage or perhaps disobeying her; if he sulks in a corner and screams in fear of punishment, his mother will certainly not forgive his fault; but if he comes to her with with his little arms outstretched, smiling and saying 'Kiss me, *I won't do it again*', surely his mother will immediately press him tenderly to her heart, forgetting all that he has done...Of course she knows quite well that her dear little boy *will do it again* at the first opportunity, but that does not matter; if he takes her by the heart, he will never be punished..."[31] This is the "little way" expressed with the humour of a child, but it is equally the way of trust and total surrender.

In all this, it cannot be said that spiritual childhood is in any way close to infantilism. On the contrary, it is a mature decision to "remain" little and to persevere in this way. It is not the mature self which is shunned by Sainte Thérèse, but the egoist self which wants to accumulate virtues: "To remain little means recognizing one's nothingness, expecting everything from the good God, *as a little child expects everything from his father*. It means not worrying about anything or being on the lookout for favors...I have always remained little, having no other ambition but to collect flowers of love and sacrifice and offer them to the good God for his pleasure. Again, to stay little means not attributing the virtues we practice to ourselves, under the impression that we are capable of such things, but to recognize that the good God places this treasure of virtue in the hand of his little child for him to use as he needs it; and that it remains God's treasure."[32]

---

[29] *Last Conversations*, 71.
[30] In *Hidden Face*, 331-32.
[31] *General Correspondence*, 2:965-66.
[32] *Saint Thérèse of Lisieux, the Little Flower of Jesus*, 295-96.

In this sense, the Theresian way is one of active receptivity. "We must do everything that is within us: give without counting the cost, practice the virtues at every opportunity, conquer ourselves all the time and prove our love by every sort of tenderness and loving attention. In a word, we must carry out all the good works that lie within our powers-- out of love for God. But it is truly essential to put our whole trust in him who alone can sanctify our work, who can indeed sanctify us without works, since he may even bring forth children of Abraham from the very stones. It is necessary for us, when we have done all we can, to confess that we are unprofitable servants, while hoping to God in his grace will give us all that we need. That is the way of childhood."[33]

After this brief reminder of the content of the little way, as refusal of heroism in the pursuit of holiness and as consent and surrender to God's love, we can now return to our question concerning the significance of all this for theology. There is not doubt that there is here a great spiritual doctrine and that Sainte Thérèse is a great teacher of spiritual doctrine. Certainly, to this extent, the theologian can profit from her teaching. But how does theology profit, in the sense of the method used by theologians in their work and the the operations they are involved in when they are involved in the activity called theology.

There are three areas that suggest themselves, all related to the theme of the "little way" as a paradigm for theological reflection. They are not directly related to Sainte Thérèse in terms of making an explicit reference to her, but they all bear witness to the same intuition. The first unlikely witness is the Canadian theologian Bernard Lonergan. Unlikely, because so much of his work on cognitional theory seems to be the antithesis of spiritual poverty. Yet, along with intellectual development towards the authenticity of the subject from below upwards, Lonergan also writes about development from above downwards, and even suggests the primacy of the latter.[34]

Another twentieth century witness is the Dominican Marie-Dominique Chenu, who early in his career worked on the nature of theology as science in the middle ages.[35] According to Thomas Aquinas, theology is a science becasue it proceeds from principles to conclusions,

---

[33] In *Hidden Face*, 281-82.

[34] Cf. Bernard Lonergan, *A Third Collection*, edited by F. Crowe (Mahwah, NJ: Paulist Press, 1985). On this see F. Crowe, *Old Things and New: A Strategy for Education* (Atlanta: Scholars Press, 1985).

[35] Cf. M.-D. Chenu, *La théologie comme science au XIIIè siècle* (Paris: pro manuscripto, 1943). The reference in Aquinas is Ia Pars, q. 1, a. 2.

but these principles are received from a higher science, a subalternating science, namely the science of of God and the blessed. In this sense, theology is a subalternated science and not in its own right because it receives its principles from another science, just like the science of optics receives its principles from physics. Now Chenu here emphasized the role of faith in theology, since it is by faith that theology receives its principles. The seemingly arcane argument of subalternation receives here a new lease on life: that by which theology is a science is also that by which it is mystical. Theology receives before it constructs, is generated before it generates. This is theology operating according a point of reference.

Lastly, there is the work of Hans Urs von Balthasar, at the heart of whose anthropology is the notion of receptivity not as an imperfection or a lack but as a characteristic of authentic creatureliness.[36]

These are but first steps in following the path traced by the newest Doctor of the Church. So many difficulties and questions remain. It is clear, for example, that a love of the truth, rather than one's own image of it, is a dominant aspect of the little way. Yet, how often we read in theological literature that too much affection for a subject diminishes one's objectivity. Is it too much to hope that the "little way" will bring a renewal of such fundamental issues?

---

[36] See for example *Unless you Become Like this Child* (San Francisco: Ignatius Press, 1991).

MAIRI COWAN

MUNGO'S MIRACLES: ST. KENTIGERN, THE CITY CREST OF GLASGOW, AND MEDIEVAL SCOTTISH TRADITIONS OF SANCTITY

ABSTRACT The city crest of Glasgow, Scotland, features a tree, a bird, a bell, and a fish with a ring in its mouth. These are representations of the miracles of Glasgow's patronsaint, Kentigern, affectionately known as St. Mungo. Kentigern was bishop of Strath clyde in the late sixth and early seventh centuries, a period of Scotland's history largely veiled in obscurity for the historian

The city crest of Glasgow, Scotland, features a tree, a bird, a bell, and a fish with a ring in its mouth. These are representations of the miracles of Glasgow's patronsaint, Kentigern, affectionately known as St. Mungo. Kentigern was bishop of Strath clyde in the late sixth and early seventh centuries, a period of Scotland's history largely veiled in obscurity for the historian

The crest, as it is now, was officially granted to the City of Glasgow District Council in 1975,[1] but the origins of the items on the crest can be traced back thirteen hundred years or more, to the life and miracles of a man named Kentigern, more commonly known as Mungo, the patron saint of Glasgow. Little is known about the historic Kentigern. His name is British – that is, from the Brittonic language. Modern scholars believe that 'Kentigern' could mean 'hound-like lord'[2] or 'hound lord'[3], while 'Mungo' might be a diminutive of Kentigern, giving a meaning of

---

[1] Joe Fisher, *The Glasgow Encyclopedia* (Edinburgh: Mainstream Publishing, 1994), p. 83.
[2] Kenneth H. Jackson, "The Sources for the Life of St Kentigern", *Studies in the Early British Church* (Cambridge: Cambridge University Press, 1958), p. 298.
[3] W. Croft Dickinson, *Scotland from the Earliest Times to 1603*. 3rd edition (Oxford: Clarendon Press, 1977), p. 37.

Saints and the Sacred - A St. Michael's College Symposium
Joseph Goering, Francesco Guardiani, Giulio Silano eds. Ottawa: Legas, 2001

'my hound'.[4] He was probably the bishop of the early medieval kingdom of Strathclyde, and he probably died in 612 or 614 and was buried at Glasgow.[5] There has survived into our time a complete vita, or 'life' of St. Kentigern, written in the later twelfth century by the Cistercian monk, Jocelin of Furness.[6] Jocelin's Life of Kentigern has been examined for information on the kingdom of Strathclyde in the early Middle Ages, and for those interested in the historical Kentigern and his time, this text presents something of a frustrating dilemma: while it is one of a very few sources available to us, it is often historically unreliable. Only a few of the historic details in Jocelin's vita can be checked against independent evidence, and many of Jocelin's assertions are flat-out contradicted by what a few more reliable sources survive.[7]

I do not intend to argue anything about the historic Kentigern from Jocelin's vita in this paper.[8] Instead, I suggest that while it may not be an especially reliable source for sixth and seventh-century Strathclyde, the Life of St. Kentigern does serve as a good source for twelfth-century Glasgow. Scholars have not yet given much attention to Scottish saints' lives as sources for later medieval Scottish history, but I propose that these texts are a very rich source. I offer as a sample this brief look at Jocelin's Life of St. Kentigern, which demonstrates, among other things, that during a time of political and religious consolidation and expansion in Scotland, ideas of sanctity in medieval Glasgow drew from traditions reaching far and wide across space and time, yet were completely at home in this small medieval burgh on the edge of Europe.

---

[4] *Ibid.* p. 37.

[5] Alan Macquarrie, *The Saints of Scotland: Essays in Scottish Church History* (Edinburgh: John Donald Publishers, 1997), pp.117, 139, 140.

[6] This text is preserved in two manuscripts, one in the British Museum, the other in the Archbishop's library in Dublin. A. P. Forbes (ed.), *The Lives of SS Ninian and Kentigern*, Historians of Scotland V (Edinburgh: Edmonston and Douglas, 1874), p. lxiv.

[7] Celtic hagiographers frequently arranged meetings between people who lived at very different times, and Jocelin can be included in this group. For instance, Kentigern simply cannot have been a disciple of St. Serf and contemporary of Rhydderch Hael, who flourished 570-600, if Serf were contemporary with Adomnan, who died in 704. See Macquarrie, *The Saints of Scotland*, p. 234.

[8] Most scholars agree that this would be very difficult. See Macquarrie, *The Saints of Scotland*, p. 2; Norman F. Shead says that all that can safely be said about Kentigern is that he flourished in the late sixth century and worked in Cumbria. Norman F. Shead, "The Origins of the Medieval Diocese of Glasgow", *Scottish Historical Review*, xlvii (1969), 221; for a more optimistic (if less up-to-date) view, see Forbes, *The Lives of SS Ninian and Kentigern*, p. 8.

Let us return now to Glasgow's city crest, and examine more closely the items featured on it to see how Jocelin's blend of traditions work in some individual stories in the vita. The bell is not directly or explicitly connected with any of Kentigern's miracles, although bells were common accoutrements of Celtic bishops, and it is possible, even likely, that Kentigern had one. The actual bell is no longer anywhere to be found, but it is clearly represented on a 15th-century seal of the city,[9] and later medieval Glaswegians seem to have believed that they had it in their possession, such as the fifteenth-century friars who rung it through the streets for the repose of souls.[10] Although some scholars have sought – and claimed to have found – Mungo's bell in Jocelin's vita,[11] I have not been able to do so. Perhaps the bell was among the ornaments of the church given to Kentigern by the pope on one of his trips to Rome, but it is not explicitly mentioned.[12] If such a bell existed in twelfth-century Glasgow, Jocelin does not mention it. Since Jocelin makes many references throughout the vita to physical reminders of Kentigern in twelfth-century Glasgow, it may be safe to suppose that the tradition of Kentigern's bell being in Glasgow was not current in the twelfth century. On the other hand, there is at least one example of a recent tradition demonstrating Kentigern's saintly powers which Jocelin did not include in his Life. This is to be found in the Carmen de Morti Somerledi, written perhaps twenty years before Jocelin's vita. It tells of how Somerled, a lord or king of Argyll and the Western Isles, attacked Glasgow. The bishop of the city implored Kentigern to pray to God. Kentigern helped the bishop bring such encouragement to the defenders of the city that the hundred of them were able to defeat Somerled's thousand. After a few impressive miracles,[13] the whole kingdom praised Kentigern with loud voices.[14] It was not long after this impressive event that Jocelin

---

[9] The bird, the branch, and the fish with the ring are also present. See David Daiches, *Glasgow* (London: Andre Deutsch, 1977).

[10] Andrew MacGeorge, *Old Glasgow: The Place and the People* (Glasgow: Blackie and Son, 1880), p. 23.

[11] Fisher, *The Glasgow Encyclopedia*, 20.

[12] Forbes (ed.), *The Lives of SS Ninian and Kentigern*, pp. 84-85.

[13] "Heather and furze-bushes, moving their heads; burnt thyme and branches; brambles, and ferns, caused panic, appearing to the enemy as soldiers".

[14] Orr Anderson (ed.), *Early Sources of Scottish History* (Edinburgh: Oliver and Boyd, 1922), pp. 256-258. For more on Somerled and the Kingdom of the Isles, please see R. Andrew McDonald, *The Kingdom of the Isles: Scotland's Western Seabord, c. 1100-c. 1336* (East Lothian, Scotland: Tuckwell Press, 1997)

wrote his vita Kentigerni, so we may well wonder why he makes no mention of it.

The robin and the tree on the crest both represent miracles from Mungo's early years as a schoolboy in Culross under the tutelage of St. Serf. The robin was a favourite pet of Serf. One day, when Serf was praying in the oratory, a group of boys began playing roughly with the little bird. So badly did they treat it, passing it around their circle, that the bird's head was torn off. Fearing their teacher's wrath, but apparently unconcerned about the poor little robin, the boys conspired to place the blame on Kentigern, who was not among the tormenters. Serf was very upset at the death of his beloved bird, but the boys rejoiced that they had escaped, that Kentigern would receive the punishment due to them, and that they had diminished the friendship between Serf and his favourite pupil. When Kentigern took the decapitated body of the bird into his hand, signed it with the sign of the cross, and prayed to the Lord, the robin revived, and flew in joy to meet Serf.[15]

Kentigern's classmates remained jealous and tried to get him in to trouble again. This is represented by the oak on the crest, which is what has evolved from the hazel branch in the legends. Serf had a rule that each of his pupils would take turns attending to the lamps in the church while the Divine office was being celebrated, and ensure that the fire be kept during the night while the others were sleeping. On Kentigern's watch, the boys, "inflamed with the torches of envy", extinguished all of the fires in the monastery and in the surrounding area. When it came time for Kentigern to light the fires, he could find no source for it anywhere. So, he took a branch of growing hazel, prayed to God, signed the bough with the sign of the cross, blessed it in the name of the Trinity, and breathed on it. It immediately sent forth flame. Jocelin draws for us a connection to this miracle in a biblical story, that of Moses and the burning bush. He tells us that it was the same God who wrought the wonder in the bush and in the twig of hazel; for the same God who destined Moses as lawgiver for the Hebrews, so that he might lead them out of Egypt, destined Kentigern as a preacher of the Christian law, so that he might rescue many nations from the power of the devil. In this part

---

[15] This was Kentigern's first notable miracle, and Jocelin tells us that by it God marked out and presignified Mungo as his own. Forbes (ed.), *The Lives of SS Ninian and Kentigern*, pp. 42-43. It has been suggested that this episode is particularly characteristic of Irish Lives of saints (Jackson, "The Sources of the Life of St. Kentigern", p. 334); the healing of birds, and of animals in general, is not uncommon in saints' lives in Europe more widely.

of the vita, Jocelin also provides us with some information about popular devotion in Glasgow of his time. He has been told by the natives that if even the greenest branch of hazel is taken from the hazel grove which has grown in the spot of Mungo's original twig, it will catch fire as if it were of the driest material.[16]

The most well-known, and perhaps the most interesting, of Kentigern's miracles is represented by the fourth item on the crest: the fish with a ring in its mouth. Queen Languoreth initiates an affair with a soldier at her court. She gives to him the ring that the king had given to her as a mark of their conjugal love, and when this ring is spotted on the soldier's finger, rumours fly about the affair which reach the king's ear. One day, while hunting with retinue, the king takes the ring off the soldier's finger as he sleeps by the Clyde and throws it into the river. When the king demands that the queen show him the ring, she claims that it is in a casket. As she feigns retrieving it, she sends a messenger to her lover to ask him to bring it quickly to her. The soldier sends back that he has lost the ring and cannot tell where, and absents himself from the court. The queen is thrown into prison, where, thinking that her death is immanent, she weeps bitterly for her sins and prays to God. She sends a messenger to her bishop, Kentigern, to tell him of her predicament, and ask for his help that he might use his influence with the king and beseech pardon for her. Kentigern, as instructed by the Holy Ghost, sends one of his men to the river Clyde, to bring back the first fish that gets pulled out of the water. The messenger returns with a salmon, and lo! when the fish is cut open, the ring is found. The queen, in the sight of all, returns the ring to the king, who thereupon feels greatly aggrieved that he had ever accused his wife of infidelity. He offers to execute or send into exile her slanderers, but the queen dissuades him. Their marriage becomes a happy one, and the queen confesses to Kentigern and makes absolution for her sin. She never commits adultery again, and while the king remains alive, she never tells anyone of what really happened, but after he dies she tells the truth openly.[17]

Stories of fish with rings inside of them are found all over the world. Herodotus tells such a tale, and versions can be found in such diverse places as Spain, Kashmir, Arabia, China, the Philippines, and the Gold

---

[16] Forbes (ed.), *The Lives of SS Ninian and Kentigern*, pp. 44-45.
[17] *Ibid.* pp. 99-102.

Coast.[18] Closer to Glasgow, the theme is frequently found in Irish literature.[19] Two stories from Ireland, one Christian and the other Pagan, are conspicuously close to the version in the Vita Kentigerni.[20] The Irish Christian version is found in a tale from the Life of St. Brigit, written by Cogitosus probably around the middle of the seventh century.[21] In this story, a lecherous man lusts after a noblewoman, but she refuses him. He tricks her by giving her a brooch for safe keeping, then steals it from her and throws it into the sea. He demands that she return it, which of course she cannot do, and threatens to make her his slave. She asks St. Brigit to intercede on her behalf, and straightaway a fisherman comes along with a fish, in which the brooch is found. Another similar tale is found in the Irish saga, Táin Bó Fraích. The daughter of a king gives to her lover a ring which had been the gift of her father. The king, disapproving of the union, steals the ring while the youth is bathing, and throws it into the water. He orders his daughter to produce the ring, and threatens to have her killed if she does not do so. Fortunately, the lover saw the ring being caught by a salmon, so he was able to retrieve it.[22]

---

[18] Jackson, "The Sources of the Life of St. Kentigern", p. 322; Jackson, "The International Popular Tale in Early Welsh Tradition", pp. 25-29; Stith Thompson, *Motif-Index of Folk Literature* (Bloomington, Indiana: Indiana University Press, 1934), N 211.1.

[19] Salmon are often repositories of otherworldly wisdom in Celtic mythology. In the Irish tradition, it gains wisdom by eating nuts of the hazel tree. Plummer speaks of a very common type of story in which lost or stolen articles are found in the interiors of fish in Charles Plummer, *Vitae Sanctorum Hiberniae* (Oxford: Clarendon Press, 1910), p. clxxxv. Some versions feature a silver brooch found in a salmon, (in a hymn of Broccin about Brigit, *Thesaurus Palaeohibernicus: A Collection of Old-Irish Glosses Scholia Prose and Verse* (Cambridge: Cambridge University Press, 1903), p. 345.) or a large ring of gold found in a salmon, which St. Moling divides into three parts, giving one-third to the poor, one-third to cover reliquaries, and one-third to do labours and works (in *The Martyrology of Donegal: A Calendar of the Saints of Ireland* (trans. John O'Donovan; eds. James Henthorn Todd and William Reeves) (Dublin: The Irish Archaeological and Celtic Society, 1864), pp. 171-173.)

[20] Comparisons with Irish literature in particular are useful for several reasons. Western Scotland and Ireland maintained a close cultural contact at this time, and so it should not be surprising to find shared stories. Furthermore, the written evidence for early Ireland is better than that for early Scotland.

[21] Jackson, "The Sources for the Life of St. Kentigern", p. 323; Ludwig Bieler, "Hagiography and Romance in Medieval Ireland", *Medievalia et Humanistica*, N.S. 6 (1975), p. 16.

[22] Jeffrey Gantz (ed.), *Early Irish Myths and Sagas* (Harmondsworth, England: Penguin Books, 1981), pp. 119-124.

It is not easy to determine the precise connection among these seemingly related tales.[23] Some think that the version in the Life of Kentigern comes directly from one or other of the Irish tales;[24] others believe that the Irish tales get the story from an early Life of Kentigern, now lost.[25] Alternatively, these stories could all be drawing on a common, somewhat vague source, a sort of widespread topos. I believe that this is the most likely relationship: one of many stories drawing from a common, deeply-placed source. Presumably, there was a good deal of unconscious popular blending of saga themes and hagiographical themes,[26] and secular and sacred literature were more closely linked at this time than we are often accustomed to think. There are many, significant, disagreements in the elements of the stories surrounding the fish and the ring – why the loss of the ring is a threat, who retrieves the ring, why it is retrieved. One way in which the story as it is told in Jocelin's vita is unique, so far as I can tell, in that here the queen is not falsely accused or tricked – she did really commit adultery, and she gave her lover her ring herself. Bishop Kentigern is a kind of accomplice after the fact, helping her to get away with her crime. We should remember, however, that the queen felt genuinely contrite over her adultery, that she confessed and made satisfaction, and that she never committed that sin again. We may be surprised that a bishop and saint would help a woman get away with adultery, but in doing so, Kentigern prevented her execution, and maintained the public dignity of the king. God had forgiven Queen Languoreth – why should not her bishop?

---

[23] For a good discussion of the difficulties involved, see Donald E. Meek, "*Tain Bo Fraich* and Other 'Fraech' Texts: A Study in thematic Relationships", *Cambridge Medieval Celtic Studies*, 7 (1984) and 8 (1984). He says, speaking of the Tain, that "much important evidence has been lost, so that one can seldom, if ever, obtain a complete picture of the development of a text from its original form to the form (or forms) in which it is known to us today. The analyst must therefore employ a certain amount of subjectivity when he attempts to explain the way in which a text has been composed, or how one version of a narrative relates to other versions of what appears to be basically the same story." p. 1. He concludes, "we should therefore be prepared to accept that a narrative may have been developed by several 'authors' over several centuries, and conceivably with several different emphases". p. 81.

[24] For example James Carney, who in *Studies in Irish Literature and History*, says that Cogitosus was the sourse of both the version in the Irish saga and in *Vita Kentigerni*; Saga Themes says that the story in the Life of Brigit has a saga origin.

[25] Carney, *Studies in Irish Literature and History*, p. 38.

[26] Bieler, "Hagiography and Romance in Medieval Ireland", p. 14.

In a discussion of Jocelin's sources,[27] we should not discount what he himself has to say about them. Jocelin tells us directly about two of his sources, both of which, unfortunately, are now lost. One of these is a little volume which he came across, "wandering through the streets and lanes of the city";[28] and the other is a life of Kentigern already in use in the cathedral. Jocelin was not very pleased with either of these. The cathedral text was tainted by something "perverse or opposed to the faith in its narrative";[29] while the little volume was made "exceedingly obscure by barbarous language".[30] Even so, it did contain at greater length the life and acts of Kentigern.[31] So, Jocelin decided to put together from either book the matter collected, and, at the command of the bishop of Glasgow, "season what had been composed in a barbarous way with Roman salt."[32]

It would serve us well to consider more closely the little volume, for it provides some insight into the different traditions of sanctity present in Glasgow. It was written, Jocelin tells us, stilo Scottico.[33] The main English translation of the legend translates stilo Scottico as "in the Scotic dialect", which perhaps has led, or misled, some into thinking this to mean that Jocelin had a Gaelic-language source for his Life of Kentigern.[34] It is perhaps unlikely that Jocelin, a monk from a monastery in England, would have been able to read a Gaelic text,[35] but possible. Although Furness was in England, it maintained a close connection with the Church in the Isle of Man; and Jocelin did later reside at Down in northern Ireland, where he composed his Life of St. Patrick.[36] It is, of course, not inherently impossible that a Gaelic-language book about Kentigern could have existed in the twelfth century. By this time in Ire-

---

[27] For more complete discussions of Jocelin's possible sources, please see Jackson, "The Sources for the Life of St. Kentigern" and the chapter "St. Kentigern of Glasgow" in Macquarrie, *The Saints of Scotland*.

[28] Forbes (ed.), *The Lives of SS Ninian and Kentigern*, p. 29.

[29] *Ibid*. p. 30.

[30] *Ibid*. p. 30.

[31] *Ibid*. p. 30.

[32] *Ibid*. p. 30.

[33] *Ibid*. p. 160.

[34] *Ibid*. p. 314 maintains that it is not unreasonable that the volume should have been written in Irish, for the influence of the Irish Church was felt along the whole west of Scotland, and the language was probably intelligible to all.

[35] Macquarrie, *The Saints of Scotland*, p. 4, suggests that Jocelin's knowledge of the Gaelic language would probably have been superficial at best.

[36] Jackson, "The Sources for the Life of St. Kentigern", p. 276.

land, Lives of Celtic saints were being composed in Irish.[37] However, based on all surviving evidence, the situation appears to have been different in Scotland: if this little volume found by Jocelin were in the vernacular, it would be unique among the Lives of saints composed in Scotland.[38] Furthermore, the terms Jocelin uses to describe the language of this little volume suggest that it was written in Latin, not Gaelic. Other examples of saints' Lives from this period can be found which bring charges of inelegance similar to that of Jocelin against their sources in order to justify writing a new text – they do not mean that the original is in another language, but rather that the Latin is somehow substandard. Ailred of Rivaulx did this when writing is Life of St. Ninian, another Scottish saint, in about 1165.[39] Perhaps Jocelin was following his example.[40] Finally, Jocelin wishes to season the text with Roman salt.[41] If he needed to translate from one language into another, surely he would require more than just seasoning. Seasoning with Roman salt would seem to imply that instead of translating Gaelic into Latin, he was editing a Hiberno-Latin text, no doubt "barbarous" to Jocelin, into a more continental Latin. Perhaps then, a better translation of stilo Scottico would be "in the style of the Scots", that is, in the style of the Irish. This source, the little volume, was probably in the Latin language, but a Celtic dialect thereof. And since its origin lay presumably in a Gaelic speaking, or erstwhile Gaelic-speaking, Celtic area, it might have represented a Celtic tradition of St. Mungo. This little volume, stilo Scottico, may well have been the source of many of the Gaelic strands in Jocelin's Life of Kentigern.

Jocelin also uses the Bible as a source, drawing on biblical stories to show similarities between the deeds of Kentigern and those of the holy people of the Bible. The mention of Solomon in his story of the fish, the connection between Mungo burning the hazel branch and Moses and the burning bush, and further examples throughout the vita tie Kentigern in to an ancient and international tradition of sanctity.[42] Jocelin

---

[37] *Ibid.* p. 276.

[38] *Ibid.* p. 277.

[39] "Hinc est quod vitam sanctissimi Niniani, sermo barbaricus obscurabat, et quo minus delectabat legentem eo minus edificabat."; "nobis liber de Vita et Miraculis ejus, barbario scriptus," Forbes (ed.), *The Lives of SS Ninian and Kentigern*, pp.137, 140.

[40] Jackson, "The Sources for the Life of St. Kentigern", p. 277.

[41] Forbes (ed.), *The Lives of SS Ninian and Kentigern*, p. 30.

[42] The story of Kentigern's founding of Glasgow is an example of this. (*Ibid.* 50 - 52 / 179) Surprisingly, this story does not make it onto the city crest. Kentigern yokes two untamed bulls to a wagon in which he had placed the body of a man. He prays to God

moreover uses oral traditions in Glasgow as sources. Sometimes even though he disagrees with what he hears, he nevertheless includes it in his vita, such as what is said by the "stupid and foolish people, who live in the diocese of S. Kentigern", who assert that he was conceived and born of a virgin.[43] (This is quite possibly that which was perverse and opposed to the faith in the Life already in the cathedral.) At other times, he cites the people of Glasgow as witnesses to Kentigern's power in their own time. Their assertions that hazel growing in the place where Mungo's hazel grew will be easily set alight is an example of this.

Jocelin also tells us why he wrote his vita: the present bishop of Glasgow requested it, since the Life of Kentigern then in use in Glasgow's cathedral was unsatisfactory for reasons already mentioned. Jocelin's more general reasons for writing a Life of Kentigern were likely those shared by other medieval writers of saints' lives: glorification of God through a recounting of the wonders and good deeds of his holy people on earth, the saints.[44] There is both literary and physical evidence demonstrating that by Jocelin's time the cult of St. Mungo was already well-established at Glasgow. Among the former is the tale mentioned earlier of Kentigern sparing inhabitants of Glasgow from Somerled. Physical evidence is to be found in the site of Glasgow cathedral, whose improb-

---

and enjoins the beasts to take the wagon to the place which God had provided for it. The bulls obediently take the wagon to Glasgow, to a cemetery previously consecrated by St. Ninian, but in which no bodies had yet been buried. Jocelin tells us that this miracle was accomplished in much the same way as God had brought the ark of the covenant from Ekron to Bethshemesh, which was placed on a new wagon and drawn by cows that had never borne the yoke. The wagon is taken to "Cathures, que nunc Glasgu vocatur" (Cathures, which now is called Glasgow). (*Ibid.* pp. 50-52; 179. There has been some debate among scholars over whether Cathures really is Glasgow, or anther town such as Govan. [see e.g. Andrew Gibb, *Glasgow: The Making of a City* (London: Croom Helm, 1983], pp. 5-8.) So far as Jocelin is concerned, there is no doubt that Glasgow is where Kentigern was led by the bulls. And so far as I can tell, medieval Glaswegians likewise had not doubt that it was in their town that Kentigern buried Fergus, and was later buried himself.

[42] Forbes (ed.), *The Lives of SS Ninian and Kentigern*, pp. 50-52.

[43] *Ibid.* 35 / 163 "populus stultus et insipiens, in diocesi Sancti Kentigerni degens"

[44] This spiritual reason for writing the life of a saint was of course not necessarily incompatible with more worldly considerations, such as the formation or enlargement of a cult of that saint, a cult whose members would go on pilgrimage to a saint's shrine and spend not inconsiderable amounts of money there. After all, by glorifying God, hagiographers are also glorifying the individual saint, the place the saint lived or was buried, the community where God chose to be glorified through his saint. Patrick Geary, "Saints, Scholars, and Society: The Elusive Goal", *Saints: Studies in Hagiography* (Binghampton, New York: Medieval & Renaissance Texts & Studies, 1996), p.15.

able site on a steeply-sloping hill is presumably due to the importance attributed to the presumed site of his tomb there.[45]

We do not know why it was at precisely this time that the bishop of Glasgow wished for a more appropriate life for the local saint, but we do know that the twelfth century was a very important time in that town's history. Glasgow was becoming a more important centre in Scotland, and Scotland was undergoing important transformations at the higher levels of secular and ecclesiastical government. In the first quarter of the century, an inquest was made by prince David (later King David I) into the possessions of the church of St. Kentigern, the findings of which established or re-established the boundaries of the diocese of Glasgow and secured considerable endowments for the church there.[46] The church was dedicated not long after, in 1136.[47] Glasgow was granted official burghal status between 1175-1178, which brought considerable benefits; it was granted the right to hold a weekly market on Thursdays, and soon after, it was given authorization to hold a fair.[48] In 1181 "Bishop Jocelin enlarged his episcopal residence, and magnificently extended the church of St. Kentigern".[49] The structure and organization of the church throughout Scotland were undergoing changes at this time, in concert with the rest of Europe. The twelfth and thirteenth centuries saw a new growth in Scotland of monasticism, during which time most of the religious houses in Scotland were founded.[50] Greater uniformity was imposed, and the peculiarities of many regional churches, including of Scotland, were removed.[51] As late as the second and third decades of the 12th century there were letters written by Popes to the Church in Scotland complaining about what were regarded as errors or

---

[45] Gibb, *Glasgow: The Making of a City*, pp. 11, 13; Norman F. Shead, "Glasgow: An Ecclesiastical Burgh", *The Scottish Medieval Town* (Edinburgh: John Donald Publishers, 1988), p. 116; G. W. S. Barrow, *Kingship and Unity: Scotland 1000-1306* (Toronto: University of Toronto Press, 1981), p. 70.

[46] Gibb, *Glasgow: The Making of a City*, p. 8.

[47] *A Medieval Chronicle of Scotland: The Chronicle of Melrose*. ed. Joseph Stevenson (Dyfed: Llanerch Press, 1991), p. 7; *Medieval Chronicles of Scotland: The Chronicles of Melrose and Holyrood*. ed. Joseph Stevenson (Dyfed: Llanerch Press, 1991), p.137.

[48] *Ibid.* p. 10.

[49] *A Medieval Chronicle of Scotland*, p. 22.

[50] Anthony Ross, "Some Notes on Religious Orders in Pre-Reformation Scotland", *Essays on the Scottish Reformation 1513-1625*. ed. David McRoberts (Glasgow: Burns, 1962), p. 190.

[51] Barrow, *Kingship and Unity*, pp. 62-64; Ian B. Cowan, *The Medieval Church in Scotland* (Edinburgh: Scottish Academic Press, 1995), p. 97; Dickinson, *Scotland from the Earliest Times to 1603*, p. 127.

abuses of an Irish type, such as lax marriage customs, the dating of Lent, and the manner of consecrating bishops.[52] This suggests that efforts to Romanize the Scottish church were not entirely successful, and Jocelin may have been trying to help the Roman cause by ensuring that Glasgow cathedral's copy of the Life of the city's patron saint contained nothing contrary to officially-approved doctrine. His insistence that Kentigern was not the result of a virgin conception, in spite of what some believed, points in this direction. So does Jocelin's careful and diplomatic justification of Kentigern's irregular consecration.[53] Although "scantly consonant with the sacred canons", Jocelin cannot judge that the consecration was invalid, for then many of Glasgow's present territorial and ecclesiastical pretentions could easily be contested; yet he must at the same time remind us that "in such times as these [the judgement of the Church] would never permit such a rite as this to be used by any one without grave censure".[54]

The variety of sources which can be traced in the vita Kentigerni are resonant of Scotland's increasing cultural diversity. By the 12th century, Scotland was a multi-national kingdom, and the Scottish kings, in recognition of this, addressed their charters to their faithful subjects, French, English, Scots, Welsh, and Galwegians.[55] We could add to this that people who now were subject to the Scottish king probably felt closer cultural connections to Dublin, Copenhagen, or Amsterdam than they did to Edinburgh. A simultaneous process was happening whereby Scotland looked both outward to wider European trends, and inward to its own past.[56] David I, who reigned from 1124-1153, is often seen as the monarch who best exemplified this. The consolidation and extension of his royal power was linked with the spread of Anglo-Norman ideas and institutions,[57] but at the same time as he was Normanizing his kingdom, David was also publicly celebrating Scotland's Gaelic past.[58]

---

[52] Barrow, *Kingship and Unity*, pp. 62-64.
[53] Forbes (ed.), *The Lives of SS Ninian and Kentigern*, pp. 54-56.
[54] *Ibid.* p. 55.
[55] Dickinson, *Scotland from the Earliest Times to 1603*, p. 33.
[56] Barrow, *Kingship and Unity*, pp. 32-35; see also Macquarrie, *The Saints of Scotland*, p.1.
[57] Ian D. White, *Scotland Before the Industrial Revolution: An Economic and Social History c. 1050-1720* (London: Longman, 1995), p. 22.
[58] David employed moneyers to strike his own coinage, established a new type of sheriffdom closely resembling that of Norman England, increased the number of royal castles constructed in Norman fashion, accelerated the process of feudalization, and founded burghs as trading communities, he also showed reverence for many native saints, and continued to be served by a Gaelic-speaking servants in traditional Celtic

Jocelin's Life of St. Kentigern can tell us a great deal about saints and the sacred in twelfth-century Glasgow, if we know what questions to ask of it. Its sources demonstrate to us something of the diversity among traditions of sanctity there. Stories in this vita draw on, or share elements with, Christian and pagan Celtic tales, biblical stories, and oral tradition. While this vita is not peculiar in Europe, and its range of sources and connections would not surprise those familiar with medieval saints' lives written at this time in other parts of Europe, it contains plenty of local, Glaswegian, detail. Time limitations have permitted me to mention only a few of the Jocelin's sources and incidental remarks about life in Glasgow. Much more could be done in this direction, and as historians of Scotland realize the historic value of saints' lives, our understanding of life and belief in medieval Scotland will be considerably enriched.

The Life of St. Kentigern also shows the enduring power of good stories. We cannot be sure when the stories associated with Mungo first appeared, but by the time Jocelin wrote them down, he was working with traditions going back, in some form, centuries. And it is clear from what Jocelin tells us that the tradition of Kentigern was strong in the Glasgow of his time. Mungo has maintained his appeal for eight centuries beyond Jocelin, surviving the Reformation, the Enlightenment, the Industrial Revolution, and the twentieth century. Glasgow cathedral still stands, housing Kentigern's tomb, and is one of the best preserved examples of pre-Reformation ecclesiastic architecture to survive in Scotland. The city crest, found in many places in the city, still bears reminders of Mungo. Glasgow University, which in the years after its founding in 1451 met in the cathedral, has adopted the stories of Mungo into its crest. This year, the university has decided to create its own tartan. The colours of the new tartan reflect those used in the university crest: blue for the river Clyde, green for the tree, white for the university mace, and gold for the bell.[59] Mungo, a bishop of the ancient kingdom of Strathclyde, is still present in his city fourteen hundred years later.

---

roles. He had a *rannaire* or 'divider of food', and doorwards in the Celtic Custom. Barrow, *Kingship and Unity*, pp. 32-35. See also G. W. S. Barrow, "David I of Scotland: The Balance of New and Old", *Scotland and its Neighbours in the Middle Ages* (London: The Hambledon Press, 1992), pp. 45-66; and Bruce Webster, *Medieval Scotland: the Making of an Identity* (London: MacMillan Press, 1997), pp. 30-35.

[59] Pamela Stephenson, "Development News", *University Avenue: The Magazine for Graduates and Friends of the University of Glasgow*, No. 27 (January 2000), p. 20.

WORKS CITED

A Medieval Chronicle of Scotland: The Chronicle of Melrose. ed. Joseph Stevenson. Facsimile reprint 1991 by Llanerch Press, Felinfach, Lampeter, Dyfed.

Anderson, Orr (ed.), *Early Sources of Scottish History.* Edinburgh: Oliver and Boyd, 1922.

Barrow, G. W. S., *Kingship and Unity: Scotland 1000-1306.* Toronto: University of Toronto Press, 1981.

_____. *The Kingdom of the Scots: Government, Church and Society from the eleventh to the fourteenth century.* London: Edward Arnold, 1973.

_____. *Scotland and Its Neighbours in the Middle Ages.* London: The Hambledon Press, 1992.

Bieler, Ludwig, "Hagiography and Romance in Medieval Ireland", *Medievalia et Humanistica.* N.S. 6 (1975). pp. 13-24.

Byrne, Francis John, *Irish Kings and High-Kings.* London: B. T. Batsford, 1973.

Carney, James, *Studies in Irish Literature and History.* Dublin: Dublin Institute for Advanced Studies, 1955.

Cowan, Ian B., *The Medieval Church in Scotland.* Edinburgh: Scottish Academic Press, 1995.

Cowan, Ian B. and David E. Easson, *Medieval Religious Houses: Scotland.* London: Longman, 1976.

Cross, Tom Peete, *Motif-Index of Early Irish Literature.* Bloomington, Indiana: Indiana University Press, 1939.

Daiches, David, *Glasgow.* London: Andre Deutsch, 1977.

Dickinson, W. Croft, *Scotland from the Earliest Times to 1603.* 3rd edition. Oxford: Clarendon Press, 1977.

Fisher, Joe, *The Glasgow Encyclopedia.* Edinburgh: Mainstream Publishing, 1994.

Forbes, A. P. (ed.), *The Lives of SS Ninian and Kentigern.* (Historians of Scotland v). Edinburgh: Edmonston and Douglas, 1874.

Gantz, Jeffrey (ed.), *Early Irish Myths and Sagas.* Hamondsworth, England: Penguin Books, 1981.

Geary, Patrick, "Saints, Scholars, and Society: The Elusive Goal", *Saints: Studies in Hagiography.* Binghampton, New York: Medieval & Renaissance Texts & Studies, 1996.

Gibb, Andrew, *Glasgow: The Making of a City.* London: Croom Helm, 1983.

Hale, Reginald B., *The Beloved St. Mungo, Founder of Glasgow.* Ottawa: University of Ottawa Press, 1989.

Heist, William, "Irish Saints' Lives, Romance, and Cultural History", *Medievalia et Humanistica.* N. S. 6 (1975) pp. 25-40.

Jackson, Kenneth Hurlstone, *The International Popular Tale and Early Welsh Tradition*, Cardiff: University of Wales Press, 1961.

_____. "The Sources for the Life of St. Kentigern", *Studies in the Early British Church*. Cambridge: Cambridge University Press, 1958.

Johnson-South, Ted, "Changing Images of Sainthood: St. Cuthbert in the *Historia de Sancto Cuthbreto*", *Saints: Studies in Hagiography*. Binghampton, New York: Medieval & Renaissance Texts & Studies, 1996.

Jolly, Karen, "Father God and Mother Earth: Nature Mysticism in the Anglo-Saxon World", *The Medieval World of Nature: A Book of Essays*. ed. Joyce E. Salisbury. New York: Garland Publishing, 1993.

MacGeorge, Andrew, *Old Glasgow: The Place and the People*. Glasgow: Blackie and Son, 1880.

Macquarrie, Alan, *The Saints of Scotland: Essays in Scottish Church History*. Edinburgh: John Donald Publishers, 1997.

The Martyrology of Donegal: A Calendar of the Saints of Ireland. trans. John O'Donovan; eds. James Henthorn Todd and William Reeves. Dublin: The Irish Archaeological and Celtic Society, 1864.

McDonald, R. Andrew, *The Kingdom of the Isles: Scotland's Western Seaboard, c. 1100-c. 1336*. East Lothian, Scotland: Tuckwell Press, 1997.

Medieval Chronicles of Scotland: The Chronicles of Melrose and Holyrood. ed. Joseph Stevenson. Facsimile reprint 1991 by Llanerch Press, Felinfach, Lampeter, Dyfed.

Meek, Donald, "*Táin Bó Fraích* and Other 'Fráech' Texts: A Study in Thematic Relationships", *Cambridge Medieval Celtic Studies*. 7 (1984) and 8 (1984). pp. 1-37 and 65-86.

O Briain, Felim, "Saga Themes in Irish Hagiography", *Feilscribhinn Torna*. Clo Ollscoile Chorcai, 1947. pp. 33-42.

Ross, Anthony, "Some Notes on the Religious Orders in Pre-Reformation Scotland", *Essays on the Scottish Reformation 1513-1625*. ed. David McRobers. Glasgow: Burns, 1962.

Sharpe, Richard, *Medieval Irish Saints' Lives: An Introduction to Vitae Sanctorum Hiberniae*. Oxford: Clarendon Press, 1991.

Shead, Norman F., "Glasgow: An Ecclesiastical Burgh", *The Scottish Medieval Town*. Edinburgh: John Donald Publishers, 1988.

_____. "The Origins of the Medieval Diocese of Glasgow", *Scottish Historical Review*, xlvii (1969). pp. 220-225.

Stephenson, Pamela, "Development News", University Avenue: The Magazine for Graduates and Friends of the University of Glasgow. No. 27 January 2000, pp. 17-22.

Thesaurus Palaeohibernicus: A Collection of Old-Irish Glosses Scholia Prose and Verse. Cambridge: Cambridge University Press, 1903.

Thompson, Stith, *Motif-Index of Folk Literature*. Bloomington, Indiana: Indiana University Press, 1934.

Tilley, Maureen A., "Martyrs, Monks, Insects, and Animals", *The Medieval World of Nature: A Book of Essays*. ed. Joyce E. Salisbury. New York: Garland Publishing, 1993.

Vitae Sanctorum Hiberniae. ed. Charles Plummer. Oxford: Clarendon Press, 1910.

Webster, Bruce, *Medieval Scotland: The Making of an Identity*. London: MacMillan Press, 1997.

White, Ian D., *Scotland Before the Industrial Revolution: An Economic and Social History c. 1050 – c. 1750*. London: Longman, 1995.

JOSEPH GOERING

THE VIRGIN AND THE GRAIL: A FORGOTTEN TWELFTH-CENTURY CULT

ABSTRACT. In the high mountains of the eastern Pyrenees a series of village churches, built or rebuilt during the twelfth century, preserve evidence of a particular devotion found (it seems) nowhere else in Christendom: Mary and the Grail. The earliest image capable of rather precise dating (AD 1123) is an apse painting in the church of S. Clemente in Taüll (Tahull) of Mary holding what is described as "a fiery grail." Similar images of Mary holding a sacred cup, bowl, or chalice are found in at least eight other churches from the same area of the Pyrenees. These images have no clear artistic antecedents, they seem not to have spread outside of this region, nor were they produced after the 12th century. The earliest of them antedate the first stories about the Grail by some fifty years, and may, in fact, have provided the particular image that would become, in the hands of Chrétien de Troyes and his successors, the legend of the Holy Grail.

It was with some surprise, a few years ago, that I found myself in search of the Holy Grail. I had assigned a group of undergraduates to read Chrétien de Troyes' story of Perceval and the Grail, and I expected to talk with them about how a young boy grows up in the Welsh countryside, learns from his Mother about angels and devils, ventures into the world against his Mother's wishes, and eventually begins to learn from painful experience. The students, however, were not to be led down that road. They wanted instead to know about the Holy Grail. Whether it was the enigmatic assertion with which Chrétien begins his romance, that "the Story of the Grail" is "the finest tale that may be told [in royal court]," or whether they had learned of the Grail and its mysteries from Malory's *Morte d'Arthur* or Tennyson's *Idylls of the King*, or, more likely, from Monty Python and Indiana Jones, I do not know, but they refused to be put off.

You will remember that Chrétien de Troyes' *Conte du Graal* (ca. 1180-1185 ?) marks the first entry of the Grail into medieval literature. Schol-

Saints and the Sacred - A St. Michael's College Symposium
Joseph Goering, Francesco Guardiani, Giulio Silano eds. Ottawa: Legas, 2001

ars agree that his romance is the starting point of all subsequent developments of the theme, and they can trace rather precisely the very rapid steps by which the enigmatic "graal" evoked by Chrétien becomes variously associated with a magic stone, the cup of the Last Supper, the vessel used by Joseph of Arimathea to capture Christ's blood after the crucifixion, and much more.[1] But before Chrétien – before about A.D.1180 – we have only silence in the sources concerning the existence, the whereabouts or the significance of the sacred vessel called the Grail. Theories abound, of course, as to its origins in Celtic myth, in indoeuropean fertility cults, and in ecclesial or para-ecclesial traditions from the earliest days of Christianity, but none of these hypotheses has been supported by any substantive evidence, whether textual or physical, dating from before 1180.[2]

Nevertheless, with the freedom granted a teacher in the classroom, I suggested to the students that the Grail was known in Spain at least fifty years before Chrétien began writing. My evidence was a pair of half-

---

[1] There is an abundant scholarly literature concerning the Grail and its development within the framework of the stories about King Arthur. For a general survey see Dhira B. Mahoney, ed., *The Grail: A Casebook* (New York and London, 2000), Norris Lacy, et al., ed., *The Arthurian Encyclopedia* (New York, 1986), and the older, but still useful collection by R. S. Loomis, ed., *Arthurian Literature in the Middle Ages: A Collaborative History* (Oxford, 1959).

[2] The theory of Celtic origins remains today the dominant scholarly view (see n. 1), but it remains only an hypothesis, based on historical and philological plausibilities which have yet to be corroborated by anything more than conjecture. The best treatment of the "Celtic hypothesis" is found in Jean Frappier's 1968 essay, "*Perceval* or *Le Conte du Graal*," (transl. Raymond Cormier) reprinted in *The Grail: A Casebook*, pp. 175-200. The strength of this theory lies primarily in the absence of any other credible theory to challenge it. Other views would see the Grail as a gnostic talisman of the true faith, whether pagan or Christian. Valuable treatments of such esoteric themes are Arthur Edward Waite, *The Holy Grail. The Galahad Quest in Arthurian Literature* (New York, 1961), and Helen Adolf, *Visio pacis: Holy City and Grail* (Philadelphia, 1960). More popular, and more credulous, is Norma Lorre Goodrich, in whose book, *The Holy Grail* (New York, 1992), one finds collected much recent speculation about the Grail and its history, but little of scholarly interest. Two modern theories perhaps deserve special mention because they associate the Grail with historical events in the area of concern to us – the French and Spanish Pyrenees – during the twelfth and thirteenth centuries. One of these theories would associate the Grail with the Order of Knights-Templars, and the other with the Cathar heretics. Both traditions seem to be the creation of nineteenth-century Romanticism and to have flourished in the twentieth century under the influence of such groups as the Society of the Friends of Montségur, and the tourist authorities of the Languedoc region. Thus far I have found no evidence earlier than the nineteenth century that would suggest a link, whether historical or literary, between the Templars or the Cathars and the Grail.

remembered pictures that I had chanced upon years ago while browsing through a book of Romanesque paintings.³ The first (fig. 1) is described as "St. Peter, and the Virgin holding a fiery Grail (early twelfth century)"; the second, (fig. 2) simply as "Virgin with the Grail (c. 1123)." The students were good; they asked all of the critical and sceptical questions: is it really the "grail"? are the dates accurate? what are the art-historical precedents? how could these paintings be associated with Chrétien de Troyes? and so on. I have been trying to answer their questions ever since.

I am now prepared to venture the following hypothesis: **That the object and the image that would become the Holy Grail in the hands of Chrétien de Troyes and his successors originated in the high Pyrenees in the late-eleventh or early-twelfth century as an otherwise-unattested attribute of the Virgin Mary.**⁴ The evidence for such an hypothesis is complex, and perhaps beyond my ability to marshall even in the best of circumstances; I certainly would not presume to try your patience with it here. Rather, I would like to describe briefly the twelfth-century evidence from the Pyrenees on which this hypothesis rests.⁵

---

³Otto Demus and Max Hirmer (photographs), *Romanesque Mural Painting* (New York, 1970), plates 199 and 210; see the discussion of these paintings, with bibliography, on pp. 477 and 479.

⁴I presume that the "Maria" who is the object of the cult or devotion described in these pages was the Virgin Mary. Readers and respondents have encouraged me to ask whether it might not be Mary Magdalene. The scholarly literature on the images discussed below is unanimous in identifying the figure in question as the Virgin Mary. Although I am unable to confirm that identification indubitably, I remain inclined to agree that it is the Virgin and not the Magdalene who is depicted. This ambiguity does not affect my argument in any substantive way, and it may reflect the historical reality. Dominique Iogna-Prat has recently drawn attention to the lively medieval interest in the "equivocity" of Mary (the Virgin Mother of God) and Mary (Magdalene, sister of Lazarus): "Les historiens," he comments, "n'ont pres prêté à cette 'équivoque' toute l'attention qu'elle mérite. On notera une curieuse concomitance des deux cultes," "Le culte de la Vierge sous le règne de Charles le Chauve," in *Marie: Le culte de la Vierge dans la société médiévale*, ed. Dominique Iogna-Prat, Éric Palazzo, Daniel Russo, (Paris, 1996) 65-107 at 97. See further, below, n. 30.

⁵Although the Grail is primarily associated with Britain and the British/Celtic King Arthur, a small but steady undercurrent has long associated the Grail with Spain. A tradition stretching back at least to the fourteenth century holds the Holy Grail came to Spain in the early days of Christianity, and that it is preserved today in the Cathedral of Valencia; see Salvador Antuñano Alea, *El misterio del Santo Grial: Tradición y leyenda del Santo Cáliz* (Valencia, 1999). See also the two stimulating (and nearly indistinguishable) books by André de Mandach , *Le "Roman du Graal" originaire*, I, *Sur les traces du modèle commun "en code transpyrénéen" de Chrétien de Troyes et Wolfram von Eschenbach* (Göppingen

One peculiarity of the images I am about to describe is their geographical and chronological distribution. The eight surviving frescoes, one wood-panel, and (perhaps) one wooden sculpture, representing Mary holding a cup or chalice or bowl, all date from the twelfth century and all are to be found in a remote and very circumscribed part of the Pyrenees. The cult which they served, or the story which they illustrated, seems not to have spread beyond the narrow confines of these mountain communities, nor to have lasted, in this form, beyond the very early years of the thirteenth century.

The images are found in small churches in the Eastern Pyrenees, in an area stretching roughly from the old boundary between Aragon and Catalonia in the West to the mountain passes of Andorra in the East. The famous pilgrimage routes to St. James of Compostella, teeming with travelers in the early twelfth century, run well to the West of this region, and the coastal routes connecting Narbonne and Arles in Southern France with the cultural and religious centers of Ripoll and Vich or the commercial centers of Girona and Barcelona are well to the East. The cities along the Ebro River valley are far to the South, and to the North are the highest peaks of the Pyrenees. Just beyond these peaks are the headwaters of the Garonne, flowing North to Toulouse, and the Ariège, flowing through Foix, but one does not cross easily here into those regions.

The place in which these images flourished is remote and inhospitable, but it is not isolated. On the basis of the artistic evidence alone, one can demonstrate an intimate familiarity with developments in the rest of Europe.[6] The Romanesque style and the iconographic programs of these churches in the high Pyrenees are in the mainstream of developments not only elsewhere in Spain, but also in France, Italy, Germany and even

---

1992), and *Auf den Spuren des Heiligen Gral: Die gemeinsame Vorlage im pyrenäischen Geheimcode von Chrétien de Troyes und Wolfram von Eschenbach* (Göppingen 1995); the second book is said to be a "New Version," although it is very little altered from the earlier French version. Mandach's intriguing, if largely unsubstantiated, thesis is that the Perceval legends originated not in northern France or in Britain, but among the ruling clans of Provence and Northeastern Spain in the time between 1120 and 1137.

[6]Still fundamental for the discussion of the paintings discussed below is Chandler Rathfon Post, *A History of Spanish Painting*, vol. 1 (Cambridge MA, 1930). See also the excellent volumes in the Zodiaque series: Édouard Junyent, *Catalogne romane*, 2 vols, (La Pierre-qui-vire [Yonne], 1960,1961) and Marcel Durliat, *Pyrénées romanes*, (La Pierre-qui-vire, 1969). For more recent discussions and bibliography see Christopher R. Dodwell, *The Pictorial Arts of the West 800-1200* (New Haven and London, 1993), and Metropolitan Museum of Art, *The Art of Medieval Spain a.d. 500-1200* (New York, 1994).

further afield. In one detail, however, they are idiosyncratic, that is in their representation of Mary holding a sacred vessel or "grail."

Perhaps the earliest representation of this image comes from the former benedictine Church of St. Peter in El Burgal.[7] The dome of the main apse is filled by a (now-damaged) depiction of "Christ in Majesty." This theme was, without question, the most common motif for apse decoration throughout Romanesque Europe.[8] On the wall beneath the apse's dome and above the level of the altar are life-size depictions of six seated figures (fragments of others remain on the adjoining walls). The four central characters, from left to right, are St. Peter with the keys, St. Mary with a radiant vessel (fig. 1), St. John the Baptist with the lamb of God, and St. Paul holding a book. Beneath these, in the lower right, is the figure of a female donor offering a large wax candle to the church. Recent scholarship has tended to identify this anonymous donor with a contessa who died in 1090; older scholarship was less certain, and was willing to date the ensemble anytime between 1090 and 1190. In my view the matter is not yet settled. None of the figures in the Burgal fresco is identified explicitly, but Peter, Paul, and John are clearly recognizable by their symbols, and likewise St. Mary, seated among them, is to be identified, at least according to local tradition as we shall see, by her symbol – the radiant vessel which she holds in her covered hand to indicate its particular sanctity. This vessel has been variously interpreted as a vase, a lamp, and a chalice; I will suggest that only anachronistically can it be called a "grail."

The earliest of the Pyreneen frescoes that can be dated with some precision is also the most renowned; it is found in the Church of St. Clement in the village of Taüll (Tahull).[9] Two churches were built within sev-

---

[7]The mural paintings of this church, like most of the others discussed here, were transferred to Barcelona early in the twentieth century, and are now beautifully displayed in the Museu Nacional d'Art de Catalunya; see Eduard Carbonell i Esteller, et al., *Romanesque Art Guide, Museu Nacional d'art de catalunya*, (Barcelona, 1998); Milagros Guardia, Jordi Camps, Immaculada Lorés, *El descubrimiento de la pintura mural románica catalana: La colección de reproducciones del MNAC* (Barcelona, 1993).

[8]"The only more or less fixed rule [in the decoration of Romanesque church interiors] applies to the painting of the vault or semi-dome of the apse. This is, almost without exception, given over to the Majesty, a representation of Christ or the Virgin and Child surrounded by members of the heavenly court," Demus and Hirmer, *Romanesque Mural Painting*, 14.

[9]Demus writes: "The master of San Clemente, the most significant artistic talent active in Spain in the twelfth century, painted the main apse ... ," Demus and Hirmer, *Romanesque Mural Painting*, 479. Dodwell calls the artist "the greatest of all wall painters of twelfth-century Spain," Dodwell, *Pictorial Arts*, 258. And Klein opines: "The towering

eral hundred yards of each other in this small village during the first years of the twelfth century. We are extraordinarily fortunate to possess a dated record of the episcopal consecration of both churches.[10] In the case of St. Clement, the act of consecration, dated 10 December 1123, was recorded in fresco, contemporary with the church's decoration, on one of the columns of the church. This happy circumstance allows us to date these paintings with something approximating certainty. (The neighboring church of St. Mary was dedicated the next day, 11 December, and the act of consecration, written more conventionally on parchment, was placed in the altar.)

A magnificent image of Christ in majesty fills the dome of the main apse. Christ is surrounded by four figures representing the Four Evangelists with their four apocalyptic symbols – the Man (Matthew), the Lion (Mark), the Ox (Luke), and the Eagle (John). On the main wall, beneath the dome, are five surviving figures. Each carries a distinguishing object, and each is further identified by an inscription painted above. From left to right they are the Apostles Thomas and Bartholomew, St. Mary ("Sancta Maria") with a radiant vessel, and the Apostles John and James. (fig. 3) Mary's vessel has been described as a cup or a dish. In its shape it resembles most nearly the depictions in neighbouring churches of the bowls used by the three wise men to carry their gifts to the Christ child.[11] Similarly-shaped vessels are also found in many Catalan depictions of the Last Supper, where they are used to serve fish to Jesus and the Apostles.[12] One may recall that Chrétien de Troyes, who says very little in his *Conte du graal* about the physical characteristics of the epony-

---

figure in twelfth-century Catalan wall painting is the Master of Sant Climent," Peter K. Klein, "The Romanesque in Catalonia," in *Art of Medieval Spain*, 194.

[10]See Cebrià Baraut, *Les actes de consagracions d'esglésies de l'antic bisbat d'Urgell (segles IX - XII)*, (La Seu d'Urgell, 1986) 179. The bishop who consecrated the Church was (St.) Raymund of Roda/Barbastre, a native of the region of Toulouse, and prior of Saint-Sernin of Toulouse before becoming bishop of Roda. The possibility that he played a part in transmitting knowledge of these frescoes to Chrétien de Troyes will be explored in a future study.

[11]See, for example, the South wall of the nave of Santa Maria in Taüll (now in Museu Nacional d'Art de Catalunya); Demus and Hirmer, *Romanesque Mural Painting*, figs. 206 and 207; and the wise men in the apse of the Catalonian church of San Juan de Tredós, now in the Cloisters Collection, New York City; *The Metropolitan Museum of Art: Europe in the Middle Ages*, (New York 1987) 63. Compare also the platter or shallow bowl held by St. Lucy in the twelfth-century murals of San Pere de Terrassa, reproduced in *El descubrimiento*, p. 39.

[12]See, for example, the Last Supper from San Baudel de Berlanga (1120 x 1140), now in the Museum of Fine Arts, Boston; Demus and Hirmer, *Romanesque Mural Painting*, fig. 213.

mous vessel, has a hermit explain to Perceval that he should not imagine that the bowl (*graal*) which Perceval had seen being carried through the dining hall "holds pike, lamprey, or salmon."[13] This well-known passage would seem to suggest that Chrétien himself imagined the sacred vessel not as a cup or chalice but rather as a serving bowl or platter.

As it happens, one of the medieval Catalan names for just such a domestic serving dish is *greala*, (an archaic form is *gradal*, in old Occitan *grazala*, old Castilian *greal*, probably from Catalan *gresa* – potter's clay).[14] Various forms of this word, from which Chrétien's "graal" (and the English "grail") almost certainly derive, are found throughout the region. The earliest attestation is in a document written in 1010 at La Seu d'Urgell, the episcopal see of all the churches discussed here.[15] Thus one may say, without fear of anachronism, that Mary is shown here holding a radiant "grail." This image antedates Chrétien's story of a radiant serving dish, borne by a maiden and called a grail, by more than fifty years. In Chrétien's story the grail contains a single eucharistic host; this mute

---

[13]"Foolish were you not to learn who was served from the bowl [graal]. ... Do not imagine that it holds pike, lamprey, or salmon," transl. David Staines, *The Complete Romances of Chrétien de Troyes* (Bloomington IN, 1990) 417.

[14]Joan Corominas, *Diccionario etimològic i complementari de la llengua Catalana*, vol. 4 (Barcelona, 1984) 637-641, ("Apèndix sobre Greala i el Greal"). Other forms of this word, used to designate one or another sort of domestic utensil in regional dialects of Catalonia, include *grasala, griala, greala, grala,* and *grela*. In Gascony and Languedoc one finds *gradau* (a salt-box) and *gradalou* (a large platter), etc.

[15]The document from Urgell reads: "Ad Sancta Fide coenobio gradales duas de argento, ad Sancto Vincentio de Castres anapos [cup, beaker] duo de argento," Coromines, *Diccionario etimològic*, 637. This is apparently not an isolated occurance; Ermengarda, daughter of Count Borrell of Barcelona, leaves the following "vessels" in her will of 1030: "vexe<l>la de auro et de argento, id sunt enapos v, et gradals ii, copes ii et cuylares v," ibid. Many scholars have sought the origin of the word *grail* in the supposed medieval Latin *gradale* (see Richard O'Gorman, "Grail," in *The Arthurian Encyclopedia* (New York, 1986) 257-260; the evidence for this erroneous etymology is the well-known description of the grail by the troubador-turned-Cistercian, Helinand of Froidmont, early in the thirteenth century. He writes: "*Gradalis* or *gradale* is the French name for a broad and somewhat deep dish in which delicacies are often laid out in rows (*gradatim*). It is also called in the vernacular, *graalz*"; cf. Frappier, "*Perceval*," p. 185 ["*Gradalis autem sive gradale gallice dicitur scutella lata et aliquantulum profunda, in qua pretiosae dapes cum suo jure divitibus solent apponi gradatim, ... et dicitur vulgari nomine 'graalz'.*"] But note that Helinand describes *gradalis* and *gradale* as French words, not Latin. That he goes on to offer a pseudo-Latin derivation of this French word, attributing to it the Latin meaning of "gradual" or "by steps," has only muddied the waters for subsequent interpreters. But Helinand's testimony squares with the evidence of the Catalan texts cited above. Both suggest that *gradalis* or *gradale* are not Latin words for the Grail, but rather transliterations into Latin letters of a vernacular term for a bowl or serving dish.

image at Taüll is less informative, but considering the position of the vessel, beneath the image of the wounded and triumphant Christ, and the strikingly red color of the radiance, one can see why scholars have had no difficulty in concluding that it is Christ's blood that Mary is holding in this grail.

Before leaving the village of Taüll I would like to introduce one further piece of evidence that may be relevant to a Pyreneen cult of the Virgin and the grail. In 1925, Harvard University's Fogg Museum acquired a beautiful, nearly-life-size, wooden sculpture which now graces the main staircase of the museum.[16] (fig. 4) It was discovered in 1907, along with a half-dozen other wooden figures, behind the altar of the church of St. Mary in Taüll.[17] This figure has been variously interpreted as one member of an "annunciation group" (the archangel Gabriel with Mary), a "visitation group" (Mary and Elizabeth), a "crucifixion group" (Jesus, Mary and John), and a "deposition group" (Jesus, Mary, John, Nicodemus, Joseph of Arimathea and the two thieves). All of these are plausible suggestions and can be paralleled with sculpture and painting in other churches in this region and period, but no companion pieces to this exquisite statue have been identified.[18] No one, it seems, has yet suggested the simpler, and perhaps more obvious interpretation, namely that the image was meant to stand alone, and to represent Mary with the Grail as depicted in the apse of the neighboring church of St. Clement. (fig. 4a) It is hard to mistake the striking similarities of form and gesture of these two contemporaneous images; only the missing left hand pre-

---

[16]See the catalogue entries by Kristin A. Mortimer, *Harvard University Art Museums: A Guide to the Collections* (Cambridge, MA, 1986) 124; Ivan Gaskell, in *Harvard's Art Museums. 100 Years of Collecting* (Cambridge, MA and New York, 1996) 162-163; Janice Mann, in *Art of Medieval Spain*, 318.

[17]The other figures found there are clearly distinct from the "Fogg Virgin" in both style and dimensions; none can have been intended originally as a companion piece. Cf. Porter, *Spanish Romanesque Sculpture*, 3, 13 (and figs. 67, 71).

[18]Porter mentions an early report that "a St. John of the same dimensions as the *Virgin* of the Fogg Museum has been found at San Clemente de Tahull," but he seems never to have confirmed the fact, nor has it been confirmed by others; *Spanish Romanesque Sculpture*, 3, 14. More recently H. Neiuwdeorp, director of the Art Museum of Antwerp, informed the Fogg Museum of "a possibly pendant *St. John* possessing the same style and dimensions," in a Belgian private collection; but no evidence to substantiate this claim has yet been published. See Mortimer, *Harvard University Art Museums*, 124; Gaskell, *Harvard's Art Museums*, 162. I wish to thank Sarah Kianovsky in the Department of Painting, Sculpture and Decorative Arts of the Fogg Art Museum for her generosity in allowing me to consult the museum files relating to this sculpture in July of 1999.

vents us from asserting confidently that this statue of Mary once held a sacred vessel or a grail.

However that may be, there are seven other undoubted examples from the same region of Mary holding a sacred vessel. In the church of St. Eulalia in the village of Estaon (North of Burgal) is an image usually dated to the middle of the twelfth century. In this representation Mary is shown in the company, not of the Apostles, but of other female saints: St. Eulalia, St. Anne and St. Lucy, and a depiction of Christ's baptism in the Jordan.[19] Mary is identified here both by a painted inscription ("Sancta Maria") and by the radiant cup she holds in her covered hand. (fig. 5)

Moving West toward the episcopal seat of Urgel, and North toward the principality of Andorra, one finds five more frescoes and one panel painting of Mary holding a sacred vessel.[20] The frescoes are usually dated

---

[19]Now in the Museu Nacional d'Art de Catalunya (MNAC). See Post, *Spanish Painting*, 1, 112-116; *El arte románico*, 89-90, 101; Junyent, *Catalogne romane*, 2, 200.

[20]The six remaining images are:

(1) From the apse of the church of St. Eugenia in Argolell (near La Seu d'Urgell); now in MNAC, Barcelona: Mary with right hand raised and holding chalice in covered left hand, with two unidentified Apostles. See Post, *Spanish Painting*, 1, 108 and 144; *El arte románico*, 30; Junyent, *Catalogne romane*, 2, 197.

(2) From the apse of the church of St. Mary in Ginestarre de Cardos; now in MNAC, Barcelona: John, Peter (keys), Mary (cup in covered left hand), Paul, Bartholomew, Andrew, and others. See Post, *Spanish Painting*, 1, 108-112, 144; *El arte románico*, 27; Junyent, *Catalogne romane*, 2, 201.

(3) From the apse of the church of St. Román dels Bons in Encamp (Andorra), consecrated in 1164; now in MNAC, Barcelona. Mary holds a chalice in covered left hand, Peter (keys), a central window, Paul and James. See Durliat, *Pyrénées romanes*, 163; Junyent, *Catalogne romane*, 2, 201; *El arte románico*, 168.

(4) From the chapel of St. Christopher in Años (Andorra); now in a private collection in USA: Mary with chalice in covered left hand between two Apostles. See Durliat, *Pyrénées romanes*, 165; Junyent, *Catalogne romane*, 2, 197.

(5) From the church of Santa Coloma (Andorra); previously housed in the Colección Baron de Cassel, Cannes, and now (?) in the Staatliche Museen Preussischen Kulturbesitz, Berlin: On the left of a window opening are Santa Coloma and Mary holding a chalice in her covered left hand; on the right are Peter (keys) and Paul. See Walter William Cook and José Gudiol Ricart, *Pintura e imaginería románicas* (Ars Hispaniae 6), (Madrid, 1950) fig. 50; Durliat, *Pyrénées romanes*, 166-167; Junyent, *Catalogne romane*, 2, 197.

(6) A painted wood-panel altar frontal from Martinet (near Urgel); now in the Worcester Art Museum, Worcester Massachusetts: A scene of the Ascension of Christ, with twelve Apostles standing beneath, each identified by an inscription: Matthias, Bartholomew, Peter, Barnabas, John and Andrew on the left; Paul, Thomas, Matthew, Luke[!], James and Philip on the right. In the middle, enclosed within an architectural niche or doorway, is Mary ("Sancta Maria") holding a chalice (unusually) in her uncovered right hand. See Walter W. S. Cook, "A Catalan Altar Frontal in the Worcester Museum,"

to the third quarter of the twelfth century (1150-1175) and the painted wooden altar-frontal to roughly the same period. In these examples the vessel is not depicted as "radiant," and it is usually given the more conventional shape of a eucharistic chalice. As far as I can determine this is a complete list of the extant Romanesque examples of Mary holding a sacred, sometimes-flaming vessel. Nowhere else, even in the immediate vicinity of these churches, and in the nearly-identical iconographic programs, is Mary depicted thus.

What, then, is the meaning of these images? How should they be interpreted? Since they antedate by at least fifty years Chrétien's romance and the stories of the Holy Grail that were invented and elaborated in the wake of his *Conte du graal*, we should be wary of appealing directly to the later stories for interpretations of these mute images. Rather we will try to understand them in their own terms, and to discover what they may have meant to the artists who first fashioned them and to the people who admired them. One way to approach this task is to investigate the historical and art-historical roots of the images, looking for sources and analogues that may have influenced the artists who made them. And here is the first surprise: the images are not only mute, but they are also, as far as I can discover, unprecedented. I have been unable to identify any antecedents or prefigurations in art or in literature. Perhaps the nearest artistic analogue is found in ninth-century Carolingian depictions of the crucifixion. (fig. 6) Here one often finds two female figures added to the traditional scene on Calvary. The woman on our right, turning away from the cross, represents the Synagogue; the one on our left represents the Church – *Ecclesia* – and she is sometimes shown holding a chalice in which she captures the blood which pours from Christ's side.[21] It is, of course, an easy step to assimilate Mary and *Ecclesia* into one, as is regularly done in the Christian teaching that Mary is an allegorical figure of the Church, but in fact all of these Crucifixion images that I have been able to examine depict Mary as a separate figure, and none shows her holding the chalice. Indeed, nowhere outside of the Pyrenees highlands, apparently, did artists depict Mary holding such a

---

Archaeologica orientalia in memoriam Ernst Herzfeld (New York, 1952) 32-38; Cook and Ricart, *Pintura e imaginería románicas*, 70 and 194, fig. 169. My thanks to Mary Zagaeski of the Worcester Art Museum for her generous hospitality during my visit to the Museum in July of 1999.

[21]Figure 6 represents a Carolingian Ivory from Metz, ca. 870, now in the Cloisters Collection, New York City; see *The Metropolitan Museum: Middle Ages*, 43. For a recent discussion of this iconography see Marie-Christine Sepière, *L'image d'un Dieu souffrant, IXe-Xe siècles: aux origines du crucifix* (Paris 1994).

vessel, and in the Pyrenees images she is not associated with scenes of the crucifixion.

Another image that might be loosely associated with the Catalan Mary and the Grail also comes from scenes of the crucifixion. In a tenth-century copy (975 AD) of the famous Spanish illuminated *Beatus Apocalypse Commentary*, and in some depictions of the miraculous *Volto Santo* of Lucca, a wooden crucifix carved, it is said, by Nicodemus, with the help of angels, one finds at the foot of the cross a chalice or other vessel which collects the blood that flows from Christ's wounds.[22] One can see the possible relevance of such an image to the sacred vessel of the Catalan images, but again there is no connection with Mary or with the decorative programs in the Pyrenees.[23] These sources and analogues can give us, at best, only a broad sense of the iconographic and doctrinal materials upon which an artist might draw; they provide no interpretive key to the specific and unusual Pyreneen images of Mary holding a sacred and often-radiant vessel, whether chalice, cup or grail/platter.

Thus far, then, it would seem that these images are something new, without clear sources or analogues in art or literature. Next we can turn to the images themselves and to their own historical milieu in search of clues for their interpretation. I would mention here three main types of

---

[22]The Beatus manuscript, called "The Girona Beatus," is in the Museu de la Catedral de Girona, Num. Inv. 7 (11), fol. 16; see John Williams, *The Illustrated Beatus. A Corpus of the Illustrations of the Commentary on the Apocalypse*, 2, *The Ninth and Tenth Centuries* (Langhorne PA, 1994) 288; and Pedro de Palol and Max Hirmer, *Early Medieval Art in Spain* (New York 1967) 54 and pl. XI. For the *Volto santo* of Lucca see Porter, *Spanish Romanesque Sculpture*, 3, 8-19, where the image is associated with the contemporaneous Catalan wood carvings such as the Fogg statue. See also *Lucca, il Volto santo e la civiltà medioevale*, Atti convegno internazionale di Studi 21-23 Ottobre 1982 (Lucca 1984). For a history of the scholarship, see Herbert Kurz, *Der Volto santo von Lucca: Ikonographie und Funktion des Kruzifixus in der gegürteten Tunika im 11. Jahrhundert* (Regensburg, 1997); and for a sensitive critical study see Michele Camillo Ferrari, "*Imago visibilis Christi*. Le *Volto santo* de Lucques et les images authentiques au moyen âge," *Micrologus* 6 (1998) 29-42.

[23]It is perhaps noteworthy that later traditions will associate this image of a chalice at the foot of the cross with Mary Magdalene. Mary Dzon has brought to my attention just such a picture, introducing the Feast of the Sacred Heart of Jesus in the *Saint Andrew Daily Missal* (Bruges, 1956) 700. The editors of the Missal provide an "Explanation of the Illustration" that concludes with the warning: "However, from this synthetical and symbolical picture, we should not infer that our Lord wore those [sacerdotal] vestments and crown on the cross, nor that the centurion was the same man who pierced our Lord's side, nor that Mary Magdalen collected Jesus' blood in the legendary 'Grail'." For possible adumbrations of this iconography in tenth-century images from southern France and from southern Italy, see Carol Heitz, "*Adoratio Crucis*. Remarques sur quelques crucifixions préromanes en Poitou," in *Études de civilisation médiévale (IXe - XIIe siècles): Mélanges offerts à Edmond-René Labande* (Poitiers, 1974) 395-405.

investigation, and report briefly on the value of each. The first way is iconological. Starting with a careful observation and description of the evidence to hand, especially the iconographical programs and the literature and liturgy of the region, one can construct several plausible, if unattested, interpretations.[24] For example, the image of Christ in Majesty accompanied by Apostles is related, iconographically, to the mystery of Christ's Ascension to heaven forty days after Easter.[25] The liturgy for the Feast of the Ascension includes the well-known verse: "When Christ ascended on high, he led captivity captive," and the Response: "He gave gifts to men, alleluia."[26] In a homily for the same feast St. Leo the Great describes how, by leaving earth and ascending to heaven, Jesus "began to be indescribably more present in his divinity to those from whom he was further removed in his humanity."[27] What are the gifts that Christ

---

[24]One such interpretation is offered by Dodwell: "Perhaps the most interesting feature of [these] paintings is the fact that they incorporate the earliest allusion to the Grail in art or in literature. ... The Grail is a subtle and complex concept which cannot be explored fully here, but it may be said that in its Christian sense it represents a relic of the Passion – usually the chalice of the Last Supper containing Christ's own blood – and in the paintings the divinity of Christ's blood is symbolized by rays of light that issue from the vessel. The Spanish artists may have associated the grail with the Virgin because they saw her as the human Grail that had carried the blood and divinity of Christ." *Pictorial Arts*, 257-8. Although there is much of value in these observations, Dodwell has been unsuccessful in avoiding an anachronistic reading of the frescoes in the light of the later stories and legends of the Holy Grail. His interpretation assumes a fully developed Grail Legend at the time that these images were painted. In fact the Grail Legend, as we know it, developed only after the appearance of Chrétien's *Conte du Graal*. The now-familiar stories that associate the Holy Grail with the cup of the Last Supper were first told, it seems, by Robert de Boron, early in the thirteenth century. On Robert, see Richard O'Gorman, *Robert de Boron, Joseph d'Arimathie: A Critical Edition of the Verse and Prose Versions*, (Toronto, 1995); for Robert's claim to be the first to relate the story of the origins and early history of the Grail, see ibid., 334-335.

[25]The classic study is by Charles L. Kuhn, *Romanesque Mural Painting of Catalonia* (Cambridge MA 1930), especially Part 2 chapter 2, "Iconography," pp. 74-88. For an excellent introduction to Marian iconography in this period see Daniel Russo, "Les représentations mariales dans l'art d'Occident: Essai sur la formation d'une tradition iconographique," in *Marie: Le culte*, 173-291, esp. 232-259; and for the uses of these images in churches Éric Palazzo, "Marie et l'élaboration d'un espace ecclésial au haut Moyen Âge," ibid., 313-325.

[26]The verse and response are taken from Eph. 4:8, where Paul works a transformation on the text of Ps 67:19 which reads: "Thou hast ascended on high; thou hast led captivity captive; thou hast received gifts in men." For a useful introduction to the liturgical rites in use in this region see Richard B. Donovan, *The Liturgical Drama of Medieval Spain*, (Toronto, 1958) 20-29 and passim.

[27]Sermo 2, de Ascensione 1-4; *Corpus Christianorum, Series Latina* 138A, tract. 74 (PL 54. 397-399).

gave to man? How does Christ begin to be more present to people after his Ascension than he was during his earthly ministry? These Pyreneen frescoes might suggest that the gifts Christ gave in his Resurrection are the Sacraments of the Church, represented by Mary, with a symbol of the Eucharist, and by St. Peter with the keys.

The problem with such explanations is not only the difficulty of demonstrating that a medieval artist or observer would have recognized them as valid, but also that, however plausible they may be as general explanations, they rarely do justice to the specifics of the case. Here, for example, such an explanation fails to elucidate the radiance or flames of Mary's vessel, the various shapes which it takes in addition to the eucharistic chalice, or the variety of iconographical contexts in which it occurs even within this narrow mountain region. In addition, by imposing a kind of normality on the images, such iconological readings may obscure or routinize that which is in fact unusual or surprising.

Another approach to discovering the original meaning of these unconventional images is to look for evidence of a local legend or cult that would help to explain them. The geographic concentration of the images lends support to a view that would see here a local phenomenon – some miracle or event which was well known in the region, but which never quite entered the mainstream of devotion and of artistic representation. If so, by the nature of the case there will be little evidence to be discovered. But local legends, folklore survivals, or the inclusion of a story among one of the many contemporaneous collections of miracles all offer some hope for discoveries.[28]

A third approach, however, has proved even more promising, that is through the study of medieval liturgical drama. Some forty years ago a colleague of ours here at St. Michael's College, Father Richard Donovan, published his still-authoritative study of *Liturgical Drama in Medieval Spain*.[29] Fr. Donovan was able to show that the churches of Spain in general, and of Aragon and Catalonia in particular, were in the forefront

---

[28]Medieval collections of the miracles and legends of the Virgin Mary (and of Mary Magdalene) flourished in the eleventh and twelfth centuries, and the scholarly literature is vast. For an introduction, see Guy Philippart, "Le récit miraculaire marial dans l'Occident médiéval," in *Marie: Le culte*, 563-589. Two twelfth-century collections in Catalan are the *Recull d'eximpis e miracles*, ed. Marià Aguiló (Barcelona, 1881-1882), and the *Miracles de la Verge Maria*, ed. Pere Bohigas (Barcelona, 1956). For Mary Magdalene, see Victor Saxer, "Maria Maddalena," in *Bibliotheca Sanctorum*, 8 (19??) 1099-1104.

[29]Donovan, *Liturgical Drama of Medieval Spain*. See also the recent study, much indebted to Fr. Donovan's pioneering efforts, by Eva Castro, *Teatro medieval*, 1: *El drama litúrgico* (Barcelona, 1997).

of the development and use of liturgical drama in medieval Europe. His book is a fascinating catalogue of discoveries in the Spanish libraries. In a fourteenth-century manuscript of the Capitular Library at Gerona, for example, one finds instructions for dramatizating the Easter Morning liturgy. They include directions that a choir-boy impersonating Mary Magdalene[30] should hold in his hands a vessel (*capça*) representing Christ's Resurrection" (*in representatione resurrectionis Christi*).[31] We are not told how this *capsa*, probably a pyx such as was used to carry the eucharistic host to the sick, was to represent Christ's Resurrection, but that it was meant to do so is beyond question.[32] Such dramatic cues might help to explain the Catalan images. It is easy to imagine that one or another of these plays called for Mary to hold some sort of sacred and radiant vessel by which sign she would be easily recognized. No such stage-directions survive in the materials studied thus far, but the liturgical manuscripts are numerous and the possibilities are by no means exhausted.[33]

Following these, and other, paths we may eventually come to a fuller understanding of the original meaning of the Catalan Virgin and her

---

[30]Donovan notices that a similar liturgical sequence suitable for dramatizing as part of the Easter liturgy, ("Dic Maria, quid vidisti contemplando crucem Christi"), usually assigned to Mary Magdalene the principal role, but that in one version, "the dominating personage in the dialogue is the Holy Virgin," Donovan, *Liturgical Drama*, 104-105, and note 18. Cf. above, note 4.

[31]"Et duo pueri cantent ... *Dic nobis, Maria <quid uidisti in uia>*. Et unus puer stans ante altare Sancte Marie indut<us> dalmatica cum alifafa [a mantle or cape] in capite, qui teneat aliquam capçam in manu in representatione resurrectionis Christi. Versa facie uersus chorum respondeat, *Sepulcrum Christi uiuentis*." Donovan, *Liturgical Drama*, 109. For the meaning of "capça" see next note. Donovan noticed the nearly identical instructions for performing this Easter play at the nearby church of St. Felix, where the word "capça" was replaced by the indefinite pronoun "aliquod": "And another boy ... who holds *something* in his hand in representation of Christ's Resurrection," ibid. 110.

[32]Eva Castro, *Teatro medieval*, 1, *El drama litúrgico* (Barcelona, 1997) 202-203, translates "capça" as "píxide" ["pyx"] and describes the object in a footnote as a: "Copón ["cup"] o cajita ["small box"] en la que se lleva la Eucaristía a los enfermos" ["in which the Eucharist is carried to the sick."] Needless to say, a vessel containing the eucharistic host and carried in procession to visit the sick would fit nicely with Chrétien's image of a "grail," containing a single mass wafer, being carried in procession to serve the wounded father of the rich Fisher King. [Medora Roe informs me that the Catalan "capça," spelled with c-cedilla as here, can also mean "cabbage"; the reluctance of scholars to go down that interpretive path is perhaps understandable.]

[33]For an excellent study of the interplay of medieval drama and artistic representation see Hélène Toubert, "La Vierge et les sages-femmes: Un jeu iconographique entre les Évangiles apocryphes et le drame liturgique," in *Marie: Le culte*, 327-360. See also the comments of Carol Heitz, "*Adoratio crucis*" (above, n. 23) pp. 403-405.

fiery Grail. In the meantime, however, we are in much the same position as any other outside observer, even one who came to see, or to hear about, these images more than 800 years ago. We are confronted by these profoundly beautiful images, full of mystery and ambiguity. May we not presume, if only for the sake of argument, that such beauty and such mystery was precisely what Chrétien de Troyes needed in order to imagine that a simple serving dish, a grail, could be transformed into the centrepiece for "the finest tale that may be told." Here, one could say, he found a vessel waiting to be filled with meaning, and the meaning with which he and others endowed it, that of the Holy Grail, was to flourish and grow for centuries to come.

ILLUSTRATIONS

Fig. 1   Virgin holding a fiery Grail; El Burgal, Catalonia, early-12th c.

Fig. 2   Virgin with the Grail; Tahull, Catalonia, c. 1123

Fig. 3   Apse of St. Clement; Tahull, Catalonia, c. 1123

Fig. 4   Statue of the Virgin; Tahull, Catalonia, 12th c.

Fig. 4a   Details of figures 2 and 4

Fig. 5   St. Eulalia, and St. Mary with a radiant grail; Estaon, Catalonia, mid-12th century

Fig. 6   Crucifixion scene; Metz, Germany, ca. 870

Figure 1.

Figure 2.

Figure 3.

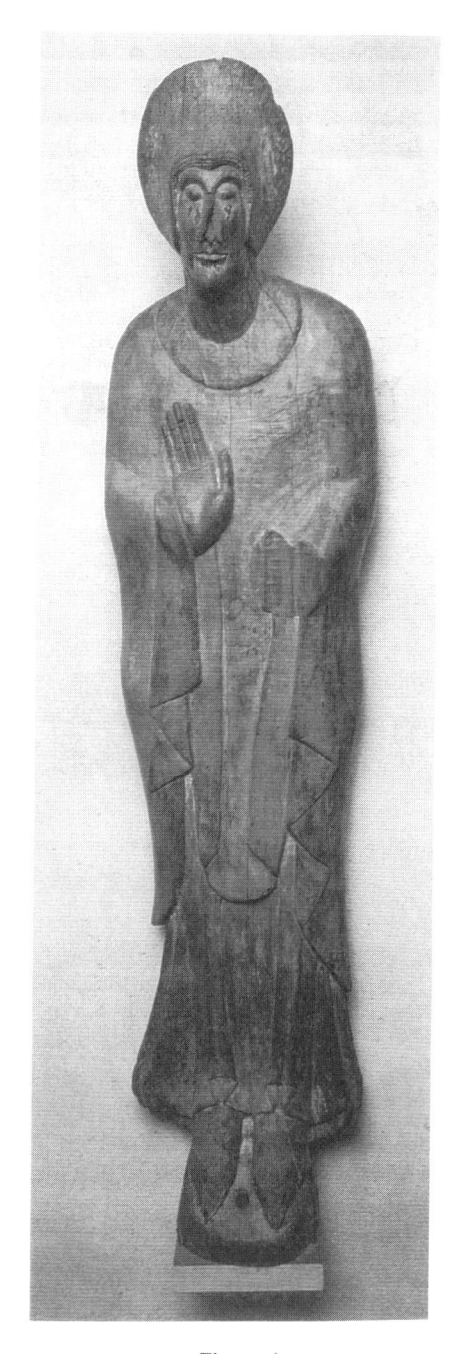

Figure 4.

Figure 5.

Figure 5.

Figure 6.

Francesco Guardiani

A Christological Metamorphosis in a Baroque Poem

ABSTRACT. Hidden between the exuberant lines (forty-two thousand of them) of the most baroque among baroque poems (*L'Adone*, by Giovan Battista Marino, first published in Paris in 1623, and soon after inscribed in the *Index librorum prohibitorum*) is the story of Christ's passion, death and resurrection. The purpose of this paper is twofold: to offer a description of all the elements leading to the identification of the protagonist, Adonis, with Christ; and to submit an interpretation of the disquieting mythological reincarnation.

The metamorphosis I will be dealing with in this paper is contained in an epic poem inspired by Ovid's work, an epic poem that is considered to be the most representative literary accomplishment of the Italian Baroque. Conceived in Naples in the early 1590's, it saw the light of print only thirty years later, in the Spring of the year 1623, in Paris, with the title, *L'Adone*, in a splendid folio edition, dedicated to (and paid by) Louis XIII and his mother, Maria de' Medici. The author was Giovan Battista Marino (1569-1625), who was already very famous at the time of the publication. He had been hailed, actually, as the greatest of all Italian, Latin, Greek, and Hebrew writers, as well as the greatest of all writers that would ever live in the future. The praise came from Claudio Achillini, a respected professor of Law in the university of Bologna and a poet himself.

It is easy for us to recognize the hyperbolic boasts of Baroque rhetoric here, but it would be a big mistake to discard as irrelevant Achillini's superlatives. Not only because for the Baroque mind there are grades of hyperbolic discourses (and here, clearly we are at the highest point), but also because this particular praise was only one of the numerous expressions of profound sympathy and admiration he received from all over

Saints and the Sacred - A St. Michael's College Symposium
Joseph Goering, Francesco Guardiani, Giulio Silano eds. Ottawa: Legas, 2001

Italy in anticipation of the *poema grande*, announced as imminent several years before its publication.

Marino knew that with his new work he could not limit himself to feed new beautiful lines to his cheering admirers. He had published already two large and immensely successful collections of lyrics, several idylls and occasional poems. It was now time for the epic, time for a new vision of society and history that he, a Neapolitan immigrant in Paris, at the Florentine court of Mary, was royally appointed to express with a *poema grande*.

The antecedent, as well as the inevitable critical term of comparison was Torquato Tasso's *Jerusalem Delivered*, the great epic moulded on revived, re-interpreted and re-defined Aristotelian poetics, and considered a truly classic, as well as Christian, Italian epic, even more so than Dante's *Divine Comedy*. Marino did not choose Homer or Vergil's works as models; he preferred the less known *Dyonisiaca* by Nonnus of Panopolis, and, in obvious opposition to Vergil's poetics, Ovid's *Metamorphoses*. While he could borrow numerous stylistic traits and mythological images and narratives from these encyclopaedic works, the new philosophy to support his creation was not to be drawn from them; it had to be completely original. All this could probably help to understand the audacity of the central metamorphosis in his poem, *L'Adone*, that he projected to be greater than the *Jerusalem Delivered*.

Marino was an instinctive, very elegant, sophisticated writer, in the sense, at least, that he wouldn't or couldn't rationalize his poetic choices; he would hint, and signify symbolically and with the full force of melodic and rhythmic expressivity, but he wouldn't say, explain, or rationalize the philosophical positions that we, as readers, are led to assume he was taking. As Giovanni Pozzi, Marino's greatest critic in modern times once remarked, for this poet first came the words, arranged in an enchanting rhetorical style, and then came the meaning of the words themselves. Marino's reluctance to speak openly on philosophical issues is also linked to the fact that the "irregularity" of his positions (such as the one we will consider in a moment) in the cultural environment of the Counter Reformation could have been highly problematic, not simply for his career, but for his own life. One of Marino's friends in France, the philosopher Giulio Cesare Vanini, was in fact put on trial and condemned by the *Tribunale del Sant'Uffizio*, in 1617; his triple execution – his tongue was pulled out, his head cut off, and his body (whatever was left of it) burned at the stake – was not very encouraging for a poet to come out of his rhetoric.

And we should not forget, at this point, to mention the famous sentence of Cardinal Sforza Pallavicino, in his *Vindicationes*, where the Roman appointed historian of the Council of Trent, from the comfort of his Vatican chair finds that Marino, already dead and condemned by the Church, but still embarrassingly famous and read and imitated, *"carebat philosophico ingenio* that since Aristotle it is required in every respectable poet." This insidious, negative comment – the *nadir* of the poet's fame, the *zenith* being Achillini's hyperboles – came from a man of the cultural establishment, the same establishment that had decreed the inclusion of *L'Adone* in the *Index librorum prohibitorum*, in 1624.

Why, one would argue, include a book by a superficial poet with no philosophical *ingenium* in the *Index*? What was the fear? Pozzi thinks that the "prelati del Sant'Uffizio" who censored the book read and understood things that were not superficial at all, and certainly would go way beyond the "common" obscenities for which the book was apparently condemned. The fact remains, however, that Sforza Pallavicino's comments helped to forge a negative image of Marino's epic which lasted for centuries.

Things have changed in the last decades of the twentieth thanks to a new appreciation of Baroque rhetoric, and also thanks to some critical work done in the area of sacred symbolism, discreetly hidden between the exuberant lines of the poem. Not counting myself, two people only have devoted considerable attention to this specific issue: Fra' Tommaso Stigliani in the seventeenth century, and Father Giovanni Pozzi twenty-five years ago. Stigliani wrote in *L'Occhiale* (an entire volume devoted to a systematic scrutiny of *L'Adone*) that Marino had a blasphemous mind and enjoyed making a mockery of articles of faith for pure perversity. For Pozzi, instead, Marino's metaphors of the sacred are part of the poet's encyclopaedic approach to literature. I submit that Marino's symbols, and especially the elements leading to the identification of Adonis with Christ, are the core of Marino's philosophy, and that they allow for a critical re-reading of the poem in a totally new and different light. I shall proceed, from now on, with a list of such elements accompanied by some brief, specific comments.

* * *

Early in the poem (canto 3, stanza 68) Adonis is assimilated to Cupid who, of course, not only is a mythological figure and one of the major characters in the poem, like Adonis himself, but also the symbolic personification of Love. He is called "Amore," in fact, with the capital "A", the name of a person as well as the name of a thing. Amore/Love is one and one only in Marino, be it *Agape, Charitas*, or pure lust. And if one reader may detect some influence here by the never mentioned by Marino but ever present in his work, contemporary philosopher of the greatest *reductio ad unum*, Giordano Bruno, the thought would certainly be well justified. As character with a described physical physiognomy, Adonis and Cupid are very different from each other; but Venus at one point cannot distinguish between her son and her lover. We can observe a typical use of symbolic language by Marino here. Whenever a character, a theme, or a situation appears to be unjustifiably unrealistic, Marino is certainly at work to emphasize the symbolic meaning. And so, when the poet tells us that Adonis *veracemente rassembra Amore* to Venus, he is telling us that Adonis is a figure of pure and perfect Love. We soon will be considering the implications of this in other passages in the poem. Meanwhile, here's the entire quote (with the English translation of Harold Martin Priest. Translations are mine when no credit is indicated).

Or giunta sotto il solitario monte,	Now having reached a solitary hill,
dove raro uman piè stampò mai l'orme,	a spot where human foot has rarely trod,
trova colà su 'l margine del fonte	she finds there at the margin of a fount
Adon che 'n braccio ai fior s'adagia e dorme;	Adonis sleeping in the flowers' embrace;
ed or che già dela serena fronte	and now, although sleep casts its shadow o'er
gli appanna il sonno le celesti forme	the heavenly features of his countenance,
e tien velato il gemino splendore,	and covers with a veil those splendors twain,
veracemente egli rassembra Amore.	even in slumber he resembles Love.
Rassembra Amor, qualor deposta e sciolta	He looks like Love, when, weary from the hunt,
La face e glil aurei strali e l'arco fido,	and having laid aside the faithful bow,
Stanco di saettar posa talvolta	the arrows and the torch, he sometimes rests
Su l'Idalio frondoso o in val di Gnido	in Gnido's vale or in Idalian slope,
E dentro i mirti, ove tra l'ombra folta	amid the myrtles where in covert shade
Han canori augelletti opaco nido,	canorous birds have found obscure retreat,
Appoggia il capo ala faretra e quivi	and on his quiver resting his fair head,
Carpisce il sonno al mormorar de' rivi.	he takes his sleep beside the murmuring brook.
(*L'Adone* 3, 68-69)	(Trans. H.M. Priest. 3.68-69)

Most of the elements leading to the identification of Adonis/Love with Christ are contained in the final cantos because only at that point in the narrative it becomes necessary for the poet to start offering an all-encompassing new symbolic significance to the re-issued mythological plot. But already in Canto 16 there is a crucial episode in the development of the *fabula sacra*. The occasion is a beauty contest in which the most handsome young man will be chosen by a number of wise men to become king of Cyprus, the island of Venus, where beauty is celebrated.

Adonis, the beautiful ("il bell'Adone") appears destined to an easy win. But Marino inserts an obstacle to the acclamation, a contestant that comes from the barbarians' land of Scythia. He is a *Saracen* ("Di Scizia un saracin") and his name is "Luciferno" (*nomen omen*: Lucifer from Inferno). Indeed, he is Satan, also called "mostro d'Averno" (monster from Hell) by one of the judges in the contest. Luciferno dares to compete with Adonis, and is killed by Cupid, whose arrows usually have only metaphorical lethal effects. But as I indicated before, traditional mythological realism, or plausibility, disappears when a particular symbolic meaning is attached to the text. In this case, the coronation of Adonis as king (which echoes the proclamation of Christ on his entering Jerusalem on Palm Sunday) can only happen with the killing of Luciferno, because Adonis/Cupid is Christ/Love and as such his power destroys Satan. Here, in Marino's own words, the appearance of Luciferno, the monster from Hell, followed by the stanza in which he is killed by Cupid. The extremely detailed description of the character with centrifugal referents that slow down the already unhurried narration is customary in Marino's rhetoric, and it shows why the poem , even when rejected by the critics in the eighteenth century, remained the favourite book of the poets of the time who saw in it an encyclopaedia of poetic imagery and rhetorical devices.

Vien Luciferno il fier dopo costui,	After him proud Lucifernus comes,
così di Scizia un saracin si noma.	A Saracen of Scythia so called.
Il Saca e 'l Battrian soggiace a lui,	Subject to him are Saca, Bactrian;
il Margo ha vinto e la Sarmazia ha doma;	Margian he won, his home Sarmatia;
e la gloria rapir presume altrui	he hopes to carry off the envied crown
per irta barba e per irsuta chioma.	because of his full beard and flowing hair.
Mostra ruvide membra, ossa robuste,	Rugged limbs he shows and robust frame,
lungo capo, ampie nari e tempie anguste.	head long and thin, full nostrils, narrow brow.
L'occhio pien di terrore e di bravura	His piercing eye, 'twixt black and greenish hue,
infra nero e verdiccio, altrui spaventa	strikes terror in the hearts of all around.
e con torvo balen di luce oscura	And with grim lightning flashes he displays
la fierezza e 'l furor vi rappresenta.	the fierce and savage gleam of those dark lights;
Portamento ha superbo e guatatura	his bearing haughty, offers signs and threats
sì feroce ed atroce e violenta,	of havoc and of dire atrocities,
che rassembra aquilon qualor più freme	which seem like Aquilon when, raging fierce,
e col torbido e Egeo combatte insieme.	he battles the wild Aegean Sea.
Su la giubba che tinta ha di morato,	Over a coat that is blackberry dyed
rete si stende d'or sottile e ricca,	is stretched a net of gold, subtle and rich,
e con puntali pur d'oro smaltato	whereon the angles of the mesh are linked
gli angoli dele maglie insieme appicca;	and intertwined with knots of inlaid gold;
porta sotto l'ascella il manto alzato,	he wears a cape suspended from one shoulder,
	which is draped under the other arm;

e'l lembo che dal braccio a terra cade,
con lunga striscia il pavimento rade.

Di lavoro azimin la scimitarra
larga, breve e ricurva appende al'anca;
dietro ha il carcasso e per taverso sbarra
l'arco serprente in su la spalla manca.
In forma di piramide bizzarra
un globo intorno al crin di tela bianca
erge, com'è de' barbari costume,
d'aviluppate fasce alto volume.

Con la test'alta e con le nari rosse,
con furibonda e formidabil faccia
sbuffando un denso fumo egli si mosse
a guisa di leon quando minaccia.
Snudò le terga ben quadrate e grosse,
brandì le forti e nerborute braccia,
di forza, di vigor, d'asprezza piene,
scropolose di muscoli e di vene.

Stanno tutti a mirarlo attenti e cheti
da Scommo infuora un vecchiarel ritroso,
de' satirici più che de' faceti,
ma carco il pigro piè d'umor nodoso
che glil tien tra gli articoli secreti
dele giunture un freddo gelo ascoso,
onde del corpo stanco il grave incarco
sovra torto bastone appoggia in arco.

Questi il capo crollò, le ciglia torse,
segni fè di disprezzo, atti di scherno:
– Vattene (disse) pur là sotto l'orse
tra le fere a regnar, mostro d'averno.
      (*L'Adone* 16, 150-56)

the border of it dangles to the earth,
and trailing wipes the pavement in long streaks.

A curving scimitar hangs at his hip,
short and broad and fancily inlaid;
a quiver at his back and curving bow
at his left shoulder on a transverse strap.
About his head a globe of snow-white cloth
arises, as the barbarous custom is,
a towering heap of convoluted bands,
in form much like a pyramid bizarre.

With head held high and nostrils showing red,
with furious and formidable face,
puffing a dense cloud of smoke he moved,
much like a lion menacing his foe.
He bared his back, which showed well set and stout,
he swung his sinews and sturdy arms,
arms threatening great force and violence,
with veins and muscles standing in relief.

All stand and gaze at him, quiet and fixed,
except for Scommus, old and ill-disposed,
a satirist more than a jester he,
his slow feet burdened with a humor vile,
which nourishes a hidden piercing chill
within his secret ligaments and joints,
whence bent and stooping o'er a crooked staff,
he leans the burden of his weary frame.

He shook his head, he creased his brow and showed
expressions of contempt and mockery.
"Be off," he said, "and there beneath the Bear
hold sway among wild beasts, monster from Hell."
      (Trans. H.M. Priest. 16.150-56)

Prima che Luciferno oltre seguisse,
strano prodigio e repentino avenne.
Quella statua d'Amor che già si disse
lo stral ch'avea su l'arco a scoccar venne.
Volando il crudo stral, l'asta gli affisse
nel costato miglior fino ale penne.
Cadde e giacque il meschin gelido e muto,
frecciato il cor di passatoio acuto.
      (*L'Adone* 16, 246)

Suddenly, before Luciferno could continue
a strange event prodigiously happened:
the statue of Cupid, that we have said,
the arrow that was ready on the arc released.
The arrow reached the left side of Luciferno's breast
And entered it all the way, deep till only the feathers
were left outside.
He fell and stayed, the wretched, mute and cold,
the heart pierced by the sharp arrow.
      (*L'Adone* 16, 246)

Other aspects of sacred symbolism we find in Amatunta, capital city of Cyprus, inside the temple of Venus, described as having architectural characteristics of a Christian church of the Renaissance. Here Adonis is presented as spending the night in prayers to prepare himself for the dramatic event in store for him the day after when the new, legitimate king of Cyprus will be crowned. He is alone, except for some soldiers, guardians of the temple, who have fallen asleep. This situation recalls the Biblical episode of Christ praying in the Gethsemane when Peter, James, and John, three apostles, "soldiers" of Christ, fall asleep.

In the temple, on the main altar, there is a statue of Venus with a crown in her hands. She will put it on the head of the future king of Cyprus. Adonis is alone in the temple; he stands in front of the statue, and all of a sudden the stone becomes flesh, Venus smiles at him and crowns him king of the island. But something else happens during the night. Adonis does not really want the crown – comparable to the bitter chalice – that Christ asks God the Father, to spare him from. And so Adonis gives the crown to Barrino, another fraudulent competitor, who will be unmasked by Venus in person during the official ceremony of the crowning, the day after.

Early in the morning , before the ceremony, two episodes take place that have unmistakable symbolic values. First, a dove that had escaped the knife of the priest for the sacrifice, appears to be circling the crowd, and finally lands on Adonis's shoulder.

Una colomba allor, che fuggitiva, del sacrato coltello avanzo solo era quel proprio dì campata viva, venne a fermargli in su la spalla il volo. Onde il buon vecchio Astreo che ne gioiva e de' presaghi aruspici lo stuolo vaticinando aventuroso stato con lieto annunzio interpretaro il fato. (*L'Adone* 16, 195)	Just then a dove that, fugitive, alone, had been that day miraculously spared from bloody, sacrificial knife escaped, upon Adonis' shoulder came to rest. Whence old Astreus, who rejoiced at this, together with a host of soothsayers, interpreted the act a fair presage, foreseeing an auspicious state of things. (Trans. H. M. Priest, 16, 195)

Later, as all eyes are fixed on the youth, an old servant of Cynira and Mirra, Adonis's parents who died tragically when he was born, recognize him as the legitimate king of the island, because of a birthmark, in the form of a rose, that he has on the left side of his chest. Pozzi explains the first episode as a reference to the baptism of Christ, and the second as a metaphor of Christ's chest wound, "la ferita del costato" which is fairly common in the language of the mystics.

At this point, as we enter canto 18 of the poem, the canto of Adonis's death, it is quite evident that Marino has been accumulating elements of Christological identification to lead his readers toward a new spiritual understanding of the old myth. Why would he not be more overt? One may ask. Again, we have to remember that we are in the middle of the Counter Reformation. The memory of Giordano Bruno, burned a few years back in Campo de' Fiori, and of the more recent execution of his friend Giulio Cesare Vanini persuaded the poet to exercise prudence. Marino certainly had no intention of becoming another martyr of the "libero pensiero". His courage was limited to expressing controversial thoughts only between the lines, in the safe compounds of his overly ornate camouflages. On the other hand, he openly advises his most sophisticated readers to look for special meanings under the external wrapping of his rhetoric. He says, in one of the opening stanzas of the poem:

Ombreggia il ver Parnaso e non rivela	(My) poetry covers the truth and does not reveal
gli alti mistery agli umili profani	(its) high mysteries to humble profane readers,
ma con scorza mentita asconde e cela	like the uncouth Silenus, it hides secrets
quasi rozo Silen celesti arcani.	of arcane knowledge under false appearances.
(*L'Adone* 1.10)	

The death of Adonis is preceded by the death of Aurilla. A name of obvious meaning: she who loves gold. Aurilla is the unfaithful servant of Adonis; she betrays him, and then, for the remorse "gitta l'oro"(18, 242); throws away the golden coins she had received from Mars, the instigator of the boar that will kill Adonis, and hangs herself. She is, unmistakeably, a personification of Judas Iscariot.

But perhaps the most obvious, as well as disquieting proof of the identification of Adonis with Christ can be found in the terminology used by Marino to indicate the anatomical area of the mortal wound inflicted by the boar. In the very elaborate narrative description of the attack, the first part of the body of the young man to be exposed to the fury of the gigantic boar is the "leg" ["un vento all'improvviso... per recargli alfin l'ultima angoscia / gli alzò la vesta e gli scoprì la coscia" (18, 94. A sudden wind to inflict on him the last anguish, lifted his skirt and showed his leg)]. Following that, the attack of the boar is aimed at the "anca" (18, 97), that is, at the "side"; and finally, with a very technical term, at the genitals: "sotto il vago galon" (16, 97. "under the iliac crest"). Pozzi in his commentary does not give particular emphasis to Marino's insistence on anatomical details, which seem to me to indicate that the poet wanted to make sure that the readers understood the sexual nature of the boar's aggression. What I find most remarkable, however, is that from this point on, and starting with the lament of Venus, the wound of Adonis is not mentioned as a wound in the genital area anymore, but as a chest wound, specifically, as "la piaga del costato," (18, 152 and 19, 358) pre-announced by the recognition of birthmark by Myrra's old maid. The expression in Italian has only one meaning: the wound in the side of Christ. To this we must add that the killer of Adonis is recognized by Venus not as a Beast of Cyprus, but as a monster from Hell.

After the death, we have the Resurrection. Marino devotes an entire canto to it, and he illustrates the rebirth of Adonis as a flower using several *exempla*, among which the most remarkable is perhaps that of Pampino, a young mythological figure like Adonis who died tragically. Pampino, who was the lover of Bacchus, after his death, Marino recalls, was transformed into "la sostanza del ciel data ale vigne" (19, 123. The substance of Heaven given to the vines), and that is the wine of the Eucharist, a metonymy for Christ himself.

Marino devotes another canto, the entire canto 20, the longest of the poem, containing more than four thousand lines, to the effects of the metamorphosis of Adonis or, better, of his resurrection: the influence of the miracle embraces all of mankind, and "the great theatre of the world" that we find here, at the end of the poem, is an epiphany of celestial beatitude, made possible by the sacrifice of Adonis/Christ.

At this point we can interrupt our series of Christological references in the poem to make a few comments, or rather, to try to make some sense of this very particular literary phenomenon. To start, why would Marino need the support of Christological symbolism for his epic poem? And why would the prelates of the Sant'Uffizio respond so harshly to the identification of Adonis with Christ, an identification that had already been accepted and elaborated on by the fathers of the Church (as a quick query into the *Patrologia latina* would indicate today to anyone)?

A quick answer to the first question would be that in some historical and cultural situations only the universal power of Christ is seen as capable of adding true metaphysical values to human events, be it a "real" power that touches the heart of the faithful, or an abstraction, a metaphorical power that appeals to the minds of those who do not believe.

In his *Discorsi del poema eroico* (1595), Torquato Tasso's own revised guide on how to write epic poems, he says that the poet must be a philosopher, a mystic and not a Thomist philosopher, one who uses reason to translate visions and not to explain them. This is a definition that suits Marino perfectly. Visions of a new world are often not pleasant projections at all, but dramatic responses to fear in a reality that has become oppressive. It was Carlo Calcaterra perhaps, in his 1940 book, *Il Parnaso in rivolta*, who more than any other critic before him, pointed to the creative anguish of the Baroque soul, "l'anima in Barocco". We see it at work in Monteverdi's sorrowful *Lamento di Arianna*, in Borromini and Bernini's ellipses and spirals, in Caravaggio's rejection of harmony and balance, just as in the Monteverdi's "stile concitato" of his "seconda pratica." Marino's "anima in barocco" includes all of this, and the pathos of his epic grows immensely as the meaning of his images become more evident, functional, and prophetic. An so we reach a point when we finally recognize that it is Christ the true protagonist of his poem.

As for the other question, of the condemnation of the book by the Sant'Uffizio, we should remember the direct, negative response to *L'Adone*, in 1623, by the new pope, Maffeo Barberini, Urbano VIII, the pope of Campanella and Galileo, a mediocre poet and a megalomaniac. He had just been elected when Marino returned triumphantly to Rome with copies of *L'Adone*, just published, *in folio grande*, by the royal print masters of Paris. Marino's presence in Rome created a sense of excitement that lasted for several months. The Oziosi Academy, the most important literary institution in Rome at the time, to which the pope himself belonged, held special festivities for Marino, who was also appointed honorary Prince of the Academy. Perhaps Maffeo Barberini, the poet, just could not stand that, and a few months after Marino's celebrations in Rome, his poem was included in the *Index*.

BIBLIOGRAPHICAL NOTE

The edition of *L'Adone* used is Giovanni Pozzi's, along with his volume of commentary (2 vols. Milano: Mondadori, 1976). I have dealt with the specific topic of this paper in other publications, in Italian, and I shall refer to them for a detailed analysis of the Christological terminology, imagery and symbols used by Marino. The issue was first discussed in my *La meravigliosa retorica dell'Adone di Giovan Battista Marino* (Firenze: Olschki, 1989, pp. 45-58). I then studied all the implications of Adonis' death and resurrection with a close re-reading of canto 18 and canto 20: "Canto 18: LA MORTE. I trastulli del cinghiale," and "Canto 20: GLI SPETTACOLI. Il gran teatro del mondo, ovvero il mondo a teatro," both in *Lectura Marini: L'Adone letto e commentato* (ed. Francesco

Guardiani. Ottawa: Dovehouse, 1989, pp 301-316 and pp. 325-347 respectively). Every passage of *L'Adone* described in this paper was considered critically by Giovanni Pozzi in his commentary (attached to the cited edition) as well as by Tommaso Stigliani in his *L'Occhiale* (Roma: Carampello, 1627). For other Baroque aspects of Marino see *The Sense of Marino: Literature, Fine Arts and Music of the Italian Baroque* (ed. Francesco Guardiani. Ottawa: Legas, 1994). The most comprehensive bibliography of Marino's editions since the seventeenth century is now available thanks to Francesco Giambonini, *Bibliografia delle opere a stampa di Giambattista Marino*. Firenze: Olschki, 2000. In terms of Marino criticism, the most reliable and complete bibliography remains the one compiled by Giorgio Fulco in his "Giovan Battista Marino," in *Storia della letteratura italiana*, vol. 5, *La fine del Cinquecento e il Seicento*. Roma, Salerno Editrice, 1977.

GIULIO SILANO

POPES AND LAWYERS ON THE PAPAL CANONIZATION OF SAINTS AND ITS REASONS

To Gianmarco
For his consolation

ABSTRACT. John Paul II has beatified and canonized an unusually large number of people – indeed, more than all his predecessors combined since the late Middle Ages. What reasons does he give for this? How do these reasons compare to those of his predecessors most responsible for the framing of the classic canonization process? This paper will examine the rationale proposed by Alexander III for asserting the necessity of papal involvement in the canonization of saints, the glosses which Innocent IV and Hostiensis produced on those reasons, and John Paul II's own view of the role and reasons of canonization in our times.

In 1171 or 1172, Pope Alexander III wrote a long letter to King Kol and to the bishops and people of Sweden. The letter opens with the assertion that an eternal and unchanging divine provision has made the most holy Roman Church the head, mother, and teacher of all the Churches and of all the faithful. Christ, by his commission to Peter, built the Church of Rome on the rock of the Catholic and Christian faith. All who are of Christ's sheepfold are to be subject to the authority and teaching of Peter and his successors. And so, whenever there is doubt about the articles of faith or ecclesiastical institutions, recourse is trustingly had to the said Roman Church, as to the mother and teacher of Christian faith, whose task it is to feed, instruct, and confirm peoples who are still tender in faith. In fulfillment of this task, Alexander, unworthy presider over the Roman Church, then proceeds to outline problematic areas of Christian observance among the Swedes.[1]

---

[1] Alexander's letter is here cited from *Patrologia latina* 200, cc. 1259-61, although in that edition it is mistakenly reported as being addressed to King Knut. Its opening sections, at c. 1259, read as follows: "Alexander episcopus, servus servorum Dei, charissimo in Christo filio K[anuto] illustri Suevorum et Gothorum regi, et venerabilibus fratribus episcopis et dilectis filiis, nobili viro duci et universo clero et populo per Gothiam con-

For one thing, they appear not to appreciate the Church's teaching regarding marriage, nor the norms touching on the respect and financial support due to clergy and religious people. Most importantly for our purposes, Alexander then proceeds to report the horror with which he has heard that some Swedes, deceived by the devil's wiles, venerate as a saint a man who was killed while in a state of crapulous drunkenness. This horrid practice befits infidels, while the Church scarcely allows prayer to be offered even on behalf, let alone to, people who die in such circumstances. And so, if Swedes hanker for God's kingdom, they must themselves abstain from drunkenness, and certainly must cease to venerate the said man. For even if many signs and miracles should occur at his intercession, it would not be lawful for them to venerate him publically as a saint without the authority of the Roman Church.[2]

This case of the drunken Swedish saint was to have a long future. Excerpted from this letter, the description of the case was to be incorporated in canonical collections and, having found a definitive place in the

---

stitutis, salutem et apostolicam benedictionem. Aeterna et incommutabilis divini consilii providentia sacrosanctam Romanam Ecclesiam omnium ecclesiarum omniumque fidelium caput, matrem et magistram esse constituit et super catholicae et Christianae fidei petram protinus nascentis erexit, dicente Domino ad Petrum: *Tu es Petrus et super hanc petram aedificabo Ecclesiam meam, et portae inferi non praevalebunt adversus eam, et tibi dabo claves regni coelorum* (Mt. 16.18). Huic enim apostolorum principi in cujus cathedra, licet immeriti, praesidemus, omnes oves suas indistincte et principaliter Dei Filius pascendas commisit. Ut quicunque de ovili Christi sunt Petri magisterio et doctrinae subjaceant, pro cujus fide specialiter rogasse se perhibet, dicens: *Ego pro te rogavi, Petre, ut non deficiat fides tua; et tu aliquando conversus confirma fratres tuos* (Lc. 22.32). Unde quoties de articulis fidei vel institutionibus ecclesiasticis dubitatur, ad praedictam Romanam Ecclesiam tanquam ad matrem et magistram fidei Christianae confidenter recurritur, cujus est teneros in fide populos verbo Dei pascere, instruere et confirmare, *sine qua fide* videlicet, testante Apostolo, *impossibile est placere Deo* (Hebr. 11.6)."

[2]The drunken saint was King Eric, who had been murdered by his successor, to whom the letter was addressed, as was concluded by Sven Tunberg, "Erik den helige, Sveriges helgenkonung," pp. 257-78. For further discussion of this case, see Eric Waldram Kemp, *Canonization and Authority in the Western Church*, pp. 99-104, and André Vauchez, *La sainteté en Occident*, pp. 29-31. The section of the letter which is of most interest here is at c. 1261, and reads as follows: "Denique quiddam audivimus, quod magno nobis fuit horrori, quod quidam inter vos sunt qui diabolica fraude decepti, hominem quemdam in potatione et ebrietate occisum quasi sanctum, more infidelium, venerantur, cum vix etiam pro talibus in suis ebrietatibus interemptis orare permittat Ecclesia. Dicit enim Apostolus quoniam *ebriosi regnum Dei non possidebunt* (1 Cor. 6.10). Unde a potationibus et ebrietatibus, si regnum Dei habere desideratis, vos continere oportet, et hominem illum de caetero colere in periculum animarum vestrarum nullatenus praesumatis. Cum etiamsi signa et miracula per eum plurima fierent, non liceret vobis pro sancto absque auctoritate Romanae Ecclesiae eum publice venerari."

Decretals of Gregory IX of 1234, it was to become the legal provision on which Catholic processes for the canonization of saints would be expressly based until 1917.[3]

It seems odd that, in 1234, this should have been thought to be the obvious text to excerpt for such a function. It is true that Alexander III is pivotal in the development of the pope's role as a canonizer of saints. He is the first pope to assume as a matter of course that he may canonize saints without a synod. He is also the one to establish a procedure of enquiry out of which the later and fuller process is to grow. And he is the first pope to assert that no public veneration may be extended to one regarded as a saint without the approval of the Roman Church.[4] And yet the compiler of the *Decretals* of 1234 had much richer and fuller texts he might have chosen.

Bulls of canonization published by Alexander himself might well seem to us as making better matter for reflection on the nature of canonization. In his declaration of the sanctity of Edward the Confessor, for example, Alexander has some nice words to say about how it is the Lord himself who, in his mercy, by miracles declares the saint to be such; the miracles serve as indication on earth that the saint, by his virtues, has deserved to be glorified by God in heaven.[5] And he speaks even more

---

[3] In the *Decretals*, the excerpt of Alexander's text, with very slight changes from the form in which we give it in the note above, under the title *Audivimus*, was placed in the title "On Relics and the Veneration of Saints," at 3.45.1; it is most usually cited in Friedberg's edition of the *Corpus Juris Canonici*, vol. 2, at 3.45.1. It might even be argued that it was not until 1983 that Alexander's text formally ceased to be the basis for the process of canonization, since, in annotating the Code of 1917, its chief compiler made clear that *Audivimus* was the first authority on which was based can. 1999 § 1 of the Code and its assertion of the exclusive papal jurisdiction over the causes of beatification and canonization: *Codex Iuris Canonici ... ab Eminentissimo Cardinali Gasparri auctus*, can. 1999 § 1 (p. 553); the importance of Alexander's provision was further pointed out by the fact that his pontificate was in effect taken in the 1917 Code to mark the beginning of legal memory with regard to the tolerated veneration of certain candidates for canonization: ibid., c. 2125 (p. 576). The stages by which *Audivimus* was received in the canonical tradition have been identified by S. Kuttner, "La réserve pontificale du droit de canonisation," pp. 196-99; Kuttner's findings are summarized by Kemp, *Canonization and Authority in the Western Church*, p. 102.

[4] For Alexander III's pivotal role in these developments, see Kemp, *Canonization and Authority in the Western Church*, especially pp. 82-92, 99-104. Fairly enough, Vauchez, *La sainteté en Occident*, p. 28, describes the process of canonization as having taken a juridical turn under Alexander.

[5] The bull of canonization of Edward the Confessor (+ 1066), of 7 February 1161, is in *Patrologia latina* 200, cc. 106-07. Similar words are used in Alexander's bull of canonization of Knut of Danemark (+ 1131), whom the pope canonized in 1169; for its text, see *Patrologia latina* 200, cc. 608-09.

wonderfully about the wonder generated by the miracles with which God has glorified the martyred Thomas Becket.[6] But even if canonists had concluded that Alexander's various bulls of canonization, for all their beauty, were too scant on the difficulties and specificities of the process, they might well have concluded that Innocent III, in bulls of canonization of the likes of Homobonus of Cremona and Empress Cunegunda, had set forth a much more mature and complete view regarding canonization of saints and the papal role in it.

Homobonus, a married merchant of Cremona, had died in 1197 in such reputation of holiness that the opportunity of canonizing him was immediately considered. Innocent III, with the openness to unusual models of Christian life and holiness that was to characterize his ready welcome of emerging religious movements such as the Franciscan and Dominican ones, proceeded to canonize Homobonus on 12 January 1199.[7]

The bull of canonization opens with the reflection that piety has the promise of both present and future life, and so the Lord glorifies his faithful ones in this life and crowns them in the next, in accordance with the prophetic promise: "I shall give you in praise, glory and honour among all the peoples (Soph. 3.10)," and with the promise which he himself makes: "Then the just ones shall shine forth as the sun in the kingdom of their Father (Mt. 13.43)."[8] By working his wonders in his

---

[6]The bull of canonization of Becket of 1173, or a bare three years after the archbishop's murder, is in *Patrologia latina* 200, cc. 901-02, and opens with these beautiful words: "Redolet Anglia fragrantia et virtute signorum quae per merita illius sancti et venerandi viri Thomae, quondam Cantuariensis archiepiscopi, omnipotens Deus operatur, et universa laetatur ubique fidelium Christiana religio, pro eo, quod ille, qui est mirabilis et gloriosus in sanctis, sanctum suum post mortem clarificavit, cujus vita laudabilis multa fulsit gloria meritorum, et tandem martyrio consummata est certaminis gloriosi. Quamvis autem de sanctitate ipsius dubitare non possit, qui ejus et laudabilem conversationem attendit, et gloriosam considerat passionem, voluit tamen Redemptor ac Salvator noster ejus sanctitatis insignia magnificis irradiare miraculis, ut qui pro Christo insuperabilis virtutis constantia necessitates et pericula pertulit, sui laboris et certaminis in aeterna beatitudine cognoscatur ab omnibus percepisse triumphum." For the exceptional importance and resonance of this canonization, see André Vauchez, *La sainteté en Occident*, p. 125 and n. 1.

[7]For a brief recounting of Innocent's canonization of Homobonus, see Kemp, *Canonization and Authority in the Western Church*, p. 105; Vauchez, *La sainteté en Occident*, pp. 42-44.

[8]For a critical edition of the bull of canonization of Homobonus, see O. Hageneder and A. Haidacher, *Das Register Innocenz' III*, vol. 1, pp. 761-64; I cite here from its more accessible edition in *Patrologia latina*, 214, cc. 483-85, where, at c. 483, we read: "Quia pietas promissionem habet vitae quae nunc est et futurae, justus et misericors Dominus fideles suos, quos praedestinavit ad vitam, frequenter in hac vita glorificat et semper in

saints, God gives a sign of charity, so that it may be renewed in others; by renewing signs and wonders in the memory of his saints, God allows the saints to be recognized by men so that the perversity of heretics may be confounded.[9] And although final perseverance is all that is required for holiness in the Church triumphant, yet the deeds of piety in this life and the power of miracles after death are required for one to be held to be a saint in the Church militant. Miracles alone are not sufficient, since Satan and his minions can also work them. It is only when miracles go with the proper virtues that one can discern the Lord at work in his saints.[10]

All these requirements appear to be met in Homobonus, according to the submissions of the bishop, many religious persons, and other honourable persons of the city and country of Cremona. They have told Innocent that Homobonus prayed day and night, except when he undertook to bring about peace in the city, or sought alms for the poor, or gave himself to other works of mercy. He cared for the poor both in his own house and elsewhere, and would bury them after their death; he held himself apart from the fellowship of worldly men, and he was a

---

futura coronat; quibus et per Prophetam promittit: *Dabo vos in laudem, gloriam et honorem in cunctis populis* (Soph. 3.10), et per se pollicetur: *Fulgebunt justi sicut sol in regno Patris eorum* (Mt. 13.43).''

[9]Ibid., c. 483: "Mirabilis enim in se ipso Dominus, mirabilis in sanctis, mirabilis in omnibus operibus suis, verum nobis exhibet suae virtutis indicium et frigescentem jam in pluribus charitatis igniculum, mirabilium suorum signis accendit, assumptis in gloriam suam qui certaverunt legitime in hoc mundo, ad memorias eorum innovat signa et mirabilia, juxta Prophetam, immutat; ut qui sanctus est apud ipsum sanctus etiam ab hominibus habeatur et in hoc praesertim haereticorum confundatur perversitas, cum ad catholicorum tumulos viderint prodigia pullulare."

[10]Ibid., cc. 483-84: "Licet autem, juxta testimonium Veritatis, sola finalis perseverantia exigatur ad sanctitatem animae in Ecclesia triumphanti, quoniam qui perseveraverit usque in finem, hic salvus erit; duo tamen, virtus videlicet morum et virtus signorum, opera scilicet pietatis in vita et miraculorum signa post mortem, ut quis reputetur sanctus in militanti Ecclesia requiruntur. Nam quia frequenter angelus Satanae se in lucis angelum transfigurat et quidam faciunt opera sua bona, ut videantur ab hominibus, quidam etiam coruscant miraculis, quorum tamen vita merito reprobatur (sicut de magis legitur Pharaonis), et etiam Antichristus, qui electos etiam, si fieri potest, inducet miraculis suis in errorem, ad id nec opera sufficiunt sola nec signa, sed cum illis praecedentibus ista succedunt, verum nobis praebent indicium sanctitatis; nec immerito nos ad ipsius venerationem inducunt quem Dominus suus ostendit miraculis venerandum. Haec autem duo ex verbis Evangelistae plenius colliguntur, ubi de apostolis loquens ait: *Illi autem profecti praedicabant ubique Domino cooperante et sermonem confirmante sequentibus signis* (Mc. 16.20); in eo namque quod ait *cooperante*, eos operatos esse demonstrans; et in eo quod sequitur sequentibus signis eos exponens imo Dominum in eis miraculis claruisse."

despiser of heretics. He died while hearing mass, and his death was followed by signs and wonders, which still continue.[11]

To remove all doubt that virtues had preceded the wonders, Innocent has investigated the matter, in particular by questioning a priest, who has come to him with the bishop's party and who had been Homobonus' confessor; this enquiry has confirmed the virtues, while the miracles are further attested by the sworn assertion of all the members of the Cremonese delegation. Since all that is required to support the petition for canonization has been proved, with the consent of his brethren, and after deliberating with several archbishops and bishops, trusting in divine mercy and the merits of the said saint, Innocent proceeds to inscribe him in the catalogue of saints and prescribes that, on the anniversary of his death, his feast be celebrated by all of Christ's faithful.[12]

Quite strikingly, of the five canonizations which Innocent III celebrated, two were of lay people; of these, Homobonus was the first, and Empress Cunegunda was the second.[13] Cunegunda was the wife of Em-

---

[11] Ibid., c. 484: "Idem etenim sanctus, tanquam lignum quod plantatum est secus decursus aquarum, quod fructum suum dat in tempore suo, prout eorumdem nobis assertio facta tam viva voce quam aliorum plurium honestorum litteris patefecit, adeo in lege Domini meditabatur die ac nocte, ut ei serviens in timore et secundum Prophetam media nocte surgens ad confitendum ei, matutinis semper laudibus interesset. Missae quoque officium et alias horas cum summa devotione frequentans, ita assiduis orationibus insistebat, ut in certis horis aut incessanter oraret aut horas ipsas aliquando praeveniret; nisi forte ipsum sollicitudo, quam super pace reformanda per civitatem tanquam pacificus vir gerebat, aut occasio eleemosynae pro pauperibus acquirendae, seu alia justa causa in aliis operibus misericordiae detineret. Qui nimirum ante crucem Dominicam ex assuetudine se prosternens, opus quodlibet faciendo, stando, sedendo, jacendo, ad orationem labia movere continuo videbatur. Inter alia vero pietatis opera quae tam circa pauperes, quos secum in domo propria tenebat, curabat et pariter procurabat, quam circa alios indigentes, quibus viventibus humanitatis officium, mortuis sepulturae beneficium consueverat devotus impendere, diligentius exercebat, ipse a saecularium hominum consortio segregatus, inter quos virebat quasi lilium inter spinas, haereticorum quorum pernicies partes illas infecit austerus exstitit aspernator. Deducto autem sic vitae sanctae curriculo, cum ad matitunale officium, prout dictum est, in festivitate sancti Brictii surrexisset, circa missae primordia idem se ante crucem Dominicam more solito in oratione prosternens, dum cantaretur hymnus angelicus, beato fine quievit."

[12] Ibid., cc. 484-85.

[13] Vauchez, *La sainteté en Occident*, pp. 295-300, offers a table of the canonical states of the saints canonized between 1198 and 1431; it makes clear how unusual this proportion was in comparison to earlier practice. In this, as in so much else, Innocent III appears to have been the setter of a trend, since the proportion of canonized lay people would continue to be relatively high throughout the thirteenth century, and even to grow in the fourteenth. But this may be somewhat misleading; unlike Homobonus, a number of the `lay' saints canonized by later popes, although they were canonically lay, in the sense that they were not clerics, monks, or nuns, yet had taken on a consecrated form of life. Such

peror Henry II, who had himself been canonized in 1152.[14] Although she had died in 1040, Cunegunda was still vividly remembered at Bamberg, where she had been a generous patroness and where she was buried. It is to the bishop and chapter of Bamberg that Innocent's bull of canonization is addressed.[15]

This bull opens with the evangelical assertion that none lights a lamp to put it under a bushel, and then quotes again the biblical verses which we saw in the earlier bull, together with the reflection on God's wonders in his saints, their use in the confounding of heresy and the confirmation of the Catholic faith.[16] Identical things, too, are said about the insufficiency of miracles for the establishment of holiness, since Satan's minions and Pharaoh's magicians were also able to do wonders; although many wonderful things have kept occurring at Cunegunda's tomb, these are not sufficient for her canonization without establishing her possession of virtues.[17] But virtues are found indeed to have existed

---

was the case, for example, with Catherine of Siena and Bridget of Sweden, whom Vauchez's table lists as lay women. Of course, this same argument militates against our presentation of Cunegunda as a lay woman, since she had spent her last years in a nunnery, but Innocent excuses our doing so since it is as a lay woman and empress that he presents her in his bull.

[14] Vauchez, *La sainteté en Occident*, p. 27.

[15] A critical edition of this bull is to be found in Jurgen Petersohn, "Die Litterae Papst Innocenz III zur Heiligsprechung der Kaiserin Kunigunde (1200)," pp. 1-25. Once more, I use its more accessible edition in *Patrologia latina*, 140, cc. 219-22.

[16] The opening of the bull, at c. 219, reads as follows: "Innocentius episcopus, servus servorum Dei, venerabili fratri Theumoni episcopo, et dilectis filiis capitulo Babenbergensi salutem et apostolicam benedictionem. Cum secundum evangelicam veritatem (Mt. 5.15) nemo accendat lucernam et ponat illam sub modio, sed super candelabrum, ut omnes qui in domo sunt videant; pium pariter et justum est, ut quos Deus merito sanctitatis coronat et honorat in coelis, nos venerationis officio laudemus et glorificemus in terris: cum ipse potius laudetur et glorificetur in illis, qui est laudabilis et gloriosus in sanctis. Pietas enim promissionem habet vitae quae nunc est, et futurae, dicente Domino per Prophetam: *Dabo vos cunctis populis in laudem, gloriam et honorem* (Dt. 26.19); et per se pollicente: *Fulgebunt justi sicut sol in regno Patris eorum* (Mt. 13.43). Nam ut suae virtutis potentiam mirabiliter manifestet, et nostrae salutis causam misericorditer operetur, fideles suos, quos semper coronat in coelo, frequenter etiam honorat in mundo, ad eorum memorias signa faciens et prodigia, per quae pravitas confundatur haeretica, et fides catholica confirmetur. Nos ergo, charissimi, quantas possumus, etsi non quantas debemus, omnipotenti Deo gratiarum referimus actiones, qui in diebus nostris, ad confirmationem fidei catholicae et confusionem haereticae pravitatis evidenter innovat signa, et miracula potenter immutat, faciens eos coruscare miraculis, qui fidem catholicam tam corde quam ore, necnon et opere tenuerint."

[17] Ibid., cc. 219-20: "Inter quos beatae memoriae Cunegundis, Romanorum imperatrix Augusta, quae degens olim in mundo magnis meritis praepollebat, nunc vivens in coelo multis coruscat miraculis, ut ejus sanctitas certis indiciis comprobetur. Licet enim ad hoc

in her, since she preserved her virginity even in marriage and was most charitable to Churches and to the poor. She and her husband had also tangibly expressed their devotion to the Holy See. Since all this has been established by an appropriate investigation,[18] the request has been made that Innocent, out of the fullness of the power which Jesus Christ granted to the most blessed Peter, should inscribe her name in the catalogue of saints, decreeing her memory to be celebrated by all the faithful. Indeed, such a sublime judgment pertains to him alone, who is the successor of Peter and the vicar of Jesus Christ.[19] Wishing to praise God in his saints, Innocent grants the request, inscribes her name in the catalogue of saints, and decrees that her memory is to be celebrated, appending to his letter the prayers to be used in her commemoration.[20] The prayer to be used at her mass is the following:

ut aliquis sanctus sit apud Deum in Ecclesia triumphante, sola sufficiat finalis perseverantia, testante Veritate, quae dicit: *Quoniam qui perseveraverit usque in finem hic salvus erit* (Mt. 10.22); et iterum: *Esto fidelis usque ad mortem, et dabo tibi coronam vitae* (Apoc. 2.10); ad hoc tamen ut ipse sanctus apud homines habeatur in Ecclesia militante, duo sunt necessaria, virtus morum, et virtus signorum, videlicet merita et miracula, ut et haec et illa sibi invicem contestentur. Non enim aut merita sine miraculis, aut miracula sine meritis plene sufficiunt ad perhibendum inter homines testimonium sanctitati: cum interdum angelus Satanae transfiguret se in angelum lucis, et quidam opera sua faciant ut ab hominibus videantur. Sed et magi Pharaonis olim signa fecerunt, et Antichristus tandem prodigia operabitur, ut, si fieri posset, in errores etiam inducantur electi. Verum cum et merita sana praecedunt, et clara succedunt miracula, certum praebent indicium sanctitatis, ut nos ad ipsius venerationem inducant quem Deus et meritis praecedentibus, et miraculis subsequentibus exhibet venerandum. Quae duo ex verbis evangelistae plenius colliguntur, qui de apostolis loquens aiebat: *Illi autem profecti praedicaverunt ubique, Domino cooperante, et sermonem confirmante, sequentibus signis* (Mc. 16.20)."

[18]To point out his awareness of the sublimity of this kind of judgment and of the necessity that the strictest means of proof be brought to bear, Innocent is careful to point out that he has received reports about all these facts under oath; he says, ibid., at c. 221: "cum hoc sublime judicium ad eum tantum pertineat qui est beati Petri successor et vicarius Jesu Christi. Nos itaque cognoscentes, quod hoc revera judicium sublimius est inter caetera judicia judicandum, in ipsius examinatione plenariam volumus habere cautelam. Et ideo praenominatos jurisjurandi religione constrinximus, ut puram nobis super hoc dicerent veritatem." On the importance of these procedural concerns of Innocent III in the definition of the canonization process, see Vauchez, *La sainteté en Occident*, pp. 44-47.

[19]Ibid., cc. 220-21.

[20]Ibid., c. 222, where the following clause is used to declare Cunegunda a saint: "Nos ergo de meritis et miraculis ejus multis et magnis non solum testimoniis, sed et testibus certiores effecti, cum secundum Prophetam laudandus sit Deus in sanctis suis; de fratrum nostrorum consilio, et pontificum multorum apud sedem apostolicam existentium, ipsam beatam virginem Cunegundem catalogo sanctorum ascripsimus, ejusque memoriam inter sanctos decrevimus celebrandam."

All-powerful and merciful God, who except no sex from your glory and exclude no state of life, we humbly beseech you that, as after the pinnacle of the earthly Empire you granted to your blessed virgin Cunegunda the throne of the heavenly kingdom, so you grant also to us, your servants, by her merits and prayers, the reward of eternal felicity. Through our Lord.[21]

Alexander and Innocent are among the highest exponents of the post-Gregorian view that the Papacy, with the whole Church, is called not simply to cultivate the memory of the early days of Christianity, but also to relive them in terms suitable to the times. In André Vauchez's words, they exercised an office which now aimed to realize *hic et nunc* an ideal Christianity.[22] The evidence of holiness in their own times was important to both of them as assurance that their efforts at the Christianization of society were blessed by God. But it was Innocent who most fully and clearly stated the reasons for this. As we have seen, Alexander, in the text that subsequent generations were to regard as the best expression of the law of canonization, had presented the papal role in this process as consisting primarily in checking the popular impulse to venerate unsuitable candidates. The exclusive papal right to include new saints in the Church's catalogue was presented primarily as a check against the exuberance of unformed Christians, who were too eager to find holiness where they ought not. Innocent III, on the other hand, sets forth a much more positive view of the matter. Saints are gifts given to God by the Church to provide patterns for the Christian life in its various states. It is a matter for wonder that God should so mercifully renew his wonders in the Church, to bolster faith and defeat heresy. It is true that people can be misled by signs and adjudge someone to be holy exclusively on that basis. The Church certainly is to beware of such a thing, and Innocent is a chief contributor to the development of procedural safeguards against such an occurrence. But fear of such occurrences is not what seems to motivate Innocent's intervention in the process of canonization; it is the teaching aspect of the process that seems to warrant the claim to a papal monopoly on the process. Furthermore, there is the desire to ensure that the glory of God manifest in

---

[21] Ibid., c. 222: "Omnipotens et misericors Deus, qui a gloria tua nullum excipis sexum, nullamque conditionem excludis, te suppliciter exoramus, ut sicut beatae Cunegundi virgini tuae, post terreni culmen imperii, coelestis regni solium contulisti, ita meritis ejus et precibus, nobis quoque famulis tuis aeternae felicitatis praemia largiaris. Per Dominum.

[22] Vauchez, *La sainteté en Occident*, p. 122.

his saints should be celebrated universally, which the pope alone may bring about.

Given the greater richness and clarity of Innocent III's canonization bulls, why did the canonical tradition prefer the brief and cantankerous statement by Alexander on the drunken saint as the better place for a discussion of canonization? Perhaps an answer to this question can only be attempted once we read what the principal commentators on Alexander's text have to say. There is no question that all subsequent exegesis on this text is dependent (usually verbatim) on the comments of two such commentators, namely Innocent IV and Hostiensis.

Innocent IV, whose reverence for Innocent III was attested by his choice of papal name, was to celebrate five canonizations of his own. Although the vicissitudes of his pontificate kept him busier than most popes, he also found time to continue his reflections on the *Decretals* of Gregory IX and published a very influential commentary on them.[23]

His commentary on the excerpt from Alexander's letter, after noting that all canonized saints are to be venerated, begins with a definition of canonization, which is said to consist in establishing "canonically and in accordance with rules that some is saint is to be honoured as a saint, that is, that a solemn office is to be celebrated for him as for other saints of the same condition - for a confessor the office of confessor, for a martyr the office of martyr, and so on for the various types."[24] Canonization is done in accordance with the rules when proofs establish the faith of the candidate, the excellence of his manner of life, and his miracles. The excellence of life and the miracles must be such that they exceed the forces and power of nature.[25]

By a gloss on Ecclesiasticus, 44.1, "Let us praise those glorious men, our ancestors, each in his generation; the Lord worked great glory in the world by his magnificence," Innocent expounds more fully the require-

---

[23]For brief introductions to the figure of Innocent IV and to his canonical achievements, see Elisabeth Vodola, "Innocent IV, pope," *Dictionary of the Middle Ages*, vol. 6, pp. 465-7; J.A. Cantini and Charles Lefebvre, "Sinibalde dei Fieschi," *Dictionnaire de droit canonique*, vol. 7, cc. 1029-62.

[24]Sinibaldus Fieschi (Innocent IV), *Commentaria Apparatus in V Libros Decretalium*, p. 457a: "Venerandi sunt omnes sancti canonizati. Canonizare est sanctos canonice et regulariter statuere quod aliquis sanctus honoretur pro sancto, puta solenne officium pro eo facere, sicut fit pro aliis sanctis qui sunt eiusdem conditionis, ut si canonizetur confessor, fiat pro eo officium confessorum, et si martyr fiat pro eo officium martyrum, et sic de aliis."

[25]Ibid.: "Et fit regulariter haec canonizatio quando per probationes constat de fide et excellentia vitae et miraculis eius qui petitur canonizari ... Et oportet tantam esse excellentiam vitae et talia esse miracula quae sint ultra vires et potentiam naturae."

ments he has just briefly set down. The verse is taken to refer to canonized saints because they alone are worthy of public praise in the Church. The mention of ancestors makes clear that only those of the faith are to be canonized. The mention of great glory makes clear that no ordinary glory is required for canonization, but that the whole life of the candidate is to be filled with glory. As for God's magnificence, it is the same as his great power, and so points to the necessity for an excellence of life and miracles which exceed natural forces and powers. Miracles without excellence of life are not sufficient because Pharaoh's magicians did many things which seemed to be above nature, and in the Gospel we read: "Did we not cast out demons in your name," etc. And yet the Lord will answer them: "I do not know you." And although one might canonize someone only on the basis of their life, yet the Church does not do so without the accompanying guarantee of signs and wonders, since such people might well lead a laxer life in private.[26]

According to Innocent, it pertains to the pope alone to canonize a saint because it is of the essence of the exercise that the saint be set before all the faithful for their veneration. But the pope alone can command such a thing universally, and so he alone can canonize. If each bishop were to do this, there would be division in the Church.[27]

---

[26] Ibid., 457a-b: "Item, non debet esse unica tantum excellentia vitae, imo oportet esse multas et continuas, ut habes in Eccles. c. 44, ubi dicitur: *Laudemus viros gloriosos et parentes nostros in generatione sua; multam gloriam fecit Dominus sua magnificentia in seculo.* Per hoc quod dicit, *Laudemus viros gloriosos,* ostendit quod canonizati erant, quia aliter non mandaretur ecclesiae quod eos laudaret. Per hoc quod dicit, *Parentes nostros,* ostendit quod nullus canonizandus est, nisi fidem habeat; soli enim parentes eius erant Iudaei, et penes quos solos erat fides canonizandi erant. Per hoc autem quod sequitur, *Multam gloriam fecit Dominus,* supple cum eis, apparet quod non sufficit quod in uno fuerit gloriosus, vel semel tantum, sed quod in multis et multoties, imo quod continue eius vita fuerit gloriosa. Per hoc quod dicit, *Sua magnificentia,* id est, sua magna potentia, ostendit quod excellentia vitae et miracula talia esse debent quae excedant vires et potentias naturales; non sufficiunt miracula sine vitae excellentia, cum magi Pharaonis multa fecerint quae supra naturam esse videntur, et in Evangelio legitur: *Quia multi dicturi sunt: Nonne in nomine tuo daemonia eiicimus,* etc., et tamen Dominus respondebt eis: *Non novi vos* (Mt. 7.22-23). Vitam tamen sine miraculis credere sufficeret quoad virtutem, tamen ecclesia non debet tales canonizare propter hoc, quia in secreto potuerunt laxiorem vitam ducere."

[27] Ibid. 457b: "Solus autem papa potest sanctos canonizare, quod ex eo apparet, quia cum costituatur omnibus fidelibus adorandum, et nullus omnibus praesit, nisi papa, apparet quod solus papa hoc potest, nec valet si dicas quod saltem cuique debet esse licitum quod in sua diocesi faciat, quia oratio eis facta debet esse communis, et ecclesia ubi debet venerari debet esse communis. Item, per hoc incideremus in illam reprehensionem qua quidam reprehensi sunt ab Apostolo, qui dicebant: *Ego sum Petri, ego Pauli.* Per hanc autem canonizationem consequitur quod ecclesia solenniter dicit officium pro eo sicut pro sancto, et in laetaniis in numero sanctorum licite enumeretur, unde in su-

– 207 –

From all this, Innocent also concludes that there ought to be no canonization of baptized infants, since great glory does not occur in such instances; the case of the Holy Innocents is a special one because they died in Christ's place.[28]

Innocent does grant that the Church's judgment in canonization may prove not to be the same as God's, and yet, if an error should occur (which is not to be believed), God would still accept prayers offered in good faith in the name of the presumed saint.[29] He concludes his commentary by not denying that anyone may lawfully pray to some deceased person, whom he believes to have been good, seeking that person's intercession before God; in such cases, God looks to the faith of the one who prays. But it is not lawful for solemn office or prayer to be offered in such cases.[30]

Henricus de Segusio, better known as Cardinal Hostiensis, was the most renowned and comprehensive commentator on the *Decretals* in the thirteenth century.[31] Raised to high honours by Innocent IV and properly admiring of his canonistic achievements, he would show great deference to Innocent's commentary on the same texts. But this does not mean that he had nothing to add to Innocent's glosses on Alexander's text.

Hostiensis produced two major commentaries on the *Decretals* of Gregory IX. The first of these is the more succinct and synthetic *Summa aurea*, which he completed while still archbishop of Embrun and whose very title (not given to it by its author) shows in what regard it came to be held by subsequent generations of canonists.

In the *Summa*, Hostiensis takes seriously the rubric of the title of the *Decretals* which concerns us, "On Relics and the Veneration of Saints." The title is composed of two chapters, of which Alexander's text is the first, and a decree of Innocent III's Council Lateran IV is the second.

---

pradicto capitulo Ecclesiastici legitur: *Sapientiam sanctorum narrent populi, et laudem eorum annunciet ecclesia.*"

[28]Ibid., 457b-458a: "Ex praedictis apparet quod pueri baptizati et incontinenti mortui non sunt canonizandi, quia nec multam gloriam fecit cum eis Dominus sua magnificentia; speciale tamen est in innocentibus, qui vice Christi mortui sunt."

[29]Ibid., 458a: "Item, dicimus quod etiam si ecclesia erraret, quod non est credendum, tamen preces per talem bona fide porrectas Deus acceptaret ..."

[30]Ibid., 458a: "Item, non negamus quin cuilibet liceat alicui defuncto quem credebat bonum virum porrigere preces ut pro eo intercedat ad Deum, quia Deus fidem eorum attendit; non tamen pro eis licet facere officium solenne, vel preces solennes."

[31]For brief introductions to Hostiensis, see Elisabeth Vodola, "Hostiensis," *Dictionary of the Middle Ages*, vol. 6, pp. 298-99; Charles Lefebvre, "Hostiensis," *Dictionnaire de droit canonique*, vol. 5, pp. 1211-27.

The latter provision notes that the sale of relics or their exposition (for gain?) frequently cause detraction to the Christian religion, and so it forbids that ancient relics be exposed outside their containers, or that they be sold. As to ancient relics newly discovered, it is forbidden that they be venerated without the approbation of the Roman pontiff. And prelates are not to allow people who come to their churches for the sake of veneration to be deceived by various fictions or false documents, as has commonly happened in a number of places for the sake of gain.[32] Hostiensis in the *Summa* begins his commentary on the title by first rehearsing the contents of the second chapter in its prohibition of the sale of relics and of their public veneration without the permission of the Roman Church.[33] It is this prerogative of the Roman Church regarding the veneration of relics which introduces the exclusive papal right to canonize, grounded in the fact that the pope is the best safeguard against someone being venerated only because of miracles.[34] It follows that diligent investigation is to be made of a candidate's life, conversation, and miracles, and the results are to be forwarded to the pope in order that he may approve or disapprove.[35]

With his distinguishing concern for being of use to practitioners, Hostiensis then pays attention to the enquiry process, providing a check-list which prospective inquisitors may perhaps use in their work. The first necessity is to investigate the life, which will be, as it were, the first witness of the many labours borne by the candidate for the sake of Christ; then the focus will shift to the candidate's chaste manner and many labours, with special regard being had for simplicity and humility. It is also relevant to ask whether the candidate suffered persecutions, and whether he did so for the sake of charity rather than in pursuit of

---

[32]The text of the canon is usually cited from Friedberg's edition of the *Corpus Juris Canonici*, vol. 2, at 3.45.2.

[33]Hostiensis, *Summa aurea*, p. 1200a: "Quoniam consecratio altaris, de qua supra dictum est, sine reliquiis fieri non debet..., dicamus de reliquiis, etc. Et sciendum est quod reliquiae antiquae et approbatae non debent venales exponi, nec extra capsam trahi; novae vero sine licentia Romanae ecclesiae publice venerari non debent ..., quia res sacrae vendi non possunt ..." The copious references to places in the body of the law which bolster each assertion are here being omitted.

[34]Ibid.: "Sed nec transferenda sunt corpora sanctorum de loco ad locum sine licentia principis, id est, papae ...; ergo ad papam pertinet approbare sive reprobare, quia quem approbat approbatus est, et quem reprobat reprobatus est... Ideo dicit quod publice non veneretur aliquis tanquam sanctus quousque sit per papam approbatus quoniam et per malos aliquando fiunt miracula ..."

[35]Ibid.: "Ideo diligenter inquirendum est de vita et conversatione et miraculis, et omnia transmittenda domino papae, ut ipse approbet vel reprobet ..."

justice. Only after these various virtues are established should the investigation proceed to the miracles, both those performed in life and the posthumous ones. To be compelling, miracles are to proceed from God, and not from human art; they are to be against nature; they are to happen by merit of the person; they are to occur for the corroboration of faith. These strict requirements are to be applied in the case of confessors, that is, in the case of candidates for canonization who have not suffered martyrdom. In the case of martyrs, the investigation into the life is not required; it is sufficient to establish the miracles and the cause for which they suffered.[36] Consistently with the way in which he began his commentary on this title, Hostiensis concludes it by again quoting Lateran IV's mandate that those who, out of devotion, go to some church because miracles occur there are not to be deceived by false and fictitious documents, as sometimes has been done in the pursuit of gain.[37]

Hostiensis returned to this same title of the *Decretals* at much greater length in his monumental *Lectura* or *Commentaria*. As he often does in this great work, he structures his discussion of canonization around Innocent IV's commentary, incorporating Innocent's glosses verbatim into his own, but introducing emphases and topics of his own. His gloss on Alexander's text opens with Innocent's definition of canonization as the decreeing of the celebration of a solemn office in honour of someone, but this is now preceded by the assertion of the centrality of the papal role in the exercise in these terms:

---

[36] Ibid., 1200a-b: "Et nota quod ad canonizandos sanctos et in sanctorum catalogo ... conscribendos, et hoc modo pervenitur. Primo oportet inquiri de vita sua, ut ipsa prior testimonium fuerat pro laboribus multis nomine Christi toleratis, pro moribus castis, pro actibus strenuis ...; oportet enim praesenti testificatione praedicari et bonae famae praeconiis non taceri ...; maxime de simplicitate et humilitate quaeri debet ... Item, utrum in vita persecutiones passus fuerit ..., et de causa persecutionis, utrum scilicet quia volebat iusticiam exercere, vel propter charitatem ... Item, quaerendum est de miraculis et in vita et post mortem factis, in quo quatuor requiruntur: primum est quod a Deo, non ex arte, procedat ...; secundum, quod sit contra naturam ...; tertium est quod non est vi verborum, sed ex merito hominis hoc contingat; hoc ideo quia panis transubstantiatur in corpus miraculose ..., sed virtute verborum ...; quartum est quod sit ad corroborationem fidei, nam et herba transit in vitrum ministerio hominis, sed propter hoc fides non corroboratur ... Et hoc intellige de confessoribus; de martyribus autem non fit tanta examinatio, sed quaeritur tantum de miraculis et causa propter quam passi sunt ..."

[37] Ibid., 1200b: "Item, hi qui causa devotionis accedunt ad aliquam ecclesiam propter miracula quae ibi fiunt, non sunt falsis vel fictitiis documentis decipiendi, sicut occasione quaestus fieri consuevit ..."

> To canonize is for the pope, to whom alone this pertains, to inscribe some saint in the catalogue of the other saints, and to declare, define, and establish publically, solemnly, canonically, and in accordance with the rules that he is to be honoured as a saint by all, and that on a day certain each year a solemn office is to be celebrated for him as for other saints of the same condition; if he is canonized as a confessor, then the office of confessor is to be done for him, and if as a martyr, then that of a martyr, and so forth for each.[38]

This variation on Innocent's gloss is followed by an extended discussion of a topic which had been absent in that gloss, but which we have seen surfacing in the *Summa aurea*, namely a description of the process of canonization.

The first step in the process is to wait for some authoritative and honourable persons to bring the matter to the Roman pontiff and to make supplication for the canonization of the saint; this is to occur not once, but several times, since it is not Roman practice to proceed quickly on such a matter. Papal reluctance is to be moved by pressing requests, a continuation of the miracles, and the growing fame for holiness of the candidate before the pope even authorizes an investigation. This reluctance is a good thing, says Hostiensis, because miracles may sometimes be done even by wicked people, and it is important to make sure that the people is not deceived.[39]

If the petition for canonization is repeated with sufficient frequency and the miracles are also said to continue, then papal custom is to bring up the matter before the cardinals and some bishops of the region of the candidate for canonization; the pope may also commission a cursory investigation regarding the candidate's fame, the people's devotion, the miracles, and other matters. This report is to be in general terms only,

---

[38] Henricus de Segusio (Hostiensis), *In tertium decretalium librum commentaria*, 172a: "Venerandi sunt omnes sancti canonizati. Canonizare est aliquem sanctum per papam, ad quem solum hoc pertinet ..., cathalogo aliorum sanctorum ascribere, et publice ac solenniter, canonice ac regulariter declarare, diffinire ac statuere quod tanquam sanctus ab omnibus honoretur et quod pro ipso sicut pro aliis sanctis eiusdem conditionis certa die fiat solenne officium annuatim, ut si canonizetur tanquam confessor, fiat pro ipso officium confessorum, et si sicut martir tanquam martirum, et sic de singulis."

[39] Ibid.: "Ad hanc autem canonizationem hoc ordine pervenitur. Primo expectatur quod aliquae personae authenticae et honestae denuntient factum Romani pontifici et supplicent pro canonizatione sancti facienda, et hoc non tantum semel, sed pluries et instanter ...; non enim consuevit moveri statim ad committendum hanc inquisitionem Romanus pontifex, sed potius expectare quod diu pulsetur et famam attendere, et utrum miracula crebrescant et continuentur, antequam inquisitionem committat, et bene, quia et quandoque per malos miracula fiunt ... Unde cavendum est ne decipiatur populus ..., et quia circa maiora periculum vertitur, cautius agendum est ..."

without any findings of fact, and it is to limit itself to reporting on fame and the opportunity of commissioning a more specific enquiry.[40] If the need for such an enquiry of fact is demonstrated, then the pope will consult with the cardinals before proceeding to commission it. Such an enquiry is to investigate the fame, life, and miracles of the candidate, in accordance with the articles and interrogatories which will be transmitted to the inquisitors under a papal bull. They will return their report on these matters under their own seals; from this report, papal chaplains or other authoritative and discreet persons will collate the information under rubrics. These rubrics will be examined by pope and cardinals to ponder whether the case for canonization has been made out.[41] If the pope decides to proceed with canonization, he will first inform the cardinals of this; then, gathering together all the bishops who may be at the Curia, he will put the case also before them and seek their advice. If their advice does not change his decision, he will summon all to meet in a specific church on a specific date. The church will be decorated with carpets and many candles will be lit in it; then pope, cardinals, and the whole clergy and people will assemble in it. The pope will preach a sermon setting out what has been proven, and he will ask the people to pray to God that he not allow the pope to err in this matter. All will kneel, and the hymn, *Veni, sancte Spiritus,* will be sung. The pope will then arise and decree that the candidate is indeed a saint, to be inscribed in the catalogue of saints, and that his feast is to be celebrated on such

---

[40]Ibid., 172b-173a: "Secundo, si continuetur supplicationis instantia et miraculorum continuatio perdurare dicatur, consuevit hoc Romanus pontifex ponere inter fratres et aliquibus episcopis patriae vel conviciniae illius, qui dicitur sanctus, vel aliis personis honestis, discretis et incorruptibilibus committere, ut inquirant de fama et devotione populi, de miraculis et aliis, quae eidem sunt nuncianda in genere, non in specie, et quo ad famam, non quo ad veritatem, et quod sibi rescribant quae invenerint, et an eis videatur quod super veritate eorundem et in specie sit inquisitio committenda."

[41]Ibid., 173a: "tertio, si rescribant talia per quae videatur quod inquisitio veritatis committi debeat, requirit iterum summus pontifex fratrum consilia, et diffinit utrum haec inquisitio sit committenda vel non. Quarto, si inquisitio sibi committenda videatur, iterum scribit eisdem vel aliis quod veritatem inquirant, primo de fama, secundo de vita, tertio de miraculis exacte, diligenter, fideliter et prudenter, secundum articulos et interrogatoria quae sub bulla sua transmittit ..., et quod invenerint sub sigillis suis inclusum remittant. Quinto, remissa inquisitione committitur examinatio in curia aliquibus capellanis vel personis authenticis et discretis, quae et formant rubricas. Sexto, rubricae sic factae examinantur cum exacta diligentia per dominum papam et fratres, et requirit papa consilia eorundem, an videantur probata talia per quae sit canonizatio non immerito facienda."

and such a day. Then the *Te Deum* is sung and the pope proceeds to celebrate mass in honour of the same saint.[42]

Hostiensis observes that this process is not always followed in every detail; particularly in the case of martyrs of the faith, it has been customary to proceed more easily.[43] He then proceeds to quote verbatim Innocent IV's text, including the gloss on Ecclesiasticus, only adding here and there fuller scriptural quotations.[44] But, on the subject of whether bishops may canonize, at least in their own diocese, while agreeing with Innocent's view that they may not, he does address the objection raised by the evidence of their having done so in the past. He explains that bishops may indeed authorize devotion to specific saints in their own dioceses, if the saints in question are such as were anciently approved and whose feasts have not yet been commanded to be celebrated everywhere. In ancient times, when saints were rare, the modern solemnity was not preserved; the modern observance is otherwise and, when someone is found to be a saint, it is proper that his feast be celebrated everywhere.[45]

---

[42]Ibid.: "Septimo, si videatur domino papae quod facienda sit, diffinit hoc secreto primitus inter fratres. Octavo, coadunatis episcopis qui sunt praesentes in curia, narrat publice in consistorio ea quae acta sunt et probata, secreta diffinitione iam facta suppressa, et requirit consilia praelatorum. Nona, assignatur certa dies ut omnes conveniant ad aliquam certam ecclesiam die certa, in qua illuminantur cerei multi, et sternitur tapetis ecclesia et paratur, et conveniunt papa et fratres et totus clerus et populus, et facit sermonem summus pontifex processum recitans et probata, inducens populum ad orandum quod Deus non permittat ipsum errare in hoc negotio. Decimo, flexis genibus, fit devota oratio et cantatur *Veni sancte Spiritus*, vel alius hymnus sive antiphona conveniens. Undecimo, surgit papa ab oratione et diffinit illum, de quo agitur, sanctum esse et sanctorum cathalogo ascribendum, et tanquam sanctum esse venerandum, et festum suum colendum tali die. Duodecimo, cantatur *Te Deum laudamus*, et celebrat missam idem papa in honorem eiusdem sancti."

[43]Ibid., 172a: "Hic autem ordo non semper ad unguem hactenus est servatus, et maxime quando agebatur de martirizatis pro fide; illi enim consueverunt facilius et levius expediri."

[44]Ibid.; the extended citation of Innocent's gloss is preceded by the wonderfully expressive phrase: "Hoc autem secundum dominum nostrum est notandum."

[45]Ibid.: "Ex hoc sequitur quod solus papa hanc venerationem universalem omnibus fidelibus indicere potest; nam et cuicunque alii possent responderi non subditi extra territorium etc. ... Nec valet si dicas quod cuique episcopo debet licere ut saltem in sua diocesi hoc facere possit, sicut hoc videtur expressum supra ..., quia illud debet intelligi de antiquitus approbatis; etenim non omnium sanctorum et singulorum festa coluntur ubique, imo aliquod festum in una diocesi colitur et non in alia. Debet et illud intelligi de illis de quibus non mandavit papa quod ubique colerentur festa eorum, quia et antiquitus haec non servabatur solennitas, quando rari erant sancti. Hodie vero aliter observatur, et mandatur ubi coli debeat festum canonizati ..., quia ex quo sanctus est non solum ab

And yet, by the tolerance of the Roman Church, Charlemagne is venerated as a saint only in his chaper at Aachen, but not elsewhere. And indeed, there are many saints, even among those canonized by the Apostolic See, who are venerated only in one diocese or province; this would seem to support the view that bishops also may canonize.[46] But Hostiensis is not convinced and lists many reasons why canonization pertains to the pope alone. First, it is one of the greater causes, and so ought to be reserved to the pope. Second, since miracles are attributed primarily to faith, it seems almost that what is involved is a question of faith, whose definition pertains to the pope alone. Third, it pertains to the pope to resolve scriptural doubts; *a fortiori* does it pertain to him to resolve doubts as to holiness, since danger is involved in the definition of such great matters. Fourth, he ought to do it lest it happen that the people be deceived by the simplicity of bishops. Fifth, it is better done by the pope lest there be an infinite multiplicity of saints, which would make for the cooling of charity and devotion and for a loss of regard for sanctity.[47] After adding these embellishments and refinements of his own, Hostiensis returns to quoting Innocent IV's text with regard to the Holy Innocents, the lawfulness of anyone seeking the intercession of any deceased whom he regards to be holy, and the possibility of the pope erring in the declaration of sanctity, which he also accepts.

It may be of some interest to note that the issue of deception, which is mentioned only in passing in the comments on Alexander's text, as we would expect, looms much larger in Hostiensis' commentary on the second chapter of the same title of the *Decretals*. The commentary is a short, but trenchant, treatise on the abuses which accompany the ven-

---

aliquibus, sed ab omnibus, non solum in una ecclesia, sed in omnibus est communiter venerandum."

[46]Ibid.: "Ex tolerantia tamen Romanae ecclesiae magnificus Carolus tanquam sanctus in sola capella sua Aquisgrani, et non in aliis ecclesiis, veneratur. Sed et multi alii sunt etiam per sedem apostolicam canonizati qui in una tantum ecclesia sive provincia coluntur, et in aliis nec laudantur, sed nec sequitur: sanctus est, ergo ubique venerandus est tanquam sanctus, ergo quilibet episcopus potest canonizare ..."

[47]Ibid.: "Dicas igitur quod multiplex ratio reddi potest quare canonizatio sanctorum ad solum papam spectat. Prima est quia haec est una de maioribus causis quae inter Christianos proponi possit; maiores autem causae sunt ad sedem apostolicam referendae ...; secunda est quia, cum praecipue fidei attribuantur miracula..., haec quaestio quasi de fide videtur, cuius diffinitio spectat ad papam solum ...; tertia quia ad papam spectat declarare dubium scripturarum ..., multofortius ergo dubium sanctitatis, quia circa maiora periculum vertitur ...; quarta, ne contingat populum decipi per multorum episcoporum simplicitatem ...; quinta, ne contingat in infinitum sanctos multiplicari, et per consequens charitate et devotione refrigescere et vilescere sanctitatem ..."

eration of relics. He is sceptical of the frequent practice of discovering new relics of old saints; he thinks this matter is better passed over in silence. But he notes that the rules regarding relics are often not kept because clerical avarice and carelessness violate all sorts of statutes. And so it happens that the worst alms-seekers are not above representing the rib of some sinful man, or even of a donkey, as being that of a saint, and others place oil in little statues of the Virgin so that she may seem to cry. The same people often preach errors and assert the truth of many fables, which are all in need of being corrected.[48]

We began with the question: why did the canonical tradition prefer Alexander's pronouncement on the drunken Swedish saint to any others, even apparently richer ones, as the locus for its discussion of the law of canonization? We can see that the answer is somewhat complicated. A short form of the answer is that the tradition did no such thing. It is a basic attitude of the medieval schools that only fools read texts without their glosses. Avoiding foolishness, we have gone to the leading glossators of Alexander's text, and we notice there that Innocent III's views, apart from the concern with the confuting of heresy, find their place in the glosses which commentators like Innocent IV and Hostiensis append to Alexander's text. The crucial balancing of life and miracles, the references to Satan's wiles and Pharaoh's magicians, the linking of canonization to papal primacy, all find their place in these glosses.

But this is only the short answer. The longer answer must begin with the acknowledgement that, indeed, these commentators too are more at ease with Alexander's laconic censorship of popular excesses than with Innocent III's more expansive search for holiness. In part, no doubt, this is because Alexander's view is more easily reducible to juridical norms and practices, and better fits the sense that law is best suited to curb vice than to enforce virtue. So both Innocent IV and Hostiensis

---

[48]Ibid., 173: "Si enim [reliquiae] venderentur, cito dicerent laici: Isti clerici decipiunt nos; ut enim extorqueant a nobis denarios faciunt sibi sanctos. Nam laici nobis opido sunt infesti ..., immo debet clericus prae caeteris avaritiam evitare ... Hoc tamen et quod praemisit de ostensione extra capsam minus bene servatur; omnia enim statuta frangit avaritia et insolertia clericorum, et ideo esset corrigendum, sed multi praelati, qui hoc ignorant, vel etiam si istud sciant, tamen vecordes vel negligentes sunt, hoc corrigere non audent vel non curant, et tamen sunt ex hoc onerati, ut sequitur. ... *Variis figmentis*. Sicut faciunt pessimi quaestuarii, qui ostendunt quandoque costam hominis peccatoris, vel asini loco sancti, quia non curant, nisi ut denarios habeant; alii ponunt oleum in oculo mariolae suae, ut videatur flere, et sic imago, quae facta erat ad imaginem Dominae nostrae, vertitur in ipsius contumeliam et derisum. *Documentis*. Quia in praedicationibus suis quandoque seminant errores, et multas fabulas asserunt veras esse, quae sunt omnino corrigenda..."

tend to view the legal process of canonization as pertaining to the discipline more than to the teaching function of the Church. It seems emblematic of this approach that Innocent IV and Hostiensis agree that the judgment of the pope in a cause of canonization is not infallible.[49] For them, the exclusive papal right to canonization is an exercise in sovereignty, and not in infallibility.

Perhaps this last point is one which bears lingering on, if our question is to find a more intriguing answer. The development of the papal role in the canonization of saints has usually been presented as a process of reservation on the part of the popes of rights and functions which used to be exercised by bishops.[50] This is a view which a more attentive reading of the texts which we have presented earlier ought to render untenable. Kemp's classic work used the very glosses which we have expounded at length as evidence of the supposed process of reservation.[51] And yet those glosses never approach the process by which popes come to canonize as one of reservation of formerly episcopal powers. Instead, they present it as an exercise of papal sovereignty over the Church.

It appears to have escaped commentators on the views of Innocent IV and Hostiensis regarding canonization that these great canonists, by casting the issue in these terms, regard the process in a way which is wholly new because it exploits a new possibility. The very fact that these eminent commentators present the existence of a *universal* calendar of saints as an obvious fact has distracted scholars from considering the extent to which such a thing is an absolutely unprecedented novelty.[52]

---

[49] That papal canonization of saints may be an exercise of infallibility appears to have been the conclusion of theologians, beginning with Thomas Aquinas; see Kemp, *Canonization and Authority in the Western Church*, pp. 151-55.

[50] This is the view underlying the fundamental work by Kemp, *Canonization and Authority in the Western Church*, and it is most explicitly presented on pp. 101-104, in which he engages in argument with Stephan Kuttner, "La réserve pontificale du droit de canonisation." The very title of Kuttner's important article makes clear the extent to which he accepts this manner of presenting the problem, arguing only that the reservation of the formerly episcopal right to canonize is later than Alexander's letter to Sweden and is primarily the achievement of the lawyers in the Schools.

[51] Kemp, *Canonization and Authority in the Western Church*, pp. 107-110, where he sets out the views of Innocent IV and Hostiensis, confirming that all subsequent discussion of papal canonization is grounded in their glosses.

[52] Kemp, *Canonization and Authority in the Western Church*, p. 116, declares it to be "usual among modern writers to say that individual bishops never could canonize because their jurisdiction was limited to their own diocese and therefore they could not authorize the veneration of anybody by the whole Church. The most any bishop could ever do was to beatify. It must be pointed out that this terminology is comparatively modern and is liable to cause confusion when applied to the period we are discussing." Because he is

At no time before the twelfth century would it have been regarded as possible, or perhaps even desirable, to have such a thing. It arises as a possibility exactly because of the juridical reflection on the nature of papal authority and the conclusion that the pope has a fullness of power over the whole Church. It is merely a corollary for the lawyers to conclude that one of the things which this full power can bring about is the elaboration of a universal calendar of saints.

If the universality of the obligation to venerate them is the pivotal effect of papal canonization of saints, then it seems indeed hard to argue that popes are engaged in a process of reservation of pre-existing rights. No one before the twelfth century – not even popes – had laid claim to the power to compel all members of the Church to venerate anyone as a saint. Certainly, no bishop or group of bishops had ever been in the position of proposing, let alone bringing about, such a thing. Perhaps that is why there is no record of any bishop protesting this supposed process of diminishment of episcopal rights. Indeed, the opposite is true. All the canonizations which we have specifically discussed earlier have bishops as petitioners. They appear to have appreciated that success before the papal court would produce a result which they were in no position to bring about: the setting of one of their own before the universal Church as worthy of imitation by all Christians. Presumably, it helped that, as we have seen in Hostiensis' description of the process, this glorious result could be achieved with the participation of local bishops at various stages of the proceedings.

It is true that the establishment of a universal calendar of saints, binding on all Christians, bears the consequence of a certain loss of importance of those holy persons whose veneration was only local. It is also true that, as we have seen, these same canonists reach the conclusion that bishops ought in future to present no competitors to the papally approved saints, at least in the sense that the celebration of such competitors ought not to be as solemn and binding as that of the saints inscribed in the universal calendar.[53] A crowding of the calendar would diminish the effect of the papal presentation of models of holiness

---

profoundly wedded to the view of reservation, Kemp appears unable to consider to what extent the lawyers had indeed been moved by the centrality of the authorization of universal veneration to the papal canonization process, and to what point this authorization is wholly new.

[53] The extent to which bishops remained free to decree local veneration of saints is disputed; see Kemp, *Canonization and Authority in the Western Church*, p. 137.

which were thought particularly relevant to the realization of Christian ideals *hic et nunc*.

The danger of (over)crowding might also have arisen if the papal process had been too generous and easy. The number of slots in the calendar that can be dedicated to the obligatory veneration of saints is necessarily limited. In any case, as Hostiensis told us, an excessive multiplication of models would not be suitable, since it would be more likely to produce a cooling of zeal rather than its increase. Hence the glee and the fullness with which Hostiensis describes the many hurdles which must be overcome in a papal process of canonization. The increasing complexity of the process constitutes both the necessary bar to make the successful cases all the more noteworthy, and the necessary guarantee that, for all the acknowledged, if implausible, fallibility of the process, one who is now bound to do so is indeed praying to a saint. It helps that, at the same time, the stringencies of the process can be presented as fences to protect the laity against the greed and lack of scruples of some clerics.

If these arguments have the validity which they claim, we should probably not rush too quickly to ascribe the restrictive nature of the canonization process to the crabbiness of jurists. It is true that Innocent IV and Hostiensis, and much of the Church with them, end up preferring Alexander's censorious approach. If a professed concern about popular tendecies to superstition has long been a strong weapon in the clerical armoury in the unending war which clerics and lay people perennially wage against each other, we see here also a concern to protect the laity. But the triumph of these views would entail the consequence that Innocent III's apparent readiness to search for holiness far and wide was not to become the norm.

André Vauchez is probably the foremost student of canonizations. In his magisterial study of the subject, he has concluded that the generous papal attempt to discern varied models of Christian holiness, which may be said to begin with Innocent III, is over by the 1260s. From then on, very few causes of canonization make it past the curial gauntlet, and most of the few candidates who pass in the fourteenth century are proposed by the Mendicant Orders and the French royal house.[54] The papacy of Innocent III and those of his immediate successors proved an interlude during which it seemed possible for popular and learned aspirations to holiness to find common ground in the papal authentication

---

[54] Vauchez, *La sainteté en Occident*, pp. 479-89.

of varied and numerous models of sanctity. The interlude proved brief and a gulf began to grow between popular veneration toward many, many saints, who were not recognized as such by a papal process of canonization, and an elite mistrustful, if not sneering, of this popular devotion. The case of Joan of Arc stands out as only the most notable late medieval example of the gulf. And the tendency to mistrust popular devotion was only to grow larger in the course of the modern era. But then came John Paul II.

At last count, John Paul II had come close to canonizing and beatifying more people than all his predecessors combined. This phenomenal pace gives no sign of easing up; by now, more than 1,000 people have been declared saints or blessed by this pope. Why is he doing this? Should we be surprised by this?[55]

In one sense, John Paul's commitment to look for holiness wherever it may be found does seem surprising. It seems to stand in contrast, for example, to Paul VI's pruning of the calendar of a number of widely popular saints.[56] It also stands in contrast to fashions in theological circles, where one has great difficulty finding any interest in saints. And yet it would be hard to say that John Paul did not inform everyone, from the very beginning of his pontificate, that he regarded saints as too important to be neglected.

Like other popes, John Paul, early in his rule, published a programmatic encyclical, *Redemptor hominis*, which informed everyone of what he regarded as important. In a section of that encyclical reflecting on the Church's core responsibility of safeguarding divine truth, he noted that "being responsible for that truth also means loving it and seeking the most exact understanding of it, in order to bring it closer to ourselves and others in all its saving power, its splendor and its profudity joined with simplicity."[57] He then added:

---

[55] For other assessments of John Paul II's approaches to canonization, see George Weigel, *Witness to Hope. The Biography of Pope John Paul II*, pp. 446-49 and passim; Yves Chiron, *Enquête sur les canonisations*, pp. 303-07 and passim.

[56] It might well be argued that Paul VI's reforms in regard to the veneration of saints constitute the logical conclusion of the attitudes and procedures which we have seen the popes and lawyers of the Middle Ages developing. The fear of people being mislead by fraudulent stories now extends to an unwillingness to require people to venerate saints whose holiness (or even very existence) cannot be established by the canons of contemporary historical scholarship. On Paul VI's harsh pruning of the calendar of saints and first simplification of the canonical process of canonizatio, see Chiron, *Enquête sur les canonisations*, pp. 76-77 and the works there cited.

[57] John Paul II, *Redemptor hominis*, c. 19.

> This love and this aspiration to understand the truth must go hand in hand, as is confirmed by the histories of the saints in the Church. These received most brightly the authentic light that illuminates divine truth and brings close God's very reality, because they approached this truth with veneration and love - love in the first place for Christ, the living Word of divine truth, and then love for His human expression in the Gospel, tradition and theology. Today we still need above all that understanding and interpretation of God's Word; we need that theology.[58]

Here is one reason, then, for papal canonizations in our time: it serves to identify for the believing community the best and surest theologians, the most effective exemplars of how to overcome the division between heart and mind that seems to afflict so many in the Church. He does not quite say, with Innocent III, that we need saints to defeat heresy, but the brunt of the argument is not distant from Innocent's. It is indeed more sublime to say that we need saints in order to proceed toward wholeness and holiness.

This exemplarity of the new saints is acknowledged even more explicitly in John Paul's encyclical of 1994, announcing preparations for the celebration of the beginning of the new millenium. There he says:

> In recent years the number of canonizations and beatifications has increased. These show the vitality of the local churches, which are much more numerous today than in the first centuries and in the first millennium. The greatest homage which all the churches can give to Christ on the threshold of the third millennium will be to manifest the redeemer's all-powerful presence through the fruits of faith, hope and charity present in men and women of many different tongues and races who have followed Christ in the various forms of the Christian vocation.[59]

But at bottom, the main reason that seems to drive this pope's generous use of the power to canonize is the conviction that holiness is much more common than many seemed to think, and that it is a necessity to recognize this, if there is to be a proper appreciation of the universal call to holiness. The preservation and growth of the holiness conferred in baptism might be said to be the reason for the existence of the Church; the joyful proclamation of the fact that the Church succeeds in this seems to John Paul a crucial element in the New Evangelization to which he has ceaselessly called the Church.

In 1983, John Paul published an Apostolic Constitution by which he reformed the process of canonization.[60] The text opens with sentiments

---

[58]John Paul II, ibid.

[59]John Paul II, *Tertio Millennio Adveniente*, c. 37.

[60]The Constitution, *Divinus perfectionis Magister*, is discussed by Kenneth L. Woodward, *Making Saints. How the Catholic Church Determines Who Becomes a Saint, Who Doesn't, and*

which are entirely redolent of those we have seen in the bulls of canonization issued by medieval popes, and by Innocent III in particular. It states:

> The divine Master and model of perfection, Christ Jesus, with the Father and the Holy Spirit, 'who alone is holy', loved the Church as a bride and gave himself for her, in order to sanctify her and render her glorious in his own eyes. And so, having given the precept to all his disciples to imitate the Father's perfection, he sent the Spirit over all of them in order to move them interiorly, so that that they may love God with their whole heart and also love each other reciprocally, in the same way in which he loved them. The followers of Christ - as the Vatican Council II exhorts them -, called and justified in Christ Jesus, not according to their works but according to his design and grace, in the Baptism of faith have truly been made children of God and sharers in the divine nature, and so truly saints.[61]

In baptism, then, all Christians are made holy. But from among them, "God in every age chooses a great number who, following more closely the example of Christ, offer a glorious witness of the Kingdom of Heaven by the spilling of their blood or by the heroic practice of the virtues."[62] After recounting briefly the development of the veneration of saints in the history of the Church, he explains that "consideration of the lives of the saints incites to seek the City that is to come and teaches a most perfect way by which, in the vicissitudes of the world, we can arrive at perfect union with Christ, or holiness, in accordance with the state and condition proper to each."[63]

Even more recently, in his *Crossing the Threshold of Hope*, John Paul returned to the question of the role of the saints under the surprising guise of answering the question: Where does the true power of the Church lie? He answered:

> Naturally, over the centuries in the West and the East the power of the Church has lain in the witness of the saints, of those who made Christ's truth their own truth, who followed the way that is Christ Himself and who lives the life that flows in Him in the Holy Spirit. And in the Eastern and Western Churches these saints have never been lacking."[64]

Why, pp. 90-99; but it might well be argued that the shift from the earlier process of canonization to that set out in the new Constitution is the subject of Woodward's whole book.

[61] John Paul II, *Divinus Perfectionis Magister*, I translate the above from the Italian. I have not seen Robert J. Sarno, tr., *New Laws for the Causes of the Saints*, nor Fabijan Veraja, *Commentary on the New Legislation for the Causes of Saints*.

[62] John Paul II, ibid.

[63] John Paul II, ibid.

[64] John Paul II, *Crossing the Threshold of Hope*, ed. Vittorio Messori, p. 176

Noting that most the saints of our century have been martyrs to various totalitarianisms (Kolbe, Stein, etc.), he also states: "They have completed in their death as martyrs the redemptive sufferings of Christ and, at the same time, they have become *the foundation of a new world, a new Europe, a new civilization*."[65]

The absolute centrality of the pursuit of holiness to the Christian life is also the crucial theme of John Paul's most recent Apostolic Letter.[66] Here he engages in an extended meditation about how gazing upon the face of Christ is the essence of the Christian pursuit of holiness. In the course of this meditation, he states:

> Faced with this mystery, we are greatly helped not only by theological investigation, but also by that great heritage which is the "lived theology" of the saints. The saints offer us precious insights which enable us to understand more easily the intuition of faith, thanks to the special enlightenment which some of them have received from the Holy Spirit, or even through their personal experience of those terrible states of trial which the mystical tradition describes as the "dark night". Not infrequently the saints have undergone something akin to Jesus' experience on the Cross in the paradoxical blending of bliss and pain. ... What an illuminating testimony![67]

It seems justified to suggest once more, then, that, with John Paul II, we see the picking up of threads and attitudes that we began to note emerging in Innocent III. There is optimism here that holiness is common. It is common because it is required for the fulfillment of the mission of the Church. It is required because it is by looking at saints that one learns the features of the Christianity which is to be realized *hic et nunc*.

This linking of John Paul II's views and actions to those of Innocent is not as gratuitous as it may seem. At least, John Paul himself would probably not regard it so. He had occasion to pronounce himself on the issue in a message to the bishop of Cremona in celebration of the eighth centenary of the death of ... St. Homobonus.[68] Unsurprisingly, the message quotes liberally from Innocent's bull of canonization, which we have examined earlier. John Paul is also generous in acknowledging Innocent's originality in having produced the canonization of the first and

---

[65] John Paul II, ibid., p. 177.
[66] John Paul II, *Novo Millennio Ineunte*, 6 January 2001. I take its text from www.adoremus.org/0601papal_letter.html.
[67] John Paul II, *Novo Millennio Ineunte*, c. 27.
[68] John Paul II, *Messaggio a S. E. Mons. Giulio Nicolini, vescovo di Cremona, nell'VIII centenario della morte di Sant'Omobono*, 24 June 1997; I take the text from www.rccr.cremona.it/campi/omobono/doc1.html.

only layman canonized in the Middle Ages who was not a member of royal or princely families.[69] He notes the continuing relevance of Homobonus, "not only because holiness is one, but for the characteristics of life and works with which this lay faithful has lived evangelical perfection."[70] He notes also that "the times are no longer those of eight hundred years ago. To the canonization of Homobonus, matured within the medieval climate and procedures, we cannot attribute the character of a 'promotion of the laity', in the sense which we today give to this concept."[71] And yet the figure of Innocent's saint can be read as harbinger of the universal call to holiness as it is now understood.

John Paul's distancing himself from the medieval procedure of canonization, even as he sings the praises of one of its fruits, can well provide matter for our conclusion. No doubt, the medieval canonization process, after a much longer run than is given to most such things to enjoy, has come to an end for many reasons. But it ought not to be neglected that what has ended with it is the very reason which the medieval canonists regarded as justifying it: the inscription of newly canonized saints in the universal calendar of the Church with the consequent obligation for the faithful to venerate them. Quite clearly, John Paul II could not have canonized or beatified so many hundreds of people, if slots had had to be found for them in the calendar of the Church. Equally clearly, it is the opening sections of Innocent III's bull of canonization of Homobonus which have now become important, and not the ones which carefully set out the extent to which strict procedural norms had been followed to assure the faithful that it was indeed a saint who was being presented for their veneration.[72]

---

[69] John Paul II, *Messaggio*, c. 1.

[70] John Paul II, *Messaggio*, c. 2.

[71] John Paul II, Messaggio, c. 7.

[72] It was fitting that, once the limitations imposed by the calendar were no longer an issue and the expectation had come about that canonizations could henceforth be numerous, the bishops should again find themselves the principal investigators of the lives of prospective candidates for canonization. That this should be the case was decreed in *Divinus perfectionis Magister*, and the norms which bishops are to follow in carrying out these investigations were set out by the Congregation for the Causes of Saints, *Norme da osservarsi nelle inchieste diocesane nelle cause dei santi*. In: *Acta Apostolicae Sedis* 75 (1983), pp. 396-403. The text of these norms can also be found at www.vatican.va/roman_curia/congregations/csaints/documents.

Works Cited

Cantini, J.A. and Charles Lefebvre. "Sinibalde dei Fieschi," *Dictionnaire de droit canonique*. Ed. R. Naz. 7 vv. Paris: Letouzey et Ané, 1935-65. Vol. 7, cc. 1029-62.

Chiron, Yves. *Enquête sur les canonisations*. Perrin: Paris, 1998.

Congregation for the Causes of Saints, *Norme da osservarsi nelle inchieste diocesane nelle cause dei santi*. In: *Acta Apostolicae Sedis* 75 (1983), pp. 396-403. The text of these norms can also be found at www.vatican.va/roman_curia/congregations/csaints/documents.

Fieschi, Sinibaldus (Innocent IV). *Commentaria Apparatus in V Libros Decretalium*. Frankfurt: 1570.

Friedberg, Emil. *Corpus Iuris Canonici*. 2 vols. Leipzig 1879. Repr. Graz: Akademische Druck-U. Verlagsanstalt, 1959.

Gasparri, Petrus. *Codex Iuris Canonici Pii X Pontificis Maximi iussu digestus, Benedicti Papae XV auctoritate promulgatus, praefatione, fontium annotatione et indice analytico-alphabetico ab Eminentissimo Cardinali Gasparri auctus*. New York: P.J. Kennedy and Sons, 1918.

Hageneder, Othmar and Anton Haidacher. *Die Register Innocenz' III*. Graz: H. Bohlaus: 1964.

John Paul II. *Crossing the Threshold of Hope*. Ed. Vittorio Messori. Alfred A. Knopf: Toronto, 1994.

_____. *Divinus Perfectionis Magister*. 25 January 1983. The English text of the constitution can be found at www.vatican.va/holy_father/john_paul_ii/apost_constitutions.

_____. *Messaggio a S. E. Mons. Giulio Nicolini, vescovo di Cremona, nell'VIII centenario della morte di Sant'Omobono*, 24 June 1997; www.rccr.cremona.it/campi/omobono/doc1.html.

_____. *Novo Millennio Ineunte*. www.vatican.va/holy_father/john_paul_ii/apost_letters.

_____. *Redemptor Hominis*. London: Catholic Truth Society, 1979. The text is also available at *www.vatican.va/holy_father/john_paul_ii/encyclicals*.

_____. *Tertio Millennio Adveniente*. Ottawa: Canadian Conference of Catholic Bishops, 1994; it is also available at www.vatican.va/holy_father/john_paul_ii/apost_letters.

Kemp, Eric Waldram. *Canonization and Authority in the Western Church*. London: Oxford University Press, 1948.

Kuttner, Stephan G. "La réserve pontificale du droit de canonisation." *Revue historique de droit français et étranger*, 4e s., 18 (1938), pp. 172-228.

Lefebvre, Charles. "Hostiensis." *Dictionnaire de droit canonique*. Ed. R. Naz. 7 vv. Paris: Letouzey et Ané, 1935-65. Vol. 5, pp. 1211-27.

Migne, Jacques-Paul. *Patrologia latina*. Paris: 1844-1855, 1862-1865.

Petersohn, Jurgen. "Die Litterae Papst Innocenz III zur Heiligsprechung der Kaiserin Kunigunde (1200)." *Jahrbuch für fränkische Landesforschung*, 37 (1977), pp. 1-25.

Sarno, Robert J. tr. *New Laws for the Causes of the Saints*. Rome: Sacred Congregation for the Causes of Saints, 1983.

Segusio, Henricus de (Hostiensis), *In quinque decretalium libros commentaria*. Venice: 1581; repr. Torino: Bottega d'Erasmo, 1965

_____. *Summa aurea*. Venice: 1574; repr. Torino: Bottega d'Erasmo, 1963.

Tunberg, Sven. "Erik den helige, Sveriges helgenkonung." *Fornvännen Meddelanden fran K. Vitterhets Historie och Antikvitets Akademien* 36 (1941), pp. 257-78.

Vauchez, André. *La sainteté en Occident aux derniers siècles du Moyen Age d'après les procès de canonisation et les documents hagiographiques*. Rome: École française de Rome, 1981.

Veraja, Fabijan. *Commentary on the New Legislation for the Causes of Saints*. Rome: 1983.

Vodola, Elisabeth. "Hostiensis," *Dictionary of the Middle Ages*. Ed. Joseph R. Strayer. 13 vv. New York: Scribner, 1982-89. Vol. 6, pp. 298-99

_____. "Innocent IV, pope." *Dictionary of the Middle Ages*. Ed. Joseph R. Strayer. 13 vv. New York: Scribner, 1982-89. Vol. 6, pp. 465-7.

Weigel, George. *Witness to Hope. The Biography of Pope John Paul II*. HarperCollins: New York, 1999.

Woodward, Kenneth L. *Making Saints. How the Catholic Church Determines Who Becomes a Saint, Who Doesn't, and Why*. Simon and Schuster